RaisingBoys
With ADHD

Secrets for
Parenting
Successful,
Happy Sons

What the Experts Say

"In this thoroughly updated second edition, Mary Anne Richey builds on the extensive resources, guidance, wisdom, and knowledge of science and experience included in the first edition to create a current, practical, readable, and useful guide for parents of boys with ADHD. This volume remains on my short list of books I recommend to parents of boys with ADHD."

—Sam Goldstein, Ph.D., Editor, *Journal of Attention Disorders*, and coauthor of *Tenacity in Children: Nurturing the Seven Instincts for Lifetime Success*

"Richey writes to parents of boys with ADHD as an experienced close friend or mentor, ready to roll up her sleeves and work toward solutions alongside the reader. She provides reassurance, facilitates acceptance, supports understanding, presents options and considerations, and outlines practical resources and action steps to manage your son's diagnosis of ADHD. This handbook covers all facets of a boy's life, even those that may not have occurred to you previously, and is accessible to parents as well as to anyone advocating for a boy with ADHD. I will be strongly recommending this read to parents and my colleagues in education, medicine, and psychology as a source of knowledge, refreshment, and perspective on supporting boys with ADHD."

—Rachel Salinger, Ph.D., Nationally Certified School Psychologist and HCPC Registered Educational Psychologist, United Kingdom

"Saving parents from endless hours of online research, Mary Anne Richey provides parents of boys with ADHD a seminal reference guide that is intelligent and compassionate, foundational and actionable. This is a book you can read cover to cover, or use as a reference, and get exactly what you need every time you crack the spine."

—Elaine Taylor-Klaus, CEO of Impact Parents and author of *The Essential Guide to Raising Complex Kids With ADHD, Anxiety, and More*

Second Edition

RaisingBoys
With ADHD

Secrets for Parenting Successful, Happy Sons

Mary Anne Richey

Routledge
Taylor & Francis Group

NEW YORK AND LONDON

Library of Congress Cataloging-in-Publication Data

Names: Richey, Mary Anne, 1947- author.
Title: Raising boys with ADHD : secrets for parenting successful, happy
  sons / Mary Anne Richey.
Description: 2nd edition. | Waco, TX : Prufrock Press Inc., [2021] |
  Revised edition of: Raising boys with ADHD / by James W. Forgan and Mary
  Anne Richey. c2012. | Includes bibliographical references. | Summary:
  "The second edition of the best-selling "Raising Boys With ADHD"
  features the latest information on research and treatment for boys with
  ADHD, empowering parents to help their sons with ADHD find success in
  school and beyond"-- Provided by publisher.
Identifiers: LCCN 2020055656 (print) | LCCN 2020055657 (ebook) | ISBN
  9781646321100 (paperback) | ISBN 9781646321117 (ebook) | ISBN
  9781646321124 (epub)
Subjects: LCSH: Attention-deficit hyperactivity disorder. |
  Attention-deficit-disordered children. | Child rearing. | Parent and
  child.
Classification: LCC RJ506.H9 F667 2021 (print) | LCC RJ506.H9 (ebook) |
  DDC 618.92/8589--dc23
LC record available at https://lccn.loc.gov/2020055656
LC ebook record available at https://lccn.loc.gov/2020055657

First published in 2021 by Prufrock Press Inc.

Published in 2021 by Routledge
605 Third Avenue, New York, NY 10017
2 Park Square, Milton Park, Abingdon, Oxon OX14 4RN

Routledge is an imprint of the Taylor & Francis Group, an informa business.

© 2021 by Taylor & Francis Group

Cover design by Allegra Denbo and layout design by Shelby Charette

ISBN: 9781646321100 (pbk)

DOI: 10.4324/9781003237464

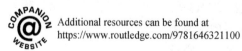

Additional resources can be found at
https://www.routledge.com/9781646321100

Dedication

I dedicate this book to a number of special people in my life. First of all, my first son, Neal, who died at 2 years of age from neuroblastoma, heightened my understanding of just how incredibly precious each child's life is. That kindled my desire to help parents recognize that in their children so that they can help them lead their best lives. Secondly, I am so indebted to my children and their spouses—Kate, Kent, Bryan, and Jessica—and to my grandchildren—Matthew, Maxwell, Molly, Cole, Teddy, and Charlotte—for all of the joy and love they have brought. Finally, but certainly not least, I thank my husband, Bill, for his love and excellent proofreading skills.

Table of Contents

Acknowledgements

Projects like this require the work of many individuals. I would especially like to thank Katy McDowall, my editor at Routledge, for her guidance and assistance. I also greatly appreciate the medical expertise of pediatrician Dr. Tommy Schechtman, behavioral health specialist Dr. Raquel Anderson, and child, adolescent, and adult psychiatrists Dr. Marshall Teitlebaum and Dr. Michelle Chaney in providing in-depth information about treatment.

Introduction

From my personal and professional experience, it seems that behind every successful boy with ADHD is a very tired parent. I bet you can relate to that! Raising a boy with ADHD can be exhausting and seem overwhelming at times, but the purpose of this second edition is to provide you the latest information about ADHD and, like the first edition, to inspire you to be fully invested in the challenge and offer support and proven strategies to help along the way. You wouldn't be reading this book if you didn't care deeply about your son. You are poised to be one of the most influential people in guiding him toward success in life. Of course, there is no *one* path to happiness and success, and it will be a journey influenced by parents, siblings, relatives, caregivers, teachers, and others. I've been down a similar path in my personal life, and I am honored to continue to work with parents and teachers of boys with ADHD in my professional life. I firmly believe that these boys often have so much untapped potential.

In this book, I encourage you to be both optimistic and realistic about your son's future by learning what you can do to make the most of his strengths and help him improve in areas that might keep him from using those strengths. There is an explosion of knowledge about ADHD. I want to present some of the most relevant research in parent-friendly terms so that you can be well-informed and intentional in your parenting.

Your son with Attention Deficit/Hyperactivity Disorder (ADHD) is unique and has his own set of strengths and skills. He may look like any other boy in many ways but has characteristics that must be looked at through the lens of ADHD, especially its neurological effects. One thing I have observed to be true for most boys with ADHD is that they are *consistently inconsistent*. Some days your son has you glowing with pride, and other days, you are scratching your head in amazement at how it could have all gone so wrong. Please be confident that you can help nurture your son's qualities to help him grow into a successful adult who will make you proud.

What Does Success for Boys With ADHD Look Like?

Everyone has their own definition of success because it is a very personal concept. When I think about success, I don't view it in terms of "things." Being successful doesn't mean owning a fancy car or a huge house or having tons of money or an extraordinary career. Although these things can be nice and often project the image of success, they don't reflect the type of success I need to feel satisfied and fulfilled. There is a saying I like that goes like this: "Do not educate your children to be rich. Educate them to be happy—so when they grow up they will know the value of things, not the price."

I've worked with enough families to know that what is portrayed on the outside does not always mirror what's happening on the inside. One client told me, "My husband works so hard to support our lifestyle that he's filled with anxiety, takes medication, doesn't sleep well at night, and barely has time to spend with me or the kids." They drive expensive cars, send their kids to an exclusive private school, own a big house, and take luxurious vacations. Everything *seemed* okay to the casual observer, but happiness had eluded them.

In my opinion, success is about being happy with yourself and with what you have and believing that you make a difference in this world. I think most parents feel that their children are successful as adults if they are happy, live independently, earn a living in a field that brings satisfaction, and contribute to making our world a better place. As the country music song "Red Dirt Road" by Brooks & Dunn goes, "Happiness on Earth ain't just for high achievers." Sure, your son with ADHD *may* become a high achiever, but that alone isn't going to make him successful. Your job as a parent is to help your son identify his purpose, develop his talents, and learn how to get along with people. It's not a high-paying or cushy job, but it is *extremely* rewarding and, in my opinion, one of the most important jobs you'll ever do.

There is no doubt that raising a son is difficult, but raising a son with ADHD is even tougher. When you have a son with ADHD, you may face issues that generally aren't on other parents' radar screens, such as:

▷ years of phone calls from his teachers,
▷ other parents' perceptions that you don't know how to discipline your son,
▷ embarrassment over the impulsive things he says or does,
▷ the intensity of your son's emotional displays,
▷ his fragile self-esteem,
▷ his automatic negativity,
▷ discouragement (yours and his),
▷ relationship issues, and
▷ severe homework struggles.

That last one struck a chord, didn't it? Homework is usually an intense endeavor for boys with ADHD. The average boy may have some difficulty getting started on his homework, but with some gentle prompting, he starts and finishes within a reasonable timeframe. The boy with ADHD? He often has to conquer a personal battle, including overcoming inertia to initiate the process and put negative thoughts about school behind him just to get started, and it goes that way every night. Parents prompt, threaten, offer rewards (sometimes they look a little like bribes), and even sit next to their son for the entire time. Sound familiar? One mom told me that because of the continual battles she has with her son with ADHD over homework, she feels that he doesn't even like her anymore. Another mother said, "I've battled him so long that I finally put him in aftercare at school so they could get him to do his homework." Helping your son take ownership of homework as his responsibility, not yours, would be a lofty goal, right?

Fortunately, there are professionals and resources to help you work through many such parenting challenges of raising boys with ADHD and put effective strategies in place that will lead to your son's independence. ***You don't have to conquer everything on your own.*** With some effort, through books and webinars and professionals like counselors, psychologists, ADHD coaches, and/or medical doctors, you can find valuable assistance and possibly even support groups with other parents of boys with ADHD. Locating the right resources and people to help you can take some energy, phone calls and emails, and research, but it *is* worth the effort. Not only will you feel less alone, but also you'll be making an investment in your son. As one wise mother of adult children told me, "You pay now or pay later." It is much better to be proactive and provide assistance to ward off problems than to be reactive when having to face even larger problems. Your son may be too young or too immature to realize and verbalize it, but he'll thank you later.

I understand the struggle of "being in the trenches" but also know how critical it is for your son's future for you to be informed and intentional in your parenting. A study of twins in Britain over 18 years showed that children with ADHD "showed poorer functioning across all domains, including mental health, substance misuse, psychosocial, physical health and socioeconomic outcomes" compared to those without ADHD (Agnew et al., 2018). Proper treatment, intervention, and informed parenting can make a real difference in the outcome. I am sharing valuable strategies from some of the most respected experts in the field and presenting the latest research on ADHD in an accessible form to fortify you on your parenting journey.

How to Use this Book

I value your time and have tried to make the information in this book easily available for the busy parent. You can read the book all of the way through, or you can turn to the chapter or part of the chapter that is most relevant to you at the time, such as treatment or need for academic support. The middle chapters are divided into the major developmental periods, including infancy and preschool, elementary years, and teenage years. In each of those chapters, I discuss topics relevant to the age band and include sections on issues you might face in school, at home, and in the community.

At the end of each chapter, you will find points to consider and action steps you can take right away to help your child. Share these with your family so that you'll have allies in choosing the best strategies for supporting your son in school and at home. And once you've finished reading the book or the chapters applicable to your son, I'll walk you through creating a personalized Dynamic Action Plan. The beauty of your Dynamic Action Plan is that it will allow you and your son to build upon today's successes while following a blueprint for his promising future. I encourage you to take the time to put your plan in writing because that will help you stay much more focused and purposeful.

ADD Versus ADHD: What's the Difference?

Before you read too far in this book, I want to explain the ADHD and ADD terminology, to make sure we are on the same page. Some professionals and parents use the acronyms ADD and ADHD interchangeably. Others use ADD to describe behaviors of forgetfulness, not paying attention, and distractibility; they apply the term ADHD to describe behaviors of hyperactivity and impulsivity. Within current professional literature, ADHD is considered the umbrella term that is used to describe both students with inattention as well as students with hyperactivity and impulsivity.

There is ADHD Predominantly Inattentive presentation, which used to be called ADD. There is also ADHD Hyperactive-Impulsive presentation, and that was called ADHD. There is also ADHD Combined presentation, meaning a certain number of symptoms from both ADD and ADHD are present. In this book, I will use ADHD as the general term that includes ADHD and ADD. The diagram in Figure 1 provides you with a visual of the variations of ADHD.

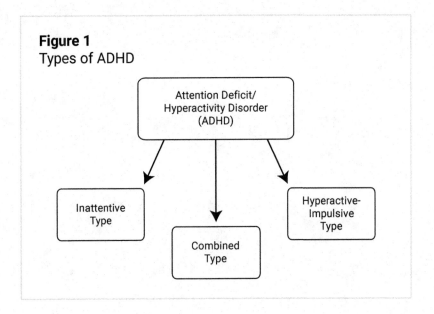

Figure 1
Types of ADHD

Chapter 1

My Son Has ADHD: Now What?

You may not always recognize boys with ADHD, but believe me, they are *everywhere*. According to the American Psychiatric Association (2013), "Population surveys suggest that ADHD occurs in most cultures in about 5% of children and about 2.5% of adults" (p. 61). The percentage of children in the U.S. who are diagnosed varies, with estimates ranging from 5% to as high as 11%, depending on the criteria used, how the data were collected, and the age span considered. According to the Centers for Disease Control and Prevention (2020), 6.1 million children in the U.S. ages 2–17 have been diagnosed with ADHD by a healthcare professional. That's a lot of kids! The CDC data show that boys (12.9%) are more than twice as likely to be diagnosed with ADHD than girls (5.6%). Dr. Thomas E. Brown (2017), a clinical psychologist who has researched ADHD extensively, suggested that the ratio is closer to 3:1, but "when adults are assessed, the ratio of males to females is closer to 1:1. This suggests that there are many girls with ADHD-related impairments who are not identified until they become adults" (p. 37). The CDC (2020) data show that three in four children with ADHD receive some kind of treatment, whether it be medication, behavioral treatment, and/or skills training.

In your son's classroom at school, there will likely be another student and maybe more diagnosed with or suspected of having ADHD. On a sports team of 12 players, there will likely be at least one with ADHD. How many kids live in your neighborhood? In addition to your own son, there are probably some boys with ADHD living around you. Boys (and girls) with ADHD are everywhere.

Did I Cause It?

In many cases, a biological parent's genetics likely contributed to a child's diagnosis. According to Brown (2017), "One out of every four people who have ADHD is likely to have a parent with ADHD, whether he or she knows it or not; the other three usually have at least one sibling, grandparent, uncle, aunt, or cousin who has ADHD" (p. 79).

ADHD is a very complex interaction of many genes located throughout the brain. Much research has gone into identifying these genes and their functioning. Dr. Russell Barkley (2016), another eminent researcher whose career focuses on ADHD, explained:

> The genes involved in causing ADHD are genes that build and operate certain regions and networks in the brain during development. Versions of genes involved in ADHD that are different when compared to typical people result in differences and even deficiencies in these structures and their functioning. (p. 13)

There is nothing to be done about genetics, so the best you can do is try to continue to learn about ADHD to help your son navigate it the best he can.

Just so you know, a much smaller proportion of cases of ADHD can result from other factors, including a mother's tobacco, alcohol, or drug use while pregnant; maternal infections during pregnancy; birth complications; and prematurity. According to Barkley (2016), "A smaller percentage of ADHD cases may be due to brain injuries suffered after the child is born, resulting from diseases, brain trauma, tumors, stroke or even poisoning, such as lead or pesticide exposure" (p. 14). Whatever the cause, the past can't be changed, so it is important to put all of your energy into learning to help your son manage his ADHD.

Because he doesn't look physically different, it might be difficult to accept that your son has a problem. This can be especially true for fathers. Often in a dad's eyes, his boy is just being a boy. He is *supposed* to be active and run around, climb things, ask a million questions, and argue. I often hear from dads, "It's the same thing I did as a kid." Pause on that thought. In many families I have worked with, ADHD had been suspected but had never been officially diagnosed in a parent. In fact, many times, a parent may be diagnosed after their child receives the diagnosis because the parent starts to realize that they have the same set of symptoms and seeks an evaluation as an adult. It doesn't help one bit to cast blame on yourself or your partner and wonder who your son "got it" from. If you do suspect a genetic link, try instead to find some sympathy and compassion for what your son is facing. I have seen many cases where the mother or father has learned to manage life with ADHD, which serves as a source of encouragement for their son.

One mistake I have seen parents make is to take the attitude that they survived without any intervention or assistance, intimating that their son should "buck up" and do the same. An important thing to remember is that school and society have become much more complex, so there will be more demands placed on your son than you experienced. Additionally, shouldn't you take advantage of all that has been learned about ADHD to help your son navigate it as successfully as possible?

Some parents feel guilt-ridden because they believe that their *actions, and not just their genetics,* may be responsible for their son's ADHD. Parents may even start to second-guess themselves by making negative assumptions. Parents have told me:

▷ "I should have breastfed him instead of using the bottle."
▷ "I should have played with him more."
▷ "I shouldn't have let him watch so much television or play so many video games."
▷ "I shouldn't have worked while leaving him in daycare or with a nanny."
▷ "If only his dad had taken more interest in him as a youngster."

Please remember that parenting style and the decisions you've made usually are not your son's main issues. Being a more skilled parent will not make ADHD go away. Poor parenting does not *cause* ADHD (but as we'll see later in the book, it certainly can aggravate the situation). Can we, as parents, improve the way we deal with our sons with ADHD? Absolutely, and I'll spend a good bit of this book sharing ways to help you do just that.

Shouldn't you take advantage of all that has been learned about ADHD to help your son navigate it as successfully as possible?

Mary L., a parent of a 9-year-old son with ADHD, expressed this: "After all these years, I was relieved to hear from a professional that my parenting style did not cause John's ADHD. I'm sure parents in my neighborhood thought his behavior was my fault, but it's not. It's his ADHD that causes him to become so emotional." Another parent, Amy S., explained it this way: "It's like a chip was missing in his brain. When Mark was young and he wanted people to go home, he would just yell, 'Make them go home!' I used to get so embarrassed and think if I was a good enough parent, this wouldn't happen."

Taking Charge of ADHD

I often advise parents not to worry so much about the label but to focus on proactive steps they can take to help their son. To raise a successful son with ADHD, you must start being more intentional in your parenting from the day you find out your son has ADHD with the ultimate goal of assisting him in learning to manage his ADHD on his own.

> *To raise a successful son with ADHD, you must start being more intentional in your parenting from the day you find out your son has ADHD.*

Recognize That ADHD Is a Disability

Even though your son may be smart and look fine on the outside, his mind is wired differently. Taking a "disability perspective" provides understanding but doesn't mean you are going to allow your son to use his ADHD as an excuse. It just means you are going to learn about how to help him manage the neurobiological functioning that makes some things more difficult for him. ADHD is now considered to involve much more than attention and/or hyperactivity. At the very heart of the disorder is difficulty with the brain's management system or its *executive function*, which refers to all of the skills needed to accomplish a task—planning, organizing, starting, focusing, sticking with it until completed, monitoring performance, using memory, and regulating emotions. Your son may know what to do but have trouble getting started or finishing a task. A reminder: ADHD has nothing to do with his intelligence but rather how he approaches tasks and manages his behavior. You are taking a great step by reading this book and teaching yourself more about ADHD. Increasing and using your knowledge about ADHD are key to raising a successful son.

Try to Become More Understanding and Patient

That doesn't mean you will let your son "get away with things," but you will need to learn to respond differently by considering his neurobiological makeup and how it impacts him. Distinct differences in the brains of those with and without ADHD have been documented time and time again. Keep in mind that reduced levels of transmitters, especially dopamine, impact communication between parts of the brain that support different functions, so information may not be exchanged efficiently to inform behavior in boys with ADHD. The end result could be that they are more impulsive, forgetful, disorganized, and/or less focused. Another important point to consider is that boys with ADHD tend to lag several years behind their peers in many cognitive and social skills. For example, even though your son is a 12-year-old, his self-regulation skills may be more like a 9-year-old's. Although you want to have standards for your son's behavior, remember that his behavior is not always under his control. Sometimes he will need additional supports or a very patient and knowledgeable parent to help him rein in some of his behaviors.

When Jack got upset or frustrated with his son, Timmy, he tended to point his index finger at Timmy and shake it up and down as he scolded him. Jack became so frustrated at himself that he was determined to stop this automatic response. One day he decided to write the letters U and P on the edge of his finger. When he got upset and pointed his finger at Timmy, Jack got an automatic visual reminder to have understanding and patience. This simple strategy worked! Jack was able to pause to think about the root of the behavior and how he might help Timmy make a better decision the next time.

Locate Support Personnel

Begin to locate different support personnel, such as educators, counselors, ADHD coaches, and doctors who can serve as resources throughout the years. Part of raising a successful son with ADHD is recognizing that it's very tough to try to do alone. If your son is going to be successful, at the very minimum you must have his teachers' support (more about that in later chapters).

Don't despair if you have limited resources at your local level or are unable to afford those that are available. There are many free online resources available through Children and Adults With Attention-Deficit/Hyperactivity Disorder (CHADD; https://chadd.org), ADDitude (https://www.additudemag.com), Child Mind Institute (https://child mind.org), American Academy of Child and Adolescent Psychiatry (https://www.aacap.org), and Understood (https://www.understood. org/pages/en/learning-thinking-differences).

Prepare for the Long Haul

Educating yourself about ADHD will equip you to be a strong advocate for your child as he moves from one developmental stage to the next. After all, if you don't go to bat for your young son, who will? (As he matures, ideally you want him to start to advocate for himself, but that will take time, support, and maturation.) No boy I have ever worked with *wants* to go to school and fail, play sports and get yelled at by the coach, or be excluded from friends' social activities because he says inappropriate things at the wrong time. Your son needs you to be strong, to be his voice when he is weak, and to encourage others to treat him fairly. Without you, your son can be at a great disadvantage in school, sports, friendships, gatherings, and life. You are a source of encouragement and support that is invaluable. Even though you will become discouraged at times, frustrated by his behavior, and embarrassed by things he does, you love your son—and your son loves you. Your hard work will pay off and you'll feel rewarded.

Educating yourself about ADHD will equip you to be a strong advocate for your child as he moves from one developmental stage to the next.

Realize that you and your son are likely going to have really good periods and possibly some really rough patches. Meaningful change occurs over time. Again, boys with ADHD are *consistently inconsistent* in their day-to-day functioning. If some of your efforts seem to have failed, I encourage you not to throw up your hands and give up. Perhaps an idea was planted or a skill was improved that will show up later. Regroup and continue moving forward with a new plan because the cost of giving up is much too high.

Sharon was told by a high school counselor to let her high school son, Jared, sink or swim on his own merits when she asked for assistance in setting up a plan to help him monitor his grades and turn in his work. She followed that advice but soon learned that he wasn't able to do that without oversight and assistance. He failed four classes that grading period, which took a toll on his self-esteem and motivation. With assistance from a caring teacher, she and Jared developed a monitoring plan for his academics. With support, he was gradually able to take on more responsibility but still needed prompting and reminders.

Remember that maturation helps many boys with ADHD. As they move from the preschool to upper elementary years, tantrums and tears tend to decrease. As they move into high school and college, they may demonstrate less hyperactivity and impulsivity but may continue to have difficulty with handling all of the demands placed on them for memory, organization, and time management. But many boys with an understanding of their strengths and weaknesses become more responsible in using strategies to help themselves and ultimately learn to advocate for themselves. So take heart that some parts of your life will become easier over time!

ADHD Is Real and More Than a Behavioral Problem

At times you still may wonder, or have to convince a skeptical family member, whether or not ADHD is a fad or made-up disorder. Rest assured that ADHD is not a diagnosis contrived by parents or professionals looking for an excuse for a child's behavior. Differences in the brains of children and adolescents with ADHD have been documented by neuroscience and brain imaging. Those diagnosed with ADHD:

> have been shown to differ in the rate of maturation of specific areas of the cortex, in the thickness of cortical tissue, in characteristics of the parietal and cerebellar regions, as well as in the basal ganglia, and in the white matter tracts that connect and provide critically important communication between various regions of the brain. (Brown, 2013, p. 5)

As a parent, the key to explaining ADHD to others is to first understand it using the latest research and thinking in the field. For some time, the core symptoms of ADHD have been considered to be developmentally inappropriate levels of inattention, hyperactivity, and impulsivity that occur across multiple settings—not just at home or at school—and interfere with academic or social progress. Mental images of children hopping around, failing to sit still while eating, or daydreaming in their own little world often come to mind.

Although these conceptions are still true, new research indicates that ADHD is a much more complex disorder with pervasive involvement of a child's neurological functioning that involves so many aspects of the self-management system of the brain. A boy's difficulties in controlling attention and impulses affect how he approaches tasks, makes decisions, maintains motivation, and manages his emotions. As I noted previously, the self-management system is referred to as *executive functioning*, or the way the brain directs us to plan and execute tasks while regulating our emotions and calling on memory to inform decisions based on past experience. The term "refers to the brain-based skills that are required for humans to *execute* or perform tasks" (Dawson & Guare, 2009, p. 13). Executive functioning includes, but is not limited to, the ability to:

▷ focus,
▷ decide what is important,
▷ set goals,
▷ use prior knowledge,
▷ initiate action,
▷ manage time,
▷ self-monitor performance,
▷ use self-restraint,
▷ remain flexible. (Forgan & Richey, 2015, p. 3)

A boy's difficulties in controlling attention and impulses affect how he approaches tasks, makes decisions, maintains motivation, and manages his emotions.

Keep in mind that these executive functions may also be delayed 2–3 years in your child, so many of them can be improved with support and training—and, of course, maturation. One parent I worked with was literally losing sleep over her middle school son's apparent inability to keep up with his belongings and his school schedule. She tried numerous interventions, from posting a schedule, having him set aside a dedicated space for crucial items, reminding and nagging, and having him use his electronics to provide reminders. When one technique failed, she and he together came up with another plan. As he matured, she could see elements of old plans starting to bear fruit and realized he was actually becoming more responsible. She had worried he would never be able to go to college and manage on his own, but as he matured, she could see that this would be a possibility.

As you can see, ADHD is no longer considered to be just a behavioral disorder but is much more far-reaching in its scope. Even though this is very complex information, understanding this can give you a new perspective on your son's behavior and diagnosis.

A Brief History of ADHD

ADHD is not unique to the postmodern era. As early as 1845, a German physician wrote a poem about "Fidgety Philip," a boy who can't sit still at dinner and accidentally knocks all of the food onto the floor, to his parents' great displeasure. This is one of the earliest records of symptoms consistent with what we now call ADHD.

A great deal of research in the 1940s and 1950s focused on disorders of the brain. Scientists described ADHD-like behavior with terms such as "minimal brain dysfunction" or "hyperkinetic impulse disorder." In 1987, the third edition of the *Diagnostic and Statistical Manual of Mental Disorders* recognized the disorder as Attention Deficit/Hyperactivity Disorder. Thus, the notion that ADHD is a disorder made up in the 1990s is a myth because behaviors related to ADHD have been recorded for more than 100 years. The rise in diagnoses can be attributed to many factors. It has to do with better understanding and greater awareness of the disorder and more availability of treatment. I personally feel that our complex, fast-moving society, with increased demands placed on children at earlier ages without taking into account their readiness and maturation, has played a role, especially for boys.

Many other myths about ADHD still exist (see Table 1). Are there any you still believe?

Table 1
Myths and Facts About ADHD

Myth	Fact
Poor parenting causes ADHD.	ADHD is neurological and often genetic.
If you have one child with ADHD, all of your children will have it.	Not all children in the same family have ADHD.
ADHD is not a disability.	ADHD is a recognized disability in the Americans With Disabilities Act (ADA) and the Individuals With Disabilities Education Act (IDEA).
Medication is the only treatment for ADHD.	Medication is only one treatment option and the one shown to have the most immediate effect. Behavior management, therapy, parent training, ADHD coaching, and neurofeedback are some widely researched interventions.
Teachers want active boys on medication.	Teachers are responsible for their students learning and want them to give their best effort. If a student is disrupting the class, it can be quite frustrating for them and other students.
If a boy is hyper, then he has ADHD.	Boys who are hyper do not always have ADHD. Other things, such as anxiety and sensory sensitivities, can cause hyperactive types of behaviors.
A boy who is quiet or can hyperfocus on activities he enjoys cannot have ADHD.	Many boys with ADHD can hyperfocus on things they like, especially video games. Boys who are quiet could have the inattentive presentation of ADHD, especially those who daydream and lose focus.

Table 1, *continued*

Myth	Fact
Schools do not know how to teach boys with ADHD.	Schools are becoming more knowledgeable about ADHD, but some teachers are much more able and willing to work with and motivate boys with ADHD than others. If a boy with ADHD has an Individualized Education Program (IEP) or 504 plan (see Chapter 6), the school is required to provide appropriate accommodations as detailed in the plan.
Only a psychiatrist can diagnose ADHD.	Pediatricians, psychologists, neurologists, psychiatrists, and other mental health and medical personnel can all diagnose ADHD.
Psychologists prescribe medication.	Only medical doctors, such as pediatricians, neurologists, and psychiatrists, and nurse practitioners can prescribe medication.
An equal number of boys and girls are diagnosed with ADHD.	More boys than girls are diagnosed with ADHD in childhood.
Boys with ADHD want to behave badly.	Boys with ADHD often have trouble behaving and controlling impulses.
ADHD is a societal fad and will go away.	ADHD has been recognized since the mid-1800s but has been called by different names.
ADHD and ADD are the same thing.	ADHD is an umbrella term that is used in the DSM-V. Three types include: Predominantly Hyperactive-Impulsive presentation, Predominantly Inattentive presentation, and Combined presentation.

Racial and Ethnic Disparities in Diagnosis and Treatment

There are some racial/ethnic disparities in the diagnosis of ADHD worth noting. Research has shown that African American and Hispanic children are less likely than White children to be diagnosed. Of those that are diagnosed, racial/ethnic minority children are less likely to be taking medication for ADHD than White children (Morgan et al., 2013). The reasons for these differences could be related to access to healthcare, cultural attitudes about ADHD and medications, fewer concerns brought to the parents' attention by school staffs, lack of knowledge about the consequences of untreated ADHD, or other undetermined factors. For these children, this means that people are not considering the neurobiological effects of ADHD on their behavior, and their treatment needs, including school accommodations, are not met.

Much study has been done on adverse childhood experiences (ACEs), which looked at the impact of things like exposure to violence, divorce, death of a parent, abuse, and neglect. Childhood exposures to two or more of these potentially traumatic experiences was more likely to result in negative outcomes in a variety of areas, including academic success and health. Studies have shown that the incidence of childhood exposures to two or more adverse experiences was higher for African Americans than Hispanics or European Americans (Mattox & Vinson, 2018). According to Mattox and Vinson (2018),

> Asking directly about traumatic exposures is an absolute necessity in working with black youth and families. While trauma-related diagnoses are by no means mutually exclusive with ADHD, if both are present, it is imperative that the family is educated about the psychological impact of trauma and that treatment interventions target both issues. (para. 5)

Otherwise, the treatment outcome could be negatively affected. Access to proper diagnosis and treatment as well as culturally sensitive efforts to communicate effectively with all parent groups are important issues going forward to ensure that all children have access to the treatment and support they need.

Typical Versus Atypical Behavior

Boys with a hyperactive component to their presentation of ADHD are often among the first to be taken for an evaluation to determine if they have ADHD. I'm often asked, "How do you determine if this is normal boy behavior or behavior that is unusual and could be ADHD or some other behavioral disorder?" Consider these three questions when deciding if your son's behavior is unusual when compared to other boys his age:

 ▷ How **frequently** does the disruptive behavior occur?
 ▷ How **long** does the disruptive behavior last?
 ▷ How **intense** is your son's behavior during this time?

Think about how frequently your son's disruptive behaviors occur. Once an hour? Once a day? Once per week? It is unusual for a child to get into significant trouble multiple times on a daily basis. I talked to one mom who felt like she had to keep her 7-year-old away from the other neighborhood boys because every time her son went out to play, he came home crying. He had an explosive temper and lashed out at the other boys when he got mad but couldn't handle it when the neighborhood kids reciprocated, and he'd run home in tears. This was unusual behavior because it happened so consistently.

How long do your son's disruptive behaviors last? Are the behaviors like a brief passing rain shower or long and drawn out? Think about an elementary-age boy who is upset because he wants to play video games but has to do his homework. Depending on their age, most boys become upset and huff and puff around, and yet recover within an age-appropriate amount of time. Time tends to heal things with most boys. Take the same situation for the boy with ADHD. You give him a 5-minute warning to prepare him for the change. Then you give a 2-minute warning that video game time is almost finished. Still, he just can't seem to stop playing or becomes visibly very upset that game time is over. It takes the boy with ADHD much longer to redirect his focus from one fixation toward something else, particularly when the next activity is something perceived as unpleasant (like homework). At home and school, boys have to shift their thoughts and activities and adapt to changes in routine, and this is often difficult for boys with ADHD.

How intense is your son's behavior during this time? If your son's temper tantrum goes on for hours and is so severe that no one wants to (or is able to) get near him, the intensity would be considered severe.

Some parents suspect very early in their son's life that he has characteristics of ADHD. Others may not suspect it until their son enters a structured educational setting when the staff calls a meeting of parents and teachers to discuss the boy's disruptive behavior in relation to frequency, duration, and intensity. At that point, parents' eyes may be opened to recognize that a potential problem exists.

> Joan's son was only 4 years old but had been kicked out of three preschools for biting, kicking, hitting, and disruptive behavior. The fourth school worked with her until Sam entered a public kindergarten, where within the first month, he was in trouble for his behavior in afterschool care and in his regular classroom. Clearly, at this point, the parent was not surprised that Sam's behavior went beyond typical boy behavior. The family sought professional help and an evaluation when Sam's parents were told he could not return to afterschool care once the month ended.
>
> A clinical psychologist completed a comprehensive evaluation and used tools to assess Sam's memory, attention, auditory and visual processing, and academics. He interviewed Sam's parents and teacher. They

also completed rating scales. At the end of the evaluation process, the psychologist sat down with Sam's parents and explained how their son met the criteria for ADHD and not other disorders that could have caused the behavior problems. Together, they set up an action plan so the parents knew exactly what to do. This was a better option for everyone—Sam, his family, his teacher, and his school—than taking a "wait-and-see" approach.

ADHD Properly Diagnosed

Have you ever asked yourself, "Why seek a professional diagnosis? Why not just begin a homeopathic or behavioral treatment?" One dad asked a colleague, a clinical psychologist, "Why should I drop a grand with you to diagnose my son when I can just start counseling?" The psychologist explained that a thorough evaluation and proper diagnosis would help determine the most appropriate treatment and interventions based on his son's profile of strengths and weaknesses.

Let's face it: You can build a house without a set of plans. It may take a lot longer, cost a lot more, and have hidden problems, but it can be done. Likewise, do you think a smart general enters a war without a battle plan? Absolutely not. So why start treating your son for something you suspect but haven't confirmed? The old saying, "Knowledge is power" holds true here.

The diagnosis serves multiple purposes. First, it may provide parents with a sense of understanding, which is often accompanied by relief. Parents may be relieved to know their son really does have something fundamentally different about his neurological makeup but something that can be managed with treatment. Many older children and teens I have worked with feel much better when they understand why controlling their behavior or staying organized may take much more effort on their part than for their friends without ADHD.

Second, and often very important—the diagnosis may enable your son to access school services if he meets the school's eligibility criteria (see Chapter 6). Most public and private schools require a professional diagnosis or an evaluation to provide any formal accommodations. Accommodations are adjustments, such as extra time to complete tests or homework, seating near the front of the class, help in breaking down complex assignments, or frequent breaks. Furthermore, as boys with ADHD prepare to take college entrance exams, a diagnosis and a complete evaluation report by a qualified individual are required to receive accommodations for extra time.

One of the secrets to success for many is that the stronger the team, the more thorough and accurate the diagnosis.

Third, the diagnosis allows you, if you desire, the option of trying medication. Not all parents want to try prescribed medication with their child and not all children need it, but research supports its effectiveness if needed when properly prescribed and monitored. If you decide to do so, you must have a proper diagnosis before obtaining a prescription. Some medical doctors will write a prescription based only on their own examination of the boy without a psychologist's written report, but many require behavior checklists from parents and teachers. (According to the diagnostic criteria, the behaviors must be present in more than one setting, so that is why a parent and teacher checklist may be requested.) As will be discussed in the next chapter, there are different professionals who can diagnose ADHD. If your finances allow and your son is having academic problems, I recommend both a psychological and medical evaluation of your child before pursuing medical treatment to properly identify all of the areas in which your son may be having trouble. For example, if learning disabilities are present, it will be important to properly identify them so that your son can get the assistance he needs. Both the psychologist and the pediatrician can become important members of your son's team. One of the secrets to success for many is that the stronger the team, the more thorough and accurate the diagnosis.

How Long Does ADHD Last?

Most researchers agree that ADHD can last a lifetime. Studies show that "ADHD is a relatively chronic disorder affecting many domains of major life activities from childhood through adolescence and into adulthood" (Barkley, 2015, p. 38). In fact, ADHD in adults is currently the topic of much research because of its impact on functioning in today's busy and hectic world.

As I noted previously, some encouraging news is that puberty or maturation changes types of ADHD behaviors for some boys. They often do not exhibit the same degree of hyperactivity, although they may continue to have that sense of restlessness. They usually gain better control over their emotions, at least in public! Inattentiveness, forgetfulness, and disorganization will likely continue but can often be managed with strategies and support.

My son loved playing school sports and became active in student government and a number of clubs in middle school and high school. His activity level remained high throughout puberty but was channeled in many different directions and became a definite positive for him. What did change was his knowledge about his strengths and limitations and his ability to work around his shortcomings, like his tendency to leave things until the last minute. He didn't engage in risk-taking behavior more than the average teenage boy and was not sensation-seeking. All in all, his teenage years were very rewarding.

Your son's experience with ADHD during and after puberty will be unique. Some of my clients have noticed decreases in their son's impulsive behavior after puberty. Sheila explained her observations: "After he hit the ninth grade, Felix did not seem as hyperactive and could actually remain seated throughout dinner and even made it through a wedding ceremony." Other parents say their son still shows excessive movement but is able to channel the energy into appropriate behaviors. One mom told me, "He still moves a lot, but now when he sits it's his leg moving up and down and not his entire body."

The important perspective is to have hope that your son's ADHD may decrease during puberty but to recognize that it may not. Regardless of the outcome, stand ready to give your son the support he needs.

Is ADHD a Gift?

The answer to this question is no. *However*, boys with ADHD often have characteristics, such as thinking outside the box or having high energy, that can lead to success with proper management.

There will be countless times when your son's ADHD seems much more like a burden than a gift. Many people you encounter tend to point out the negatives about ADHD. You'll hear comments like these:

- ▷ "He talks too much."
- ▷ "He won't sit still."
- ▷ "He annoys other students around him."
- ▷ "He won't listen."
- ▷ "He makes inappropriate comments."

The list goes on and on, and you can almost certainly add to it. I've found that most kids with ADHD hear 3–4 times as many negative as positive comments daily.

Especially when your son with ADHD is in preschool and early elementary school, he may likely have difficulty conforming to school rules, expectations, and behavior. He won't consider his ADHD a gift, and you probably won't either. Most elementary schools are not set up to accommodate active boys. For example, in kindergarten, kids are expected to sit on the carpet in front of the teacher and listen to a book being read. This was difficult for Ricky, for example, because his body needed to move. He preferred to shift around on the carpet, lie down, then get up again, often inadvertently touching his neighbor.

His teacher found this bothersome; not only did he get in trouble, but also he was moved to the back of the carpet or made to sit at his desk. In the elementary classroom, his ADHD was definitely not a gift.

So when *can* ADHD become a positive? When your son's natural talents are harnessed in the right direction, the way his brain functions can lead to success at any age. For many boys it becomes a gift in the outdoors; while building; when participating in sports, extracurricular activities, art, music, or academic subjects that interest them; or when they're interacting with people. Some reasons people have considered ADHD to be a gift is because individuals with ADHD may:

 ▷ have talents that others lack,
 ▷ think outside the box,
 ▷ hyperfocus on things of interest, and/or
 ▷ have a high energy level that enables them to accomplish many things.

> When your son's natural talents are harnessed in the right direction, the way his brain functions can lead to success at any age.

You understand your son with ADHD best, so think about his talents. What are they? Your insight will help you identify his strengths. Ask yourself these types of questions:

 ▷ What comes naturally to my son?
 ▷ What does he enjoy spending time doing?
 ▷ If asked, what would family or friends identify as his talents?
 ▷ What type of career do I picture for my son?

Our sons may be described as being social, exciting, funny, loving, risk-taking, and energetic. These positive qualities should not be overlooked and can become huge assets when they are adults. Dr. John C. Maxwell (2007), an international leadership expert, advised parents not to focus on weaknesses but to find, build, and nurture their children's strengths. Buy books on topics your son enjoys, talk with experts, attend seminars, and take field trips. Maxwell stressed that your child's strengths will carry him through life. If your child is a C student in reading, perhaps you should be okay with that as long as he continues to develop his skills. Instead of spending an inordinate number of hours and hours working with tutors, online learning, and worksheets in an attempt to mold him into an A-level reader, spend time building on his strengths instead. If you like this notion, you may enjoy Maxwell's (2007) book *Talent Is Never Enough* or a book I coauthored with Dr. James W. Forgan, *The ADHD Empowerment Guide: Identifying Your Child's Strengths and Unlocking Potential* (Forgan & Richey, 2019).

My son demonstrated strengths in leadership and athletics. He was not detail-oriented and did not enjoy academics, but did the required work. He had high energy, a quality that many other teens enjoy. We encouraged him to pursue scouting and student government. He was able to see the big picture and organize people toward a common goal, something he currently does in his career. My husband, his sister, and I worked with him to find areas that interested him while helping him acquire self-discipline and perseverance that would lead to success. When he signed up for a sport or activity, he knew he couldn't quit until the season ended but didn't have to sign up again if it wasn't something he wanted to pursue.

You will spend time and energy in helping a boy with ADHD develop his interests and strengths. But that time and energy pays big dividends in self-esteem, helps him form a basis for friendships, and provides him with constructive ways to spend his time. Your son has more strengths than you and he have probably identified. Look at the list in Figure 2 and check off all of the areas of strength that apply to your son.

Now that you've identified some of your son's strengths, build upon them. Together with your son, make a list of his talents and special qualities, and post it where you both can be reminded of them. Provide various opportunities for your son to develop these strengths

Figure 2
Identifying Your Son's Strengths

❏ Creative	❏ Artistic	❏ Outdoorsy
❏ Intuitive	❏ Exuberant	❏ Sensitive
❏ Emotionally expressive	❏ Funny	❏ Flexible
❏ Kind	❏ Considerate	❏ Thoughtful
❏ Energetic	❏ Humorous	❏ Imaginative
❏ Smart	❏ Attractive	❏ Curious
❏ Athletic	❏ Friendly	❏ Visual
❏ Intuitive about building	❏ Clever in designing	❏ Musical
❏ Spontaneous	❏ Effective in problem solving	❏ Leadership
❏ Resilient	❏ Fast processor	❏ Out-of-the box thinker

as well as discover new hidden talents. Your son has gifts that can take him far and help him have a happy and satisfying adult life. It's our job as parents of boys with ADHD to nurture those talents.

Explaining ADHD to Others

If your son has ADHD, should you tell other people? Has your son's behavior embarrassed you? Do you worry about people judging your parenting skills and your son? Are you concerned with your child having a label? These are some of the issues parents often bring up to me, and they are questions that don't always have easy answers.

If your son has ADHD, then chances are excellent that you have been embarrassed by his behavior at one point or another. Sometimes parents wish they could hide in a shell. One mother of a 9-year-old boy told me, "I got a call from the school principal. She said my son was saying inappropriate sexual things during car line. I don't have a clue where he heard them because we never use such talk around him."

Marco found himself embarrassed when his son Javier's behavior was less than perfect. He remembered picking Javier up from Sunday school—a place you really want your child to be at his best—and being faced with reports of the various ways Javier had misbehaved. In fact, sometimes Marco and his wife took turns picking Javier up, just so one of them could be spared the discomfort of hearing the rundown of things that had gone wrong that particular week.

As a parent of a son with ADHD, you may have to develop what some people call a "thick skin" at times, because others may judge *you* based on *your son's* behavior. Most boys with ADHD are active, energetic, and enthusiastic children who love excitement. They would much rather play with toys they can smash, crash, and trash in ways that seem to defy logic. Parents who only have girls or have quieter, more subdued boys don't seem to understand this and often become annoyed by this type of play.

Years later, Joseph can finally laugh when he remembers the Christmas when 6-year-old airplane-crazy Jamari got three Playmobil toy sets. The sets were too advanced for Jamari to build alone, so Joseph spent 3 hours building an airport and airplanes, adhering the tiny stickers, and arranging the furniture and accessories. Jamari couldn't wait to fly his planes. "What I didn't expect," Joseph recalls, "was that instead of landing the airplane next to the airport, Jamari landed it in the airport with a huge crash and smashed it to pieces! Three hours of building were destroyed in seconds. Then he flew his airplane right into his sister's brand-new Playmobil grocery store and just about annihilated it." Jamari's mom stared in disbelief. After everyone regained control,

Joseph had Jamari apologize and decide how he would make amends, which included rebuilding the destroyed items. Later when Jamari was out of earshot, Joseph explained that boys, especially boys with ADHD, like this type of smash-and-crash play and often act before thinking about the impact of their actions. Joseph acknowledged it was hard work, but he and his wife were continuing to work very hard at helping Jamari stop and think about consequences before he acted and needed his family's understanding.

It is up to you to decide whether or not your son would benefit from those close to him, such as grandparents, teachers, and sports coaches, knowing that he has ADHD. In many cases, the sooner you can explain ADHD to others, the sooner you will help pave your son's road to success. I have found that boys with ADHD are very sensitive to disapproval. It is almost like they have antennae that pick it up easily and are highly sensitive to it. If another adult has no understanding about ADHD, they might be harshly critical about your son's impulsiveness, rambunctiousness, or need for activity. If you're comfortable, you can have a heart-to-heart conversation about your son's ADHD, but sometimes those kinds of talks just aren't possible. Figure 3 is a sample letter you might use to explain your son's diagnosis to loved ones. Rewrite it, insert your son's name, and customize it so it has the right feel for the recipient and for your situation.

Depending on the relationships, it may be helpful to make sure significant family members have some knowledge base about ADHD, especially if they could become part of your team in helping your son learn to manage his ADHD. You might even avoid some unwanted advice from relatives if they understand how proactive you are in seeking out information. You know your family structure and dynamics and can decide if it would be helpful or not. Sometimes communicating in writing gives them time to digest the information, but you might decide it would be too formal.

Figure 3
Letter to a Family Member

Dear _____,

This isn't an easy letter to write, but it is an important one—and you're a very important person in (insert son's name)'s life. Not long ago I took _____ for a series of tests and activities to find out how he learns best and whether there were any areas of concern. The psychologist gathered input from me, from _____'s teacher, and from observing _____. Based on the evaluation results and the input from everyone, they concluded that _____ has Attention Deficit/Hyperactivity Disorder or ADHD.

There are a lot of myths about ADHD, so I wanted to make sure you have good, solid information about it. ADHD is a medical condition and one of the most well-researched childhood disorders. It is not a fad or an excuse for bad behavior or lack of motivation. His brain is wired very differently from most other children's, which means that although he's a bright boy, he'll have to work much harder than others his age at staying focused, completing tasks, and thinking before acting. Learning does not always come easily to him in all areas.

Many of our daily struggles are related to his ADHD. _____'s ADHD behaviors occur in school, at home, and with friends. This is why life is tough for him. He never gets a break from having ADHD. We've learned that _____'s brain is actually understimulated in the areas that maintain focus, deal with frustration, and apply what he knows consistently, predictably, and independently. This is why _____ can focus on something he really likes but has such a hard time focusing on things that don't interest him. It also explains why he can be so inconsistent in his behavior. It's all related to ADHD. We are now using strategies at school and at home to try to minimize the effects of _____'s ADHD to help him and the whole family. It's a long road ahead and we all need your support along the way. There will be ups and downs as we teach

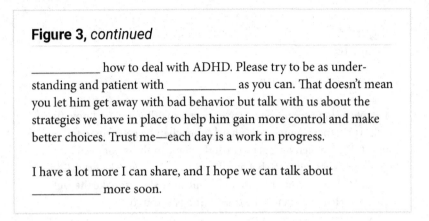

Figure 3, *continued*

_____ how to deal with ADHD. Please try to be as under-standing and patient with _____ as you can. That doesn't mean you let him get away with bad behavior but talk with us about the strategies we have in place to help him gain more control and make better choices. Trust me—each day is a work in progress.

I have a lot more I can share, and I hope we can talk about _____ more soon.

Depending on your family dynamic, you might choose to discuss your son's diagnosis in person with his siblings, share it with them in a letter, or some combination of the two. Figure 4 is an example of how you can explain ADHD to siblings. It is not uncommon for the siblings of boys with ADHD to be resentful of the additional time their parents have to spend in helping their son learn to manage his ADHD. Many times children without ADHD feel parents are being unfair because they have a different set of expectations and toler-ances. It is important to spend time with them, help them understand the problems caused by ADHD because they are often invisible, and show how everyone can work together to create a better life for the whole family.

Figure 5 is a letter a client gave to her son's first-grade teacher before the school year started. It highlighted Julian's strengths and potential areas of weakness and also offered suggestions of strategies that had proven to be effective. Each year through elementary school, they wrote a letter like this. Additionally, they met with the teacher either before the first day of school or within the first week of school. They also met with the administration in the spring to encourage Julian's placement in a classroom with a teacher who had the proven ability to work with students with ADHD for the following year.

Figure 4
Letter to a Sibling

Dear (insert sibling's name),

I want to share something very important with you. You know that (insert brother's name) has a hard time when he gets frustrated or upset. You've seen him get mad and say mean things or even hit you. He doesn't want to behave that way, but his mind works differently. He knows what he should do but can't always make the right choices. He reacts before he thinks things through.

I took _____ to a doctor who said he has Attention Deficit/ Hyperactivity Disorder or ADHD. It means his brain works differently because of its connections but not that something is wrong with his brain. This is something he was born with, and no one person or thing caused it. Lots of people have ADHD, even famous people. Some people even think Albert Einstein may have had ADHD. It's something that _____ is learning to deal with, and so are we. We are working with his teacher at school to make sure he does well there.

At home we're going to be trying some things to help _____ and everyone get along together. It's going to take a lot of work, and there are still going to be missteps along the way, but we're on the right track. You can help by being patient with _____ and guiding him to make right choices. I'm always here for any questions you have, and if you can't think of any now, you can always ask me later.

Love,
Mom/Dad

Figure 5
Letter to School/Teacher of an Elementary Student

Dear (insert teacher's name),

(Insert child's name) is outgoing and athletic. He is a gifted athlete and excels in most physical sports. This summer he learned to water-ski and got up on his third try. He loves insects and is the expert lizard catcher in our neighborhood. He also knows a lot about fishing. He really enjoys hands-on projects and kinesthetic learning.

_____ learns and remembers best when he has the opportunity to learn through multiple modes, such as hearing, seeing, and moving. He has really taken to reading using the multisensory approach based on Orton-Gillingham principles. This summer _____ worked with a tutor who uses that system, and he is good at "tapping" out sounds. Ask him to tap out a word for you like "hot" or "tub." Because of his ADHD, _____ works best when he can take short breaks during and between assignments. It may be helpful to have him repeat the instructions back to you (without embarrassing him, as he is very sensitive to criticism).

_____ has an older sister, and they get along very well. We are glad _____ is off to a great start in your class.

Sincerely,
Jack and Michelle Smith

Explaining ADHD to Your Son

You need to tell your son about his ADHD. Of course, it is up to you as to when you want to do this. You want him to understand

ADHD, but you don't want him to use it as a crutch or an excuse for failing to behave or achieve his potential.

The Younger Child

We believe you can explain ADHD to elementary-age children. Little boys I have worked with often recognize they are different than classmates in some ways and find it reassuring that difficulties they may be having can be helped and don't have anything to do with how smart they are. It opens the door for them to come to you when they have questions or are feeling confused and upset.

You may find it easier to explain by reading a children's book about ADHD to your son. Your son may identify with the book's character and realize that he is not alone with his ADHD. A book also becomes a nonthreatening way for you to have a simple conversation about school and behavior. These are a few books currently available to explain ADHD to younger boys arranged according to age:

▷ *Baxter Turns Down His Buzz: A Story for Little Kids About ADHD* (ages 4–8) by James M. Foley
▷ *Otto Learns About His Medicine: A Story About Medication for Children With ADHD* (3rd ed., ages 4–8) by Matthew R. Galvin
▷ *Sparky's Excellent Misadventures: My A.D.D. Journal, By Me (Sparky)* (ages 5–11) by Phyllis Carpenter and Marti Ford
▷ *Cory Stories: A Kid's Book About Living With ADHD* (ages 6–11) by Jeanne Kraus
▷ *Learning to Be Kind and Understand Differences: Empathy Skills for Kids With AD/HD* (ages 8–12) by Judith Glasser and Jill Menkes Kushner
▷ *Putting on the Brakes: Understanding and Taking Control of Your ADD or ADHD* (3rd ed., ages 8–13) by Patricia O. Quinn and Judith M. Stern

The Tween or Teen

If your middle school or teenage son has just been diagnosed with ADHD, you'll handle it a bit differently. Ideally, the person who officially diagnosed your son will give him an age-appropriate explanation of his ADHD. An appropriate sample might go like this:

> (Teen's name), the testing and interview you completed showed that you have quite a few strengths, and some of them include (*fill in the blank with his strengths*). The testing also showed there are some things that are much harder for you, compared with other boys your age. For example, you mentioned that it is difficult for you to (*fill in the blank: complete your homework, turn in your homework, stay seated for a length of time, remain organized, study for tests, etc.*). This difficulty is related to Attention Deficit/Hyperactivity Disorder or ADHD. Have you heard of ADHD? The evaluation confirmed that you have ADHD. This does not mean that something is wrong with your brain or that you can't be successful, but it has to do with the way your mind is wired, which causes you to have difficulty with (*fill in the blank*). This difficulty is not going to stop you from being successful in school; it won't stop you from going to college or technical school or having a good career. You can be successful, but you are often going to have to work harder than many boys. It also means that you may need more support, like having a counselor, coach, or person to help guide you. You and your family may consider trying medication to help you. The important thing for you to remember is that you can't use your ADHD as an excuse not to do well in school. As I already said, you can be successful, but it takes hard work. There are many successful men

with ADHD, such as Michael Phelps, Ty Pennington, Jim Carrey, and lots of others. What questions do you have?

If the professional you worked with did not explain ADHD to your son, you can provide the explanation, and books can fill in the gaps. Here are resources you can share with your older son:

▷ *The ADHD Workbook for Teens: Activities to Help You Gain Motivation and Confidence* by Lara Honos-Webb

▷ *ADHD and Me: What I Learned From Lighting Fires at the Dinner Table* by Blake E. S. Taylor

▷ *Learning Outside the Lines: Two Ivy League Students With Learning Disabilities and ADHD Give You the Tools for Academic Success and Educational Revolution* by Jonathan Mooney and David Cole

▷ *Take Control of ADHD: The Ultimate Guide for Teens With ADHD* by Ruth Spodak and Kenneth Stefano

Once your son understands his ADHD, he can begin to learn to work through and around it. An age-appropriate explanation provides relief for many boys and affirms that they are not weird or crazy—they just have a brain that is wired and communicates differently. The explanation and label can create understanding around your son's weaknesses so that he can move forward with an attitude of hope and optimism.

After learning about his ADHD diagnosis, 16-year-old Chad said, "It makes me feel better to know that what causes me so much trouble at school has nothing to do with how smart I am. I believed kids when they called me 'dumb' and my teachers when they said I was 'lazy.' Now I understand my difficulty with staying focused causes me to miss lots of what my teachers say and my trouble with organization causes me to miss deadlines and not turn in work."

Promoting Self-Advocacy

Self-advocacy is always very difficult, for tweens and teens especially, but it is very important. Students I work with are very reticent to approach teachers to let them know how their ADHD affects their academic work, but it can be a long-term goal to help them gain self-confidence to advocate for themselves. When you think about it, middle and high school teachers may see five or six different classrooms of students. Learning what works most effectively for each student would be an impossible task. As a rule, teachers want their students to be successful and appreciate a student taking the initiative to let them know what supports might be helpful. For example, if a student knows he gets lost in the directions, he might let the teacher know that and ask if the teacher can show an example of what the finished assignment should look like or check with him once he has started the assignment to make sure he has understood what he was expected to do. Even though this takes courage and maturity, I have occasionally had students who have asked teachers if they could come by after class to talk about their challenges and what helps them. Others are more comfortable emailing the teacher or writing a short letter of introduction and listing their challenges and modifications that help. If your son has a 504 plan or an Individualized Education Program (IEP; discussed in Chapter 6), accommodations will be listed on those documents. However, it is still better for your son to communicate directly with his teacher because the teacher might remember his needs much better than just seeing them on a document.

Sometimes teachers welcome information on managing ADHD in the classroom. It is up to you to decide if they would welcome the information or be offended by it. Chapter 4 includes helpful information you can share with your child's teacher if they are open to the information. If you think your son's teacher might appreciate it, some books are:

> ▷ *Managing ADHD in School: The Best Evidence-Based Methods for Teachers* by Russell Barkley

▷ *How to Reach and Teach Children With ADD/ADHD: Practical Techniques, Strategies, and Interventions* by Sandra Rief

Points to Consider

1. Have you accepted your son's ADHD as a disability?
2. What ADHD myths do you still believe?
3. Who will you tell about your son's ADHD, and what words will you use?
4. How will you explain ADHD to your son?

Action Steps to Take Now

1. Remember that your son has probably heard far more negative comments than positive ones. Look for areas where you can offer genuine encouragement.
2. What are your son's natural strengths or talents? List them, let him know, and post them where they are visible. Together, identify one activity or experience you can provide to build upon those strengths.
3. Write a letter about your son's ADHD and deliver it to all appropriate individuals or have a discussion with the people who need to know.
4. Begin to establish a support system for yourself by enlisting the help of caring professionals (e.g., counselors, physicians, teachers), researching the availability of any support groups, and continuing to read and learn about ADHD.

Chapter 2

Management and Treatment Options for ADHD

From the day your son is born, he is learning and picking up information from his environment. If he doesn't stay focused long enough to take in, process, and store information, his development will be negatively impacted. Likewise, if his behavior results in persistently negative interactions with those around him, his self-concept will suffer. As parents, we must try to make sure supports and treatment are in place to enable our boys to be successful while helping them to be as independent as possible.

Behavior is often one of the most difficult aspects of ADHD for parents to manage. From my work with boys with ADHD, it appears that their behavior often breaks down when the demands placed on them exceed their ability to complete the requested task. As a parent, you have seen this play out over and over. Your son melts down when he can't do something, and he doesn't yet have the skills to handle it a better way. Your son may impulsively knock his head against a table when feeling frustrated with his schoolwork because he just can't figure it out. He may become the class clown to avoid feeling dumb. Or the stress of holding himself together in school may exhaust him to the point that he becomes a little wild man at home because he just can't maintain control any longer.

As parents, we must try to make sure supports and treatment are in place to enable our boys to be successful while helping them to be as independent as possible.

There is no question that our boys with ADHD face challenges that other boys don't. A study by McConaughy and colleagues (2011) showed that 15%–55% of children with ADHD "exhibited 'clinically significant' impairment in academic performance and 26–85% exhibited 'clinically significant' impairment in social behavior, depending on the measure" (p. 221). When your son can't perform, he'll let you know in a good or bad way. Your child is fortunate to have a parent like you who is concerned enough to research and learn about the best treatment options.

You know that the subject of ADHD treatment is a highly charged topic. Strong opinions run the gamut, from those who believe medication is the only truly effective treatment to those who advocate only natural, holistic interventions, to those who support a combination of medication, environmental modification, parent training, coaching, and behavior therapy. I believe there is no one treatment that fits every boy and that often a combination of treatments works best. Every boy and the services and supports available to them are unique. Figuring out what is best for your son will require time and research but will be well worth the effort.

I am not a medical doctor and can only speak from my own personal and professional experience and my review of the literature. There is no question that medication can improve the chemical imbalance of the ADHD brain. Some parents are skeptical about the influence of the drug companies that manufacture the various medications, and others worry about the long-term effects of medication. Later in this chapter, three well-respected physicians, including a pediatrician and two psychiatrists who treat children with ADHD, provide solid information and the latest treatment approaches. Learning about treatment options will help you sort out fact from false narratives.

CHADD (n.d.-a) recommended a multipronged, comprehensive approach to dealing with ADHD dependent on your son's presentation, which can include:

▷ education regarding the ADHD diagnosis, causes, and treatment for parents and child;

▷ behavioral therapy to help manage deficits and acquire new skills if needed;

▷ medication when necessary with careful monitoring;

▷ mental health counseling if needed;

▷ parent training or coaching if needed; and

▷ educational support when needed, which could include tutoring, a 504 plan or IEP.

CHADD suggested that a comprehensive evaluation will inform you about the areas where your son needs support and that often, more than one intervention will be helpful. The treatment plan should address *each area where your son is struggling*. Some parents think that medication alone is sufficient, but it has been said time and time again that medication doesn't teach skills, which are so critical to helping our sons manage ADHD most effectively.

Starting Point

Many people who seek treatment for their son begin with their pediatrician, especially if their son has a long-standing relationship with the doctor. Pediatricians have strong knowledge of developmental sequences and see children of various ages on a daily basis. One thing to keep in mind is that your pediatrician is seeing your son in an individualized setting where little is required of him—very different from school with lots of children, noise, and demands to complete tasks that may be uninteresting to your child—so the pediatrician must consider all aspects of your son's functioning and not just the way he presents in the office. When concerns arise, some pediatricians refer to school psychologists, clinical psychologists, neuropsychologists, neurologists, developmental pediatricians, or psychiatrists. Pediatricians are often interested in knowing the level of your son's intellectual and academic functioning, as well as his executive functioning skills, in order to rule out learning problems or other issues as the root cause of the behavior. Most parents are very confused about the roles of the different specialists, so a brief overview is included in Table 2.

Many pediatricians are willing to treat a child with moderate ADHD with medication if they believe it is warranted. A developmental pediatrician would be a good choice if your son also has complicating developmental issues, such as Pervasive Developmental Disorder–Not Otherwise Specified or autism. A neurologist may be recommended if there are any concerns about brain functioning, such as seizures or tics. A psychiatrist should be consulted for complicated cases where there are accompanying problems with anxiety, mood, or oppositional behavior. All of the above have gone to medical school and can prescribe medication. A nurse practitioner may work under the direction of a doctor and also can prescribe medication.

There is no one assessment instrument that determines the presence or absence of ADHD, but a diagnosis can be made based on a comprehensive examination.

Clinical psychologists, neuropsychologists, and school psychologists approach ADHD from the functional, educational, and neurobiological aspects. They focus on the impact that the behavior has on learning and general life adjustment. Their training involves using various assessment measures to provide information on the child's

Table 2
Roles of Professionals in Treating ADHD

Specialty	Training	Function
Pediatrician	M.D. or D.O., general practitioner	Oversees wellness of children, diagnoses medical conditions, and prescribes medication
Developmental Pediatrician	M.D. or D.O., specialist in developmental issues	Is consulted for anomalies in development, diagnoses medical conditions, and prescribes medication
Neurologist	M.D. or D.O., specialist in neurology and the brain	Is consulted for neurological problems, diagnoses medical conditions, and prescribes medication
Psychiatrist	M.D. or D.O., specialist in mental disorders	Is consulted for and diagnoses behavior/mental health issues and prescribes medication
Nurse Practitioner	Advanced Practice Registered Nurse (APRN)	Works under the direction of a doctor and prescribes medication
Clinical Psychologist	Ph.D. or Psy.D.	Diagnoses conditions and provides therapy, can't prescribe medication
Neuropsychologist	Ph.D. or Psy.D.	Diagnoses conditions, often does testing, can't prescribe medication
School Psychologist	Master's, Specialist, Ph.D., or Psy.D.	Provides testing and consultation regarding problems that impact education and some can diagnose ADHD, can't prescribe medication
Licensed Clinical Social Worker	MSW or Ph.D.	Diagnoses conditions and provides therapy, can't prescribe medication

Table 2, *continued*

Specialty	Training	Function
Behavioral Therapist	Master's or Ph.D.	Provides behavioral therapy, can't prescribe medication
Coach	Training varies	Guides management of daily activities, plans for the future

functioning and clinical interviews with the child, parents, and sometimes teachers. There is no one assessment that determines the presence or absence of ADHD, but a psychologist can make a diagnosis based on a comprehensive examination, including clinical interviews and often behavior rating scales. They provide an overall picture of the child in terms of his intelligence, academic strengths and weaknesses, processing abilities, and emotional adjustment. Psychologists do not prescribe medication but often work closely with medical personnel who can. Some psychologists also provide counseling for both the child and the family as well as behavioral therapy.

A psychologist would be a good place to start if you are unsure about the role your child's intellectual functioning plays in his behavior. For example, it is not unusual for gifted children to get into trouble at home and school because they are curious about how things work or their boredom causes misbehavior as they seek out stimulation. On the other hand, some children who refuse or can't do schoolwork have a learning disability and need specialized instruction for success. Ruling out contributing problems in your child's overall picture is important.

Malik was frequently in trouble with his preschool teacher. He balked at doing routine tasks that were aimed at teaching colors and shapes. He was constantly wandering around the room. When doing a standard preschool checklist, his teachers determined that he had mastered all preschool concepts. His parents made an appoint-

ment with a school psychologist for an intellectual evaluation. He scored in the gifted range and was ultimately
placed in a more stimulating environment. His behavior
improved instantly when he had more challenging activities and peers to interact with who were on his level.

If you are concerned about the presence of a learning disability
or processing problems, a psychologist can evaluate your child's intelligence, academic skills, and processing capabilities. For example, a
child may appear to be inattentive when, in reality, he is not capable
of doing the schoolwork he has been given and feels completely lost
in the curriculum. Or a child who is not processing language may
appear to have attention issues while, in actuality, he is not following
the instructions because he doesn't understand them.

Juan never seemed to be doing what his kindergarten
teacher asked him to do. When his group was engaged
in story time, he stared around the room. When ques-
tioned about a story, his answer usually did not match the
question asked. His teacher noticed that he was much
more attentive when she used visuals. Juan received a
comprehensive neuropsychological evaluation and was
diagnosed with a learning disability as well as auditory
processing problems. His behavior improved when he
received special education services to address his learning disability and accommodate his auditory processing
difficulty. From then on, his teacher always used visuals with his instruction, spoke to him in short sentences,
and provided him with an example of what his finished
product should look like.

Licensed clinical social workers and behavior therapists may provide therapy, such as cognitive behavioral therapy, behavior modification, or family therapy. Sometimes behavior therapists work in
conjunction with the classroom teacher, providing support in imple-

menting behavior management plans designed to increase a student's motivation to comply with teacher requests and complete assigned tasks. Neither social workers nor therapists prescribe medication.

> Troung's family found help from working with a therapist. He had more difficulty at home than at school, where the structure was much tighter. His parents experienced frequent tantrums when he did not get his way, as well as dangerous, risk-taking behavior like running out into streets and climbing on furniture. They recognized that they could use some assistance in improving the way they dealt with Troung's behavior, so they contacted a therapist with training in behavior modification who assisted them in creating a more structured home environment, with consequences and incentives for behavior, and helped them improve their communication. The therapist worked with Troung on stopping and thinking before acting and learning to identify his feelings as the first step in controlling them.

A Quick Synopsis of the Two Most Widely Reported Treatment Studies

As you can imagine, research on the effectiveness of treatments for ADHD is difficult because of so many variables—control groups; ages of the subjects; type of diagnosis—predominantly inattentive, hyperactive-impulsive, or combined type; how the diagnosis was made and documented; who the respondents were who reported results; how results were collected; dosages and types of medication if used; and variables involved in therapy if used—just to name a few. One of the most widely reported studies released in 1999 that looked at psychosocial treatments (behavior therapy and community care) for ADHD with and without medication was The Multimodal Treatment Study of ADHD (MTA), which was run by the National Institute of Mental Health (NIMH, 2009). It looked at:

▷ medication only,

▷ medication plus behavior therapy,

▷ behavior therapy only, and

▷ community care and support—the control group treated with lower doses of stimulant medication.

Nearly 600 children ages 7–9 across the country were included in the study, which took place over a 14-month period. There has been much analysis of the results and some follow-up studies, but the most important findings were that medication alone was more effective than behavior therapy alone and that there were positive effects of medication in conjunction with behavior therapy (Pliszka & AACAP Work Group on Quality Issues, 2007).

NIMH (2006) also funded the Preschool ADHD Treatment Study (PATS), which involved more than 300 preschoolers who had been diagnosed with ADHD. The study found that low doses of the stimulant methylphenidate were safe and effective for preschoolers but that they were more sensitive to the side effects of the medication, including slower-than-average growth rates. If behavior is severe enough to require medication, preschoolers should be closely monitored by their doctor while taking ADHD medications.

Most physicians consider Ritalin, the drug studied in the MTA and which is a central nervous system stimulant, to be effective, safe, and to have relatively few side effects. As reported by DuPaul (2007), "Numerous studies have shown methylphenidate and amphetamine compounds to improve classroom attention, behavior control, and peer interactions as well as to enhance productivity and accuracy on academic tasks and curriculum-based measurement probes" (pp. 185–186). (Medications are discussed in depth later in the chapter by a pediatrician and two psychiatrists.)

Treatment Is Not All About Medication

The key is figuring out what the treatment plan should look like for your individual child and family based on the impact of his symptoms on his daily life. Some boys with ADHD do not have symptoms severe enough to warrant medication. Nonmedical treatments, like behavioral therapy, coaching, and/or home and classroom supports, may enable them to manage relatively well. Other boys would be doomed to failure without medication. If medication would make the difference between success and failure for your son, how could you pass on that option? Even in children who take medication, it is important to realize the value of other treatments that build skills and teach strategies as an adjunct. For example, if your child's presenting problems are significant impulsivity and hyperactivity as well as a lack of social skills, he may need social skills training in addition to medication.

One thing to keep in mind is that ADHD is a very complex disorder with unique presentations. What works for your friend's child may not work for yours. That is one reason it is so important for you to be aware of all of the supportive options for your son so that you can be an educated partner in choosing the right treatment program for him so he can develop his strengths and minimize his weaknesses.

When looking at treatment, take a deep breath and try to make the best decision you can with the information you have gleaned from trusted professionals.

For example, if your son is depressed and withdrawn, he may benefit from cognitive behavioral therapy (CBT) to teach him to look at things in a different way. If being hopelessly disorganized is part of your son's ADHD, he may need coaching to teach him some skills. At the preschool age, most practitioners agree that behavior therapy should be a key part of any boy's treatment. At this young age, it often takes the form of play therapy. Children with ADHD have varying degrees of difficulties with their executive functioning—those skills required to get tasks done—which may require the intervention of specially trained teachers or ADHD coaches if their problems are impacting their performance. Unfortunately, ADHD is often accompanied by other conditions, such as anxiety, oppositional behavior, and/or depression. When these conditions are present, they should be addressed either through counseling, behavioral therapy, medication, or a combination of several treatment strategies. Many children with ADHD also have learning disabilities and may need specialized tutoring and educational accommodations.

Studies have shown that therapy in combination with medication can result in the need for lower doses of medication (Dawson, 2007). Pelham and Fabiano (2008) found in their research that treatment does not have to center around medicine when behavior modification strategies are taught to children, parents, and teachers. There is general consensus that although medication addresses symptoms, it doesn't address specific impairments such as planning, organization, and social skill deficits. Medication can improve functioning but does not teach skills so often lacking in children with ADHD. Therefore, it is advantageous if you can work with a professional who can see your son's complete picture and help you choose the best treatment for his unique needs.

Try not to be overwhelmed, especially if your child is complex. Hopefully you can locate a trusted professional who can help you prioritize your son's needs so you don't feel you have to try to do everything at once. That would be too taxing for you and him. When looking at treatment, take a deep breath and try to make the best decision you can with the information you have gleaned from trusted professionals.

The Future of Treatment

Various studies have shown that if the correct match is made, then less intensive treatments can be as effective as more intensive ones. The goal of much of the current research is to predict which types of interventions will produce the most effective results for different types of ADHD. In other words, you want to identify your son's main challenges and then match them to the most effective treatment. Dr. Ben Vitiello (Vitiello & Sherrill, 2007) acknowledged that an important direction for research is to figure out if "it is possible to *predict* whether children with certain characteristics might benefit from certain specific treatments or to lower intensity intervention, whereas others might require different treatments or higher intensity intervention" (p. 288). Dr. Russell Barkley (2007) suggested the possibility "that different genotypes of ADHD may have different medication responses but also different responses to psychosocial treatment" (p. 284). Thus, medications and treatment for ADHD could become highly customized as more is learned about the specific genes involved.

> *The goal of much of the current research is to predict which types of interventions will produce the most effective results for different types of ADHD.*

The Bottom Line

The bottom line is that one type of treatment does not work for all boys with ADHD. Because each boy has unique characteristics, his treatment needs to be comprehensive, customized, and carefully monitored. Although researchers have documented that certain treatments work for the majority of children with ADHD, there are always exceptions.

> *Because each boy has unique characteristics, his treatment needs to be comprehensive, customized, and carefully monitored.*

As an informed parent, it will be up to you to consider the big picture—any additional problems with academic, executive functioning, language, anxiety, depression, or oppositional behavior that your son may have in addition to ADHD, as well as any family or school stressors that exist. Keep in mind that medicine in general seems to be going in the direction of very individualized treatment protocols for many types of medical conditions, and ADHD is no exception. If this is overwhelming, you may be able to identify a professional—a doctor, psychologist, or therapist—who takes the time to understand your son within the context of his family and school and select treatments that work for him and you. Try to stay informed about research underway about specific areas of the brain impacted by ADHD, as well as studies of the effectiveness of treatments and combinations of treatments. It will be up to you along with your physician as to what treatments or combinations will prove the most effective for your son.

I have found it is always very helpful to have a written plan to ensure better follow-through. Chapter 7 will help you develop a Dynamic Action Plan, which will include the support you need to obtain for your son. Sometimes it helps if you have something concrete to show for your efforts in learning all you can about ADHD and what supports will help your son maximize his skills. Lots of planning and intentional parenting can go a long way!

Advice From Doctors

Because I am not a medical doctor, I asked Dr. Tommy Schechtman, pediatrician, and Dr. Raquel Anderson, a behavioral health specialist in his office in South Florida, and Dr. Marshall Teitelbaum and Dr.

Michelle Chaney, both child, adolescent, and adult psychiatrists in Jupiter, FL, to write about medication and ADHD.

A View From the Pediatrician's Office

With Dr. Tommy Schectman and Dr. Raquel Anderson

Q: What Questions Should Parents Ask Their Pediatrician?

Dr. Schechtman and Dr. Anderson recommend that parents ask their pediatrician five important questions, and they also explain the importance of asking each question.

1. **What are the risks if I decide not to treat my child?** Everything we do in medicine should be based on constantly assessing the benefits of treatment versus potential side effects of our therapeutic interventions. Although most parents are appropriately concerned about the short-term and long-term side effects of medication, what often is not asked is, "What is the risk of not treating my son?" Not treating ADHD when it is evident can be risky. This can have a negative impact on academic performances, self-esteem, motivation, future success, and emotional stability. ADHD permeates into several areas of one's life and can impact not only your child's performance in school, but also, due to the impulsive nature of these individuals, their social skills and personal relationships. In addition, more studies show that those who go untreated have a higher propensity to self-medicate later in life. This can take the form of substance use or addiction. Most importantly, without treatment, we are depriving the child of the opportunity to meet or exceed their own expectations. When we do treat a child, we afford the child the ability to achieve their optimal success both in school and in life. When we treat a child, we do not change who they are or who they want to be, but rather provide them with the "toolkit" to maximize their potential, whatever that potential is.

2. **Are there comorbidities?** Comorbidity is the simultaneous appearance of two or more diagnoses. There are several conditions that can co-occur with ADHD. The common ones include anxiety, depression, obsessive-compulsive disorder (OCD), a tic disorder, sleep disturbances, learning disabilities, and oppositional defiant disorder (ODD). For example, one might meet the diagnostic criteria for ADHD and anxiety. Some comorbidities happen alongside the diagnosis of ADHD and are separate from it. Some comorbidities are caused by the ADHD and may go away, or the symptoms may disappear, when the individual is adequately treated for ADHD. When there is a separate or underlying issue in addition to the diagnosis of ADHD, this is a more complicated issue and requires a different approach to address all of the presenting issues.

3. **What happens when my child does not respond to medication?** If your child appears to not be responding to the medication prescribed, there are several possible explanations. First of all, this may indicate that the right dose has not been achieved yet. This may require the medication be titrated up to reach optimal clinical effectiveness. Secondly, this could indicate that this is not the right type of medication. There are two forms of medication to consider in the treatment of ADHD, stimulants and nonstimulants. Stimulants have been shown to be the most clinically effective and are commonly used as a first course of treatment. If your child is experiencing severe mood changes or increased anxiety, for example, this may be an indication that there is a separate comorbidity at play that needs to be addressed and treated in addition to or separately from ADHD.

4. **How are you going to monitor my child's progress?** It is important to have routine periodic visits with your child's physician while they are regularly taking any form of medication. It is always important to monitor the child's growth and development as well as their vitals throughout the course of

treatment. Also, we should never expect "perfect" results, but neither should you accept "good" results. Your doctor should be constantly monitoring and assessing your child's progress. Each child responds differently to different medications, and your child's regimen needs to be custom tailored for them in order to achieve "great" results.

5. **On what evidence are you basing the ADHD diagnosis?** Oftentimes a diagnosis of ADHD is made or assumed by an individual who is untrained or unqualified to do so. When it has been suggested to you that your child may have attention issues, make sure you address this from a comprehensive approach. Although there are several national standardized tests (e.g., Vanderbilt, Connors) for ADHD, these are not perfect assessment tools. There are not any blood or imaging (X-rays) tests or physical exam findings that help with the diagnosis. The diagnosis is one of exclusion (ruling out other neurological, physical, and psychological disorders), and one of profiling of commonly associated symptoms (e.g., lack of focus and short-term memory, poor organizational skills, impulsivity). The diagnosis needs to be made by a qualified and experienced mental health professional and/or a physician. However, because ADHD can permeate into so many areas of one's life, it is recommended to seek the service of both. Ideally it would be best if these professionals had access to each other so that there could be the best coordination of treatment.

Q: How Do You Explain to Parents How Stimulants Work?

Many parents are confused about how stimulants work for their already hyperactive or distracted child, and they are apprehensive to use them. This is a complex decision and understandably a difficult one to make. Parents rightly should seek all of the answers they need to make a confident decision. Part of having that confidence is partnering with a physician and mental health provider who can educate you and walk with you through the diagnosis and treatment process. We try to explain the mechanics of the use of stimulant medication for the treatment of ADHD in very simplistic terms. The ADHD brain craves to be stimulated due to deficiencies or developmental issues. That is why children are so easily distracted or appear to be hyperactive. These are the ways that the brain is attempting to get the stimulation it needs. When we can satisfy the brain's craving through medication, the brain can then focus on the material at hand (e.g., the teacher's lecture, the book your child is reading, the test they are taking). ADHD does not affect one's ability or intellect. Take, for example, a child who wears glasses. We can all agree that wearing glasses does not affect the student's ability to read or their intellect. When they remove their glasses, they have not lost the ability to read nor has their IQ dropped, but they can no longer read the words on the page. The student's glasses are the tool their eyes need to focus on the paper they are reading or object they are looking at. In the same way, stimulant medications are a tool used to help the individual focus on the task at hand.

A View From the Psychiatrist's Office

With Dr. Marshall Teitelbaum

Q: Is Medication for ADHD Essential?

Whether medication is necessary is often perceived as controversial. Usually the decision is clinically straightforward, however. The issue is truly more one of evaluating what the true diagnoses are first, if ADHD is either *the* diagnosis or among the diagnoses, and how the symptoms are interfering in the boy's life. If there are biologically associated diagnoses present, such as obsessive-compulsive disorder, a chronic tic disorder (including Tourette syndrome), or bipolar disorder, then consideration has to be given toward the potential risk of using a medication for ADHD in combination with the related condition. If there are behaviorally associated comorbid conditions present, such as oppositional defiant disorder, conduct disorder traits, and/or low self-esteem/depressive disorders, then the likelihood of a more aggressive measure, such as using medication, becomes practically essential. The bottom line is that ADHD presents differently in different folks, and how it specifically is affecting the given person is what needs to be considered the most when it comes to treatment decisions. If there are significant effects, or a near-term expectation of one or more of these, on behavioral, social, or academic function, the ADHD symptoms have to be addressed immediately. The goal is to avoid the future consequences for what happens if these problems are allowed to evolve, such as lower school and/or career achievement, higher risk for legal or substance abuse problems, more relationship challenges, and more injuries, ER visits, and moving traffic violations. In other words, we all worry about the potential risks of medications, but we also have to worry about the potential risks of not using medications. There are a number of ADHD medications available, which I will summarize here.

ADHD medications are primarily categorized into two groups, *stimulants* and *nonstimulants*. The FDA-approved nonstimulants are Strattera (atomoxetine), Intuniv (long-acting guanfacine), and Kapvay (long-acting clonidine formulation). These options are typically slower to take effect and less potent, although they can be used in combination with stimulants when necessary to augment treatment, as well as to assist with later day stimulant rebound. All except atomoxetine are based on alpha-2 agonist blood pressure medications that have been used for years off label to treat ADHD, but longer acting versions came out on label and with greater ease of use (as the prior ones often required three to four dosages per day). The alpha-2 agonists can be helpful with ADHD-associated insomnia and tic disorders, thus assisting when this genetically linked condition is part of the equation. Given the potential for blood pressure effects, they have to be increased slowly and, after having been used for a sufficient length of time, have to be reduced gradually. Atomoxetine works by way of blocking uptake of the neurotransmitter norepinephrine. Any of the medications described here can be of value if a stimulant is not considered a safe medical option or if the necessary adequate dosage of stimulant medication is not tolerable, thus sometimes requiring a combination.

The stimulant medications are the more well-known FDA-approved ADHD treatments. This class is predominantly broken down into two types, those related to methylphenidate (i.e., Ritalin) or amphetamine (i.e., Adderall or Dexedrine). They all tend to cause appetite suppression, but for most children, it can be managed well with the appropriate interventions.

Methylphenidate-based medications include shorter acting (usually no more than 4 hours) and longer acting (upward of 8 hours) medications. The shorter acting medicines include methylphenidate (Ritalin) and dexmethylphenidate (Focalin).

The longer acting methylphenidates include Concerta, Ritalin LA, Metadate CD/ER, Ritalin SR, Aptensio XR, Adhansia XR, Jornay PM, Cotempla XR-ODT, Quillivant, Quillichew, and Daytrana, along with the related dexmethylphenidate (the right chemical half of the methylphenidate molecule), Focalin XR. Daytrana is a patch that goes on the hip, rotating sites daily to lessen the risk of skin irritation. It can allow for better morning symptom management if applied while your son is still in bed, and it can allow more active management of the wear-off time based on when it is removed, regardless of the time it is applied (e.g., if you have a teenager who likes to sleep in on weekends). Jornay PM is provided at night with the goal of delaying its effect until the next morning while still having a full day of efficacy. Concerta, Ritalin LA, Metadate CD, Aptensio XR, Adhansia XR, Cotempla XR-ODT, Quillivant XR, Quillichew XR, and Focalin XR are medications with differing delivery technologies that increase the likelihood of ongoing benefit throughout the day. Concerta may last longer for some, although Focalin XR may kick in faster. There are various deliveries with fruit flavorings, such as dissolving in the mouth rapidly (Cotempla XR-ODT), liquid (Quillivant XR), and chewable (Quillichew XR). There are others that can be opened and sprinkled, such as Focalin XR, Adhansia XR, and Aptensio XR. The goal for many is to make dosing easier if unable to swallow pills, but some can also allow easier finessing of dosages for those who do best on "in-between" strengths. The times of day that require better medication coverage need to be kept in mind when using these.

Shorter acting (up to 4 hours) amphetamine-based medications (admit it—the name is scary) include Adderall (mixed dextroamphetamine at 75% and levoamphetamine at 25% salts), Evekeo (regular and orally disintegrating tablets with mix of 50/50 proportion of dextroamphetamine and levoamphetamine salts, and for some may have a longer duration), Dexedrine (dextroamphetamine), Zenzedi (dextroamphetamine), and ProCentra (liquid dextroamphetamine), with ProCentra being useful at times for kids who cannot swallow pills. Longer acting versions include Adderall XR, Dexedrine spansule, Vyvanse (capsule and chewable versions), Dyanavel XR, and Adzenys ER and XR-ODT. The longer acting medications are more likely to allow better full-day coverage, with Dexedrine spansule typically lasting 6–8 hours, Vyvanse lasting from 10–14 hours, and the others usually being effective for 10–12 hours. Vyvanse is a prodrug, meaning it is turned into its active product (lisdexamfetamine into dextroamphetamine) only after the body begins to metabolize it. Some can be opened and sprinkled into food, such as Adderall XR and Dexedrine spansule, although typically this should be done in a tablespoon to ensure full medication ingestion. Vyvanse capsules can be opened while pouring the powder into a few ounces of water, yogurt, or orange juice to dissolve. For those with difficulty swallowing who don't want to open capsules, Vyvanse also has a chewable version, Dyanavel XR is available in liquid (allowing greater ease for those needing unusual dosages), and Adzenys XR-ODT dissolves rapidly in the mouth.

As I'm prone to reminding parents, nonschool hours are often as or more important, as these can be times of higher risk. Driving while distracted can be a major danger, for instance, and the GPA is irrelevant when someone is in the emergency room. There can be more difficulty getting homework completed independently, social disruption, family conflict, defiance, higher risk behavior experimentation, and self-esteem problems, with all over time leading to much larger challenges, even if only occurring a few hours per day or a few days per week.

There are a variety of other medication classes still being researched, as well as medications that are used for off-label treatment (medications that are thought to be of value at times but that are not formally approved by the FDA for the given medical indication) of ADHD. It is always of the utmost importance that the risks for both treating and not treating ADHD medically are fully explored to help dictate the appropriate treatment course.

Q: How Do You Know When to Stop Using ADHD Medications With Your Son?

The issue of knowing if or when it might make sense to stop ADHD medication is often quite challenging to decide, especially if the boy is doing well.

There are many considerations. First, if your son is on a faster acting medication such as a psychostimulant, have there been days of missed dosages, and if so what transpired on these days? If the boy had a miserable day with the original symptoms of ADHD seen prior to medication initiation, in all likelihood the medication needs to be continued. If he has been doing really well for an extended time, it is usually wise to reassess the medication need at least annually, and usually at a time when it would be the least problematic if reduction causes symptom recurrence. For instance, stopping a boy's medication just prior to final exams or some other type of big event would be silly. Often lowering the dosage when there is less going on at school, and possibly with the teacher's awareness, makes it easier to assess the efficacy. Other times it can be less risky to reduce when school is out, although if the main issues of ADHD are on the inattentive (vs. impulsive) spectrum, it can be more challenging to evaluate.

The most important issues have to do whether the symptoms of ADHD are still there, which is usually the case to at least some degree for the majority of affected individuals, and what ways the residual symptoms are still interfering. A boy who has problems with socialization or behavior when off of medication is likely to have a variety of problems if taking an extended break from medication over the summer, for instance. If he is either having no further life interferences without medication or is having minimal enough disturbance that can be addressed in other ways (e.g., organizational coaching, psychotherapy), then it may be reasonable to stop medication.

It is hard being a parent. It is even harder when you have a son with ADHD, as often you do not get the support of others like you do with a child with other medical problems. However, it is your responsibility to make the decisions that are in the best interest of your child, regardless of whether they are easy or popular. I often compare the condition to severe allergy or vision problems, as none are thought of as immediately life threatening, but the quality of life and potential risks going forward, if ignored, can be severe. If the medical issue is interfering with your son's life, then it is your responsibility as a parent to make decisions, even those that you do not like. Keep in mind that your son is not choosing to have ADHD (i.e., be distracted, disorganized, hyperactive). So, take advantage of all of the resources that this modern society has to offer!

A View From the Psychiatrist's Office

With Dr. Michelle Chaney

Q: Can You Explain How the Two Different Classes of Medications, Stimulants and Nonstimulants, Work?

Stimulant medications appear to normalize biochemistry in the parts of the brain involved with ADHD. When a child takes a stimulant, the neurotransmitters dopamine and norepinephrine are released more effectively. Stimulant medications enhance nerve-to-nerve communication by making more neurotransmitters available to boost the signal between neurons. In addition, they block the recycle mechanism or reuptake of the sending nerve cell, leading to an accumulation of the neurotransmitter. Overall, enhancement of dopamine and norepinephrine actions in certain brain regions are thought to improve attention, concentration, and wakefulness, as well as decrease hyperactivity.

The nonstimulant treatments vary in their mechanism of action. Strattera (atomoxetine) is a highly specific presynaptic (sending neuron) noradrenergic reuptake inhibitor. This ultimately makes more norepinephrine available for nerve-to-nerve communication. The alpha agonist medications (including guanfacine and clonidine) have action on receptors in the prefrontal cortex of the brain, which is thought to be responsible for modulation of working memory, attention, impulse control, and planning.

Q: Could You Provide Information About Comorbidities Often Seen in Boys With ADHD?

Comorbidities are often seen in boys with ADHD, as approximately 75% of children diagnosed with ADHD have at least one additional mental health or learning disorder during their lifetimes (American Academy of Child and Adolescent Psychiatry & American Psychiatric Association, 2013). Some of the more common comorbidities include oppositional defiant disorder, learning and language disorders, anxiety disorders, Tourette syndrome, and depressive disorders. These comorbidities are diagnosed by having a comprehensive evaluation by a skilled practitioner, who is often a psychiatrist, a neurologist, a clinical psychologist, or a neuropsychologist depending on the presenting symptoms. Only psychiatrists and neurologists can prescribe medication, but they often work collaboratively with clinical psychologists and neuropsychologists. Typically this evaluation will include an extensive diagnostic interview and may incorporate rating scales, often completed by the child's parents and teachers. Because many psychiatric conditions have symptoms that can overlap (e.g., poor concentration may be seen in an individual struggling with depression and anxiety as well as with ADHD), it may be beneficial to treat the condition that appears to be having the greatest adverse effect first and then reassess. Psychological testing can be important to better understand emotional and cognitive functioning as well as possible learning disorders.

Thanks to Drs. Schechtman, Anderson, Teitelbaum, and Chaney for sharing their valuable insight with us. It's not often that a parent is afforded the time during their son's doctor's visit to learn this type of information because many doctors are pressed for time. And even if we had the time to hear this from a doctor, it would be too much to quickly take in, so it is nice to have an explanation in writing to read and reference as needed.

Really, Should I Medicate My Son?

Some risk accompanies almost all medications, and most have some side effects, which can usually be managed. Concerns parents sometimes have about medication for ADHD include decreased appetite, impacted sleep, growth retardation, potential for addiction, and heart problems. These concerns are understandable, but having good medical information from research and your doctor can alleviate some of the concerns and allow you to weigh the benefits against the side effects.

Issues with appetite can often be addressed by working with your doctor on timing of medication, dosages, and/or adding calories. Insomnia may be addressed through helping your child establish an appropriate routine conducive to sleep prior to bedtime, such as limiting screen time or exciting activities, and/or consulting your physician.

Much research has been done on the issue of growth retardation. Brown (2017) summed up some of the research on children on ADHD medication and their delays in reaching their full height: "Most of those delays were minor and transient, involving differences of 1 centimeter or less, relative to predicted height for age, differences that almost always disappear in later childhood or adolescence" (p. 199). Brown recommended having your son's height and weight monitored while on medication, and modifications to treatment investigated if your son is very small for his age.

Numerous studies have *not* found increased risk of drug abuse by those who were taking their stimulant medication properly as prescribed. According to Chang et al. (2014), "If anything, the data suggested a long-term protective effect on substance abuse." Many believe that proper treatment with medication when needed leads to improved self-esteem and better overall functioning, which can be protective factors against self-medication and use of illicit drugs.

Large-scale studies have reviewed the possibility that medications for ADHD might be related to cardiovascular problems. In discussing his review of research related to this topic, Brown (2017) said, "Results provided no evidence for increased risk of cardiovascular problems among those treated with ADHD medications." Certainly if your child has any cardiac defects or a family history of any, you could ask your doctor about ordering an electrocardiogram (EKG) before starting stimulant medication.

Many parents I have worked with have grappled with medication's side effects and ultimately concluded that the discomfort of the side effects was worth the gain they saw in their son. If your son is not thriving and is having a tough time with attention and focus, why wouldn't you work with a trusted physician to find a solution?

Jack and his wife, Susan, were confronted with the dilemma about whether or not to use medication when Timmy was diagnosed at age 6. They asked themselves, "Should we medicate our 6-year-old?" They considered two main factors before making the decision to try medication. First, Timmy was aware that he was getting in trouble from his teacher. Second, his inability to concentrate was affecting his learning, and he was falling behind in reading. After consulting with the pediatrician, a medication trial was started. Right away Timmy's teacher noticed an improvement in his behavior and schoolwork. The Friday after he started the medication Susan was helping in the class and a student spontaneously said, "Timmy's mom, he hasn't been getting in trouble lately." Even his peers noticed the improvement. So, despite initial hesitations, medication helped Timmy improve his confidence, behavior, and academics.

If your child is or may soon be taking medication, an honest discussion with your doctor is important so that they can explain the cautions and help you feel comfortable with your decision. There's no doubt that you have already been influenced by the media, family, and friends, so it is important to seek the best available medical advice you can. Be sure to ask your doctor for any clarification you may need, so you are not worrying needlessly about questions that could be answered. If you choose medication, be assured that there is much research to back up its benefits and safety when it is prescribed judiciously and carefully monitored by you and your physician.

An honest discussion with your doctor is important so that they can explain the cautions and help you feel comfortable with your decision.

As a concerned parent myself, I am presenting the facts to you as straightforwardly as I can, but it is your decision. My perception is that some mainstream media can sometimes portray ADHD medication in an unfavorable way when the reality is that medication helps a lot of boys work up to their potential. I know this from my professional and personal experiences.

When to Stop Medication

Dr. Teitelbaum provided some good advice for you to consider (see p. 63). Some families I have worked with are reluctant to start medication because they don't want their sons to take it forever. It is hard for a doctor to predict the long-term need for medication because it is dependent on so many things—maturation, effectiveness of interventions and accommodations provided, degree of development in executive functioning skills, situational demands, and your son's motivation. I have seen boys who have learned to use strategies effectively, relied on their strengths to supplement their weaknesses, and found themselves in supportive educational environments where they no longer needed medication in their current situation. When demands increased, such as when they entered high school or started college, some found they needed to restart medication until they could learn to handle their responsibilities. On the other hand, there are others who need to continue medication into adulthood in order to be successful. Of course, medication isn't something that you and your son should start and stop without medical supervision.

One colleague and her husband had expended lots of time and effort in getting their son, John, the help he needed for his ADHD, combined type. He had a comorbid reading disorder and had had years of specialized reading instruction, which had brought him to grade level. They had identified his weaknesses in getting his assignments done on time and keeping up with his belongings and had been proactive in helping him learn to use organizational strategies to improve in those areas. He had accommodations at school through a 504 plan. They communicated with their doctor about their desire for John to have a trial of stopping his medication to see how it worked. The doctor agreed that with the type of medication John was taking, he could not take it on weekends, holidays, and during the summer leading up to his sixth-grade year. It went fairly smoothly, but they and the doctor felt John needed to restart the medication at a reduced dosage when school started. He continued on the medication when school was in session but did not take it on weekends or holidays. They decided to stop having him take any medication altogether near the end of his sixth-grade year after a successful transition to middle school. They considered the following points when deciding when to stop ADHD medication:

1. Was he mature enough to try going without medication?
2. Were the side effects of medication worth the benefit?
3. How were his grades?
4. How was his school and home behavior?
5. What was he saying about how it helped?
6. What was he like when the medication wore off?
7. If he stopped now, would he have to start again later?
8. What did the medical doctor say about stopping?

If you feel that your son's functioning and self-control have improved to the point you could consider stopping the medication, talk to the prescribing doctor. During this process, one thing I advise parents against doing is stopping medication just because your son puts up a fuss when it is time to take his medication or if he complains that he doesn't want to take it anymore. Boys can be compelling and badgering, but this alone is not a valid reason to cease treatment. I recommend that there be a medical reason or other compelling reasons to stop. If your son is resisting, often the doctor can help work through problems he may be experiencing with the medication. I have also seen ADHD coaches and therapists help a reluctant teen understand the benefits of medication and assist them in developing a plan to get off the medication responsibly with the assistance of their doctor.

If you desire more information about medication, the following resources are very helpful:

> *Outside the Box: Rethinking ADD/ADHD in Children and Adults* (2017) by Thomas E. Brown (especially the chapter entitled "Practical Aspects of Medication Treatments for ADHD," which provides a good explanation about how medications work), and

▷ *Straight Talk About Psychiatric Medications for Kids* (4th ed., 2016) by Timothy E. Wilens and Paul G. Hammerness.

Nonmedical Treatments: Evidence-Based Interventions to Improve Behavior and Functioning

Counseling, coaching, parent training, and behavioral and academic interventions at home and in school can be highly effective components of your son's treatment, depending on his needs. Numerous studies have verified the benefit of such interventions. For example, Pelham and Fabiano (2008) noted studies that show the value of behavior-related therapies and parent training. When you consider the nature of ADHD with accompanying deficits in many areas of executive functioning, it is very logical that these types of interventions could be advantageous. Some or all of them may be helpful at various times in your journey to help your son be the best he can be. In my work, I have seen very positive results from counseling, coaching, parent training, and school supports, especially when tailored to the boy's specific needs. Your journey can be complicated enough; you don't need to go it alone without support if you can have access to help. There are costs associated with some of them, some of which may be covered by some insurance, but there are also several supports available for free.

> *Your journey can be complicated enough; you don't need to go it alone without support if you can have access to help.*

Counseling

Many boys with ADHD, especially those with self-esteem issues or an explosive temper or depression, find help working with a counselor or mental health therapist. If your son has been diagnosed with anxiety, a behavior disorder, or some other mental health issue, counseling may be especially critical. Sometimes it is much more appealing to a boy if he thinks of the therapist as a "coach"—especially if he is involved in sports and understands a coach's role in improving performance. If your child is younger, the sessions will be structured around play therapy rather than talk-centered. Keys to success will be having a counselor with a good knowledge base about ADHD and how it can impact functioning and one who can connect with your son. Sometimes you have to try several different counselors to find the right fit for your son and your family.

Although counseling does not cure ADHD, it can teach boys how to better manage their ADHD. Counseling often helps boys whether or not they are taking ADHD medication. Those taking ADHD medications still need to learn how to harness their strengths and work with their ADHD. I have said many times, "Pills don't teach skills." Medication alone won't teach your son the valuable life skills he'll need for success, so that's why counseling can be an effective treatment. Because each boy is unique, your son will have his own specific needs. Many boys use counseling to learn how to develop and maintain a positive mindset, appropriately express their frustrations, and/or deal with anger. What skills could your son use help developing?

In my experience, parents typically seek counseling when they feel they have done everything they know how to do, yet there are still problems. When your son's challenges reach crisis level, it may prompt you to reach out for a professional's support. As one mom told me, "I just couldn't take one more phone call from the school telling me about his bad behavior. I had to do something." It is often more advantageous to seek counseling when problems first begin cropping up rather than waiting until they have reached a flash point and your son's self-esteem has been damaged. Habits develop quickly.

Remember that it is much easier to change behavior before it becomes an ingrained pattern. To have the most benefit, counseling usually involves you, your son, and the immediate family. One benefit of counseling is that families often figure out some of their own solutions when talking about things with a nonjudgmental third party.

Types of Counseling. There are several types of counseling, including cognitive behavioral therapy (CBT), dialectical behavior therapy (DBT), and school counseling.

Cognitive Behavioral Therapy. CBT is one of the most common therapeutic approaches used with those with ADHD. It is based on the premise that a person's thoughts, not external events or people, cause feelings and behaviors. The goal is to change behavior by changing thoughts about what is happening. Cognitive behavioral therapy has a solid research base and is short term, goal oriented, and instructive. It can be as short as 12 weeks or as long as a year or more, depending on motivation to change and circumstances that brought your son to therapy. During counseling, boys are taught how to identify and express concerns, problem solve, and apply what they learned. The sessions also involve the boy evaluating how well he applied the newly learned skill. As part of the counseling process, parents also learn how to change their thoughts and behavior.

Dialectical Behavior Therapy. DBT includes mindfulness; emotional regulation, including developing tolerance of uncomfortable feelings; and interpersonal effectiveness. Both CBT and DBT are behaviorally focused therapies, but DBT also adds the mindfulness component. Like CBT, DBT can be anywhere from 12 weeks to a year. It may also involve some group therapy.

School Counseling. Some schools have mental health counselors, guidance counselors, or school psychologists who offer some counseling, whether individual or group, at no cost. It may be more generic, of shorter duration, and focus more on school-related issues than outside counseling. Mental health seems to be becoming more of a priority in schools following the increased incidences of depression and anxiety in the general population, so be sure to inquire about any supports available at your school, especially if your son is having difficulty, primarily at school.

Finding the Right Counselor. A secret to making counseling work for you and your son is finding the right match between your son and his counselor. Having a strong relationship will make or break how well his counseling works. Therefore, you must talk to the counselor about this from the start. You should know after three or four sessions if it's the right pairing. Ask your son questions such as, "How do you like the counselor? Do you feel like the counselor listens to and understands you? Are you becoming comfortable talking to the counselor?" Likewise, ask the counselor if your son is expressive, open, and honest. From this point you can make the decision to stay or find another counselor. Please don't give up if the first or even second counselor you try isn't the right match if your son really needs counseling. These are questions to ask when choosing a counselor for your son:

▷ What is your philosophy toward helping make meaningful change?
▷ What type of counseling is used?
▷ Is there a specific curriculum?
▷ How long does the average client remain in counseling?
▷ What are common causes for leaving?
▷ What is the most frequent age range of boys you counsel?
▷ How are parents and/or family involved?
▷ Do you communicate with teachers or school staff if we give permission?

The goal of counseling is to help children with ADHD learn to manage their emotions.

One parent of an 8-year-old told me, "I feel lost as a parent. I feel like I can't get control of his behavior. He's out of control, I'm not in control, and I'm not sure how to rein in his behavior." In this case,

Joey's behavior was much worse at home than at school because he responded to the tightly structured environment provided for him at school and had strong academic skills. His family was reluctant to engage in family therapy but realized they had no other choice if they were to help Joey. They chose a counselor who used dialectical behavior therapy because they felt the mindfulness component would resonate with Joey. His parents were not organized people themselves but realized they had to "tighten up" their ship, provide consistency, and hold Joey accountable for his behavior. It went against their nature to be so scheduled, but they knew it was what Joey needed. They found that the techniques they had used when he was younger no longer worked, so they had to acquire new tools and strategies. They learned he needed cues and prompts to guide his behavior. Even these didn't always work but were generally helpful.

To summarize, counseling is a proven way for your son to learn to manage his ADHD and build a skill set for life. The goal of counseling is to help children with ADHD learn to manage their emotions. Goals would be for them to stay calm and in control, have a plan in place to manage their impulsivity, and avoid situations that bring on misbehavior. If you have tried it in the past and it didn't work for your son, perhaps it wasn't the right time for your son to take advantage of it or wasn't the right counselor. Don't give up on it all together if it sounds like something he may still need.

Coaching

Coaching generally deals with more practical aspects of management of ADHD and involves assistance with tasks, such as organization, scheduling, goal setting, and time management. Research (Kubik, 2010; Merriman & Codding, 2008) indicates that it is an effective and complementary approach for helping people with ADHD develop or improve these skills so necessary for success in everyday life. Older elementary students, teenagers, and adults are the most likely candidates to find success with coaching. Coaching is often more action oriented than counseling and is most effective when the boys are motivated to make changes in their daily life and don't have emotional problems that would be better served through counseling. It is often of shorter duration than counseling, depending on the issues involved and your son's willingness to implement strategies. The coach will often assist the person with ADHD in breaking down tasks into short-term goals and will check in frequently to see how the person is progressing toward those goals. If coaching isn't available in your area or if you feel it may be more beneficial because of travel time or preference, many coaches offer video-based coaching. Impact Parents is a comprehensive resource for parents offering virtual group coaching as well as parent training, which is referenced in the later section on parent training.

Coaching as an industry has been evolving over time and becoming more organized and consistent in delivery. As noted, it can be in person or accessed virtually. There are now several organizations involved in disseminating research and information about coaching and, most importantly, establishing certification and delivering training for coaches. Some of the organizations offering coach training and certification are ADD Coach Academy, JST Coaching & Training, and ADHD Coaches Organization. Some programs confer titles like Professional ADHD Coach, which means that the coach has met the requirements of the International Coaches Federation and has additional hours in ADHD-specific training. Jodi Sleeper-Triplett is a nationally recognized authority on ADHD coaching and authored a valuable book entitled *Empowering Youth With ADHD: Your Guide to Coaching Adolescents and Young Adults for Coaches, Parents, and Professionals.*

Like with finding a counselor, you should interview the coach to ensure they are trained, have an understanding of ADHD and accompanying executive functioning problems, can address your son's issues in a way that will resonate with him, and will develop a plan so you can monitor progress. Make sure to ask questions like:

▷ What is your training specific to coaching ADHD?

▷ How many boys with ADHD have you worked with, and can you provide some examples of successes you have had?

▷ Describe your approach and how you monitor progress.

▷ What changes could I expect to see in my son?

▷ Do you offer check-ins between sessions through texts or calls if needed to prompt boys to change their patterns?

▷ How do you communicate progress with parents, and will we be involved in the coaching?

▷ What are your fees?

Counseling or Coaching for Low Motivation

When parents and teachers come to me for help I often hear them describe the boy with ADHD as unmotivated, lazy, not applying himself, or having no interest in school. Some counselors or coaches are very effective in helping boys with these issues individually and in small groups to improve their academic motivation.

A helpful book for these types of counseling or coaching sessions is *Enhancing Academic Motivation: An Intervention Program for Young Adolescents* by Norman Brier (2010). It was designed for classroom use for children in grades 5–8 but can be adapted for younger students and could be used by a parent. This book contains 16 lessons on goal setting, discussion, role-plays, and homework—things boys need to work on after the session. This program also has a parent component so parents can reinforce the information their son has learned. This program works well because its format is not what a boy typically thinks about when he hears he is going to counseling or coaching. Most boys perceive counseling as it is seen in the movies, with the patient lying on a sofa talking to a counselor. This book's lessons are interactive and engage boys in a way that seems to make the time pass quickly. Boys who are initially reluctant to participate in counseling may end up looking forward to the sessions.

Parent Training

If you are like most parents of boys with ADHD, you cannot even begin to count the times you have thrown your hands up in dismay at the daunting task of parenting. You want the best for your son but are at a loss as to how to make that happen. Dr. Phyllis Teeter (1998), author of *Interventions for ADHD: Treatment in Developmental Context*, suggested that parent training will be essential, especially to increase the likelihood that your child will comply with your rules and structure. She noted the purpose of the programs was to "incorporate techniques to improve parent-child interactions, to decrease noncompliance and to facilitate family communication patterns" (p. 155). Elaine Taylor-Klaus's (2020) book *The Essential Guide to Raising Complex Kids With ADHD, Anxiety, and More* focuses on supporting parents as they develop a "coach approach" in collaborating with their children to create a more peaceful household. How many times have you wished for just one skill that would make you feel like you had some impact on your son's behavior?

> *Your son needs to know you want the best for him and will never give up on helping him develop his strengths.*

You may be surprised to realize that your knowledge about ADHD and how it impacts your son's functioning is a very important part of his treatment plan. After all, you are with him probably more than anyone else. The structure you provide for him when he can't provide it for himself, your knowledge about what behavior he is able to control and where he still needs support, and your ability to help him problem solve will be invaluable. And don't underestimate the value of the relationship you build with him. He needs to know you want the best for him and will never give up on helping him develop his strengths and determining how to manage the challenges ADHD brings to his life.

Fortunately, parent training to assist in the understanding and management of ADHD is widely available online. Some in-person training may be available in your community, often offered through schools or other organization supportive of children. The following is a list of a number of resources, some of which are free.

▷ **Children and Adults With Attention-Deficit/Hyperactivity Disorder (CHADD)** (https://chadd.org) is a nonprofit organization that disseminates information about ADHD and offers a number of parent resources, including e-learning, webinars, virtual support groups for dads, and in-person training, and a valuable resource directory of coaches, psychologists, and other services. The National Resource Center on ADHD (NRC) is a program of CHADD that provides updated, evidence-based information on ADHD.

▷ **ADDitude** (https://www.additudemag.com) disseminates information on ADHD and related conditions and offers webinars, a magazine, and many articles and videos on behavior, schooling, treatments, and parenting.

▷ **Impact Parents** (https://impactparents.com/help-for-parents) is a coaching and advocacy program that offers Sanity School modules for parent learning, as well as group and individual coaching, home study, videos, webinars, and blogs.

▷ **Triple P Parenting** (https://www.triplep-parenting.com/us/triple-p) is a self-directed, evidence-based program parents can do online. It provides guidance in preventing and treating behavioral problems in children and teens.

▷ **Incredible Years Parenting Program** (http://www.incredibleyears.com/programs/parent) is an online program out of Australia designed to treat behavior and emotional problems in children from birth through age 12. It does not specifically address ADHD, but does have a program called Stepping Stones Triple P designed for parents of children with disabilities.

▷ **Parent-Child Interaction Therapy** (http://www.pcit.org) is an international evidence-based program designed for children ages 2–7 with behavior problems whereby a therapist coaches parents in interactions with their child through play and behavior therapy.

Treatments Considered Alternative or Requiring More Research

The media is full of claims for the effectiveness of treatments, such as omega-3 supplements, diets, computer training programs including working memory training, and neurofeedback, on ADHD. In 2020, the U.S. Food and Drug Administration (FDA) even approved an interactive video game called EndeavorRx under an emergency release, which has a randomized controlled trial to support its effectiveness. Often testimonials and research are included for many of these areas, but current *peer-reviewed* research does not yet widely support these treatments. Some of these are gaining in popularity and may be promising in the future, so continue following the research.

Neurofeedback/Biofeedback

Neurofeedback (also called EEG biofeedback or biofeedback) is a type of brain exercise or training based on the premise that people can learn to control brain wave patterns and thus impact their inattention, hyperactivity, and impulsivity. Simply stated, the goal is to mediate the symptoms of ADHD by decreasing theta (slow) waves often seen during daydreaming and increasing beta (fast) waves present when a person is thinking and interacting with their environment, often through specialized games. Electrodes are attached to the head or to a cap to monitor wave patterns while the subject engages in a computer-based activity designed to teach them how to alter their brain rhythms. The subject is notified through beeps or a visual when they have reached a desired level. The goal is to teach the subject how to become aware of and modify their brain rhythms with the goal of normalizing them. The hope would be that children can translate this to their everyday environment to improve behavior and schoolwork by normalizing their brain rhythms.

But does it work? That answer depends on who you ask and what research studies support their claims. There have been and continue to be many studies in many different countries that show mixed results. Historically, concerns about the studies have focused on inadequate research methodology, such as too few children in the sample sizes, lack of a randomized design, inadequate control group, and/or use of raters who had a vested interest in the outcome (like parents who had put in effort and money for their children to receive neurofeedback or researchers who had a relationship with a company offering the services). Another problem is that the treatment doesn't have an established protocol, such as the number of sessions per week, length of treatment, and overall design. The bottom line is that some recent studies have shown some promising results, especially with inattention, but more large-scale well-designed studies are needed to establish conclusive proof.

Logistics and cost are important considerations. Estimates of the number of treatment sessions range from 20–40 sessions lasting between 30–50 minutes. Costs are variable but can range from $50–$125 per session. There are home-based treatment systems that are initially more expensive because they require buying equipment, but you don't have to travel. Negatives on a home-based system are that you don't have the benefit of a clinician to guide you and your son, and difficulties might arise in getting your son to follow through with a schedule of usage directed by the parent. We all know our kids often perform much better for others than their parents!

If you are interested in learning more about the research being done, researchers at Ohio State University received National Institute of Mental Health funding for a pilot study on neurofeedback. Based on their pilot study, the results were promising enough for them to launch a large-scale, multisite research study completed in 2019 with a 13-month follow-up in 2020. The results did not support a specific effect of neurofeedback at treatment end or during the 13-month follow-up, but findings will be reassessed in a 25-month follow-up (The Neurofeedback Collaborative Group, 2020).

Some professionals, like Dr. Vincent Monastra (Monastra, 2014; Monastra et al., 2002, 2005), author of numerous articles and books on ADHD, such as *Parenting Children With ADHD: 10 Lessons That Medicine Cannot Teach*, suggest that neurofeedback could be helpful. However, Dr. Russell Barkley (Loo & Barkley, 2005) is not as optimistic based on methodological errors he sees in the research and suggests that no conclusions as to its effectiveness can be drawn at this time. CHADD's (n.d.-b) Professional Advisory Board concurred that strong empirical evidence is lacking, but the board rated neurofeedback as an option based on emerging empirical evidence.

The bottom line is: Investigate any neurofeedback program you may be considering very carefully and proceed at your own risk because, at this point, the transference of the benefits to daily functioning has not been widely and consistently proven. I have not personally had any clients who felt it was particularly helpful to them in the long run. Some have liked it because it is often presented in a game format but have not felt that it helped them concentrate more effectively in the school setting. It is an area to continue to monitor as it develops.

Charles and his wife believed neurofeedback had enough validity behind it, so they had their son partake in about 30 neurofeedback sessions. At the time Todd started neurofeedback, he was 10 years old and halfway through his fifth-grade year. He had been taking ADHD medication since kindergarten. While taking an extended-release ADHD medication, his mornings went well, but it was harder for him to concentrate and complete his schoolwork during the afternoon. Before beginning neurofeedback, Todd and his parents consulted with his teacher, and she supported the decision and agreed to help by monitoring his performance. Todd continued taking his ADHD medication as he progressed through the neurofeedback sessions. Overall, his teacher reported an improvement in his ability to concentrate, stay on task in the morning, and complete his class work, but she did not notice any improvement during the afternoon. Charles and his wife did not notice any significant improvement at home after completing 30 sessions.

EndeavorRX

EndeavorRX is an iPad and iPhone game designed by Akili Interactive for children ages 8–12 with ADHD, Combined presentation and Predominantly Inattentive presentation. It is legally prescribed as medicine as part of a therapeutic program directed by a clinician and purports to increase focus. It has been in randomized controlled clinical trials for 7 years with its effectiveness evaluated through an objective measure. It was approved by the FDA as digital therapy for ADHD in April 2020 with the caveat that EndeavorRX should not replace existing treatment. It is time-consuming, requiring 25 minutes per day, 5 days a week for 4 weeks or more.

Working Memory Training

Researchers have supported the importance of working memory in a child's ability to remain attentive (Alderson et al., 2010; Kofler et al., 2010). There has been some interest in using computer-based memory training programs to facilitate recall, but no widely accepted research supports them even though programs like Cogmed Working Memory Training cite research studies and testimonials of its effectiveness. The American Psychological Association (2012) stated that "working memory training is unlikely be to an effective treatment for children suffering from disorders such as attention-deficit/hyperactivity." It will be an area to continue to watch as advances are made in technology as well as in ways to monitor its effectiveness. Currently, the programs available are expensive and time-consuming. Training is often done at home, which can lead to a power struggle between parent and child.

Elimination Diets

There is no question that children with and without ADHD will benefit from a well-balanced diet of proteins, fats, and carbohydrates, as well as adequate vitamins and minerals. The organic food movement has been gaining momentum with its emphasis on decreasing the amount of processed food in diets. CHADD provides information on diets for children with ADHD and also a cookbook on its website featuring healthy meal suggestions and recipes.

However, there is significant controversy about the role of diets in children with ADHD. There are proponents of elimination diets and/or supplementation with nutrients as treatments for ADHD, neither of which have wide research support but have anecdotal endorsements. If you choose any of these elimination or supplementary diet approaches, first discuss it with your pediatrician.

The Feingold Diet, developed during the 1960s by Ben Feingold, a San Francisco allergist, focuses on eliminating "artificial flavorings, preservatives, dyes, and other additives, as well as food containing naturally occurring salicylates (such as oranges, apples, apricots, berries, and grapes)" (Armstrong, 1995, p. 72). However, most studies have not verified the effectiveness of the diet even though anecdotal reports indicate some children with sensitivities to these substances have benefited from it. I don't recommend this diet.

If you feel that your child may be sensitive to food additives, such as red food dye, you might want to keep a log of food your child is eating and note adverse effects. Many doctors recommend 2 weeks on and 2 weeks off for any substance you are checking for sensitivities. Monitor any specific behavior changes in your son during that time and report them to your doctor or other professional. Some parents feel that their children's behavior worsens when they have too much sugar, but there is no consensus on this based on the research.

General Behavior Strategies

Behavior is such a critical issue for parents that it will be mentioned throughout the book. In upcoming chapters, I will discuss behavioral techniques that have proven successful with specific age groups, but I also mention behavior in this chapter because the behavioral support you give your son can be a key part of his treatment. After all, you are probably with him more than anyone else. Strategies applicable across the age span include:

▷ establishing structure—children with ADHD need this but usually can't provide it for themselves;

▷ creating an environment engineered for success—encouraging proper sleep, nutrition, exercise, and support when you know your son is likely to be overwhelmed;

▷ understanding what your son is capable of controlling and what he needs help managing;

▷ setting realistic expectations for him within his capabilities;

▷ helping him develop resilience and understanding that mistakes present an opportunity to try a different approach next time;

▷ consistently administering consequences closely following the misbehavior;

▷ serving as his role model for problem solving and behavioral control; and

▷ maintaining a relationship with your son—spending time having fun with him and having open, honest communication with him.

For older children, strategies also include:

▷ encouraging your son to learn to value long-term over short-term outcomes of behavior, and

▷ establishing a collaborative approach to problem solving—getting your son's buy-in for any behavior change is critical to its success.

The following are some specific behavioral strategies you may also want to implement that I have found useful with clients.

Establishing Clear, Firm Boundaries

One of the secrets of effectively parenting boys with ADHD is to provide clear and firm boundaries for what types of behaviors are and are not acceptable in your home. Remember that most boys with ADHD can't provide these for themselves but need them to help organize and manage their behavior. If you don't establish and continually remind your son about these acceptable behaviors, he may take advantage of you and his siblings and see how far he can push the limits. Then you will find yourself yelling at your children and feeling like they don't listen to or respect you.

Try to complete a plan with your partner or other adult(s) in the home who will be involved. If your son is old enough, it will be helpful to have him participate. The more buy-in you get from him, the greater the likelihood the plan will be successful. Ideally, you want everyone on the same page and responding consistently. Consider the following process:

1. Identify and write down your five most important rules for the children.
2. Write down the consequences for not following the rules (e.g., first infraction, second, third).
3. Schedule a family meeting.
4. Discuss the rules and consequences and clarify expectations.
5. Implement the new plan and revise as needed.

When deciding on your five most important rules, try to keep them short. One parent I worked with, Tom, set up the following rules with 10-year-old Victor:

 ▷ no cursing,
 ▷ no name calling,
 ▷ keep hands and feet to yourself,
 ▷ no talking back, and
 ▷ complete assigned chores.

Victor's consequences included a verbal warning for the first infraction, time in his room for the second infraction, loss of privileges (e.g., video games, phone, or computer) for repeated offenses, and grounding as a last resort. When Victor was grounded, it meant he couldn't play any video games, watch TV, use the computer, or see or talk with friends. He was allowed to read, draw, or play outside by himself. Tom tried to put supports in place so that grounding wasn't necessary because he realized Victor's social skills needed continuing development, so time with his friends was important and playing video games was a way for him to regroup after a tough day at school. When Tom did take away privileges, he made sure Victor had a way to earn them back in a reasonable amount of time.

As you sit everyone down for the family meeting, structure the conversation by saying something similar to this:

> You may have noticed that things have not been running so smoothly in our family lately and there has been a lot of yelling and arguing. It's time to get our family back on the right track and get us working together as a team. After all, if we don't take care of our family, who will? It's up to us to make our home run smoother. We need and want everyone to contribute their fair share, so let's come up with new rules. We've always had family rules, but they might not have been so clear. (*Note*: Try to get suggestions from your children on new rules. If they are reluc-

tant, question them about certain things, like taking others' things without permission, hitting, etc. Of course, you, as the parent, will have to insist on rules you think are critical, but the more buy-in you can get from your children, the better.) Now we've clearly listed the rules along with the consequences of not following them. Let's go over them together and see if we can all agree to try to follow them so we can have a better time when we're at home. None of us are perfect, so we will slip up from time to time, but it is up to us to help each other get back on track.

By having this type of talk and agreement with your family, you hopefully will have removed some of the emotion that will occur the next time you discipline your son or other children. The clear consequences help you remain neutral because everyone has agreed upon the rules and consequences. So, if one of your rules was that cursing wasn't allowed and your son bellows out a curse word, you can confidently state the warning and inform him that the next consequence is a loss of a privilege. When things have calmed down and you can talk with him, explore more effective ways he could have communicated his dismay that might have ended in a much better resolution. After all, his ability to resolve conflicts will be very important to his future success. These conversations can be difficult to have but can be effective in helping both of you improve your communication. By the way, when you slip up and curse, admit it and talk with your child about strategies you are going to use to avoid it next time.

Expect your son to test you on the new rules and consequences for two reasons. First, he is impulsive and he will know the rule but won't consider it before acting and breaking the rule. Second, he wants to test you to find out if you are serious about enforcing the rules. This plan will work, but as I have stated before, you must be consistent in using it and following through. When my children were younger, I used to think to myself, "If you don't follow through, you are going to pay for it next time the situation occurs." It is critical for your son to know that you mean what you say.

Using Behavior Plans

Behavior charts and plans can also work to modify a boy's behavior when used consistently. In my experience, parents are challenged to maintain and monitor the plans over time. Most parents start out strong and then fizzle out within a week or so.

Behavior plans can work well for children who do not yet have the natural ability to self-monitor their own behavior and need to be held accountable. As described in Chapter 3, young boys with ADHD are not able to self-reflect very effectively, so they benefit from the external control that a behavior plan provides.

Carol used behavior plans with her son while he was in kindergarten and first grade. Although she did not use them continually throughout these two grades, she faded them in and out as needed. Carol identified and wrote five important behaviors to be practiced at home and at school on Joe's behavior plans. At the end of each day, Carol reviewed each behavior with her son based on her observation, his teacher's note, and Joe's input. She found that this review became valuable, as Joe gradually opened up about problems he was having because he realized his mom and teacher were trying to help life go better for all. If he followed the individual behavior, then Carol drew a smiley face in the square, but if he did not follow the behavior, then Carol wrote, "Try again tomorrow." Each day Joe needed to get four out of five smiley faces in order to earn a reward, which included things like selecting a dinner menu for the following evening, a special snack, 15 extra minutes of play, special time with a parent, or a sticker for his sticker book. At the end of the week, if he had 4 out of 5 days with four or more smiley faces, then he picked a larger reward from the prize box that Carol and her husband created, which contained activities as well as concrete items. This external control and reinforcement helped Carol's son improve his overall behavior.

You can create a behavior plan or chart on the computer. If you need samples, enter "sample behavior charts" in a search engine, or go to Pinterest to find many examples of behavior plans you can customize for your own use. Your son might even enjoy the process of helping to create one.

If a behavior plan that encompasses the whole day is not effective, your child may need more immediate reinforcement for exhibiting good behavior. Token reinforcement systems provide immediate reinforcement, whether in the form of something tangible like a sticker or checkmark or an intangible like verbal praise, after the desired behavior is displayed.

Incorporating the Element of Time and Novelty

I have found that many younger boys with ADHD improve their performance when they are challenged with the element of time or provided with a game-like atmosphere for completing tasks. Some boys like to do things fast and within a certain amount of time. For example you might say, "I'm going to time you to see how fast you can pick up your clothes off the floor and put them in the clothes hamper. Ready? Go!" The element of time and necessity often motivates them to complete tasks.

Motivating With Visual Timers. I recommend using a visual timer that your son can view. A simple kitchen timer, microwave timer, or an app for your smartphone all work well. Give your son a reasonable amount of time to complete his task and set the timer. If he has to write spelling sentences, say, "Let's see if you can write five good sentences using neat handwriting in 15 minutes. Do you think you can do it? Remember, the sentences must be good and neat. Go."

Teachers can also use timers in the classroom with your young son. You or the teacher can purchase small timers that fit on a desk. When it's time for your son to complete independent seatwork, he can set the timer for the designated time. This provides him with a visual reminder to remain on task. Timers are a versatile tool that can help him at home or school.

Utilizing a Game Format or Introducing Novelty. I find that some young boys with ADHD complete tasks better when part of the task is turned into a game-like experience. If your son resists when you tell him it is time to take a bath, then make a game about getting to the tub. Ask him if he can hop like a bunny to the bathroom. Can he crawl like a turtle or lumber like an elephant? Many boys enjoy the novelty and readily comply. I've seen teachers apply this concept within the classroom by asking the class to line up from tallest to shortest or vice versa. Other teachers encourage their students to walk in line by having them walk with their hands in their pockets, their hands folded behind their backs, or one hand behind their backs and one in front of them. Again, this provides novelty. I caution you that this strategy works but not if you use it over and over. You must use your creativity and vary the game. So, the next time your son whines when you ask him to complete a simple task, try altering it into a novel game-like experience.

Offering the Two-Seat Method

Think back to the last time you took a class or seminar where you had to study for a test. Where did you like to study? Was it at a desk, sitting at the kitchen table, or on your comfy couch? I bet there were at least two places where you concentrated and studied best. Those two places had the right feeling to get you into study mode. The same goes for the boy with ADHD, and this is the premise behind the two-seat method. Sometimes it feels best to have the choice between two places to complete school- or homework. If you like this idea and your son is eligible for accommodations at school, then you can ask to have the two-seat method written into his IEP or 504 plan. Then, he will have the choice of sitting at his desk or in another location, such as an empty table in the back of the room, to do his work. At home you can provide him with the choice of working at a table or another designated spot. Providing your son with choices helps empower him and may allow him to create better work.

Providing Choices

Which do you prefer, waking up early or sleeping in? Working in the evening or working in the early morning? Getting paid once a month or every other week? People like choices, and the same holds true for boys with ADHD. As a parent I found my son usually responded better when presented with two choices. For example, I've given choices such as, "You can cut the grass in the morning or after lunch, but it will be cut today," "You can wear this shirt to school or this one," "You can learn to play the piano or guitar," and "Would you like to do your spelling words now or right after dinner?" Giving your son choices does not excuse him from the task.

As parents, we should provide our sons with age-appropriate decision-making opportunities.

Think about what providing choices does for him. First, it helps him learn to problem solve. For instance, if he is presented with the choice of vacuuming out the car on Saturday before or after he watches a favorite cartoon, then he must think about the benefits. If he completes the task before his show, then he does not have to think about it and can enjoy the show. Yet, vacuuming before the show starts could take longer than anticipated, and then he might have less time to watch the show. Waiting until after the show presents a different set of potential problems. Even though this seems like a simple decision, it requires him to apply problem-solving skills.

Next, providing choices helps your son learn to make decisions. Some boys become indecisive because choices are made for them. As parents, we should provide our sons with age-appropriate decision-making opportunities. If choices are made for him as a child, then your son may mature into an adult who can't make his own decisions. He may be easily swayed into unhealthy habits or relationships.

Finally, giving your son choices can help empower him and make him feel valued. For example, one birthday Eddie was given the choice of celebrating his birthday by spending the night at a local dude ranch with his grandparents and cousins or having a party with lots of friends at a local venue. He chose the family birthday celebration at the dude ranch, and the weekend turned out fantastic, with many laughs and memories. He felt great about the decision, and everyone thanked him for inviting them.

The main points to remember are that you want your son to learn to problem solve and to make his own good choices. In order to do that, he needs three things from you: opportunity, instruction, and helpful feedback. You can get started today.

Giving Second Chances

I strongly urge you not to get into an all-or-nothing situation with your son when it comes to behavior. He should be given a way to "earn it back," or else he has nothing to work for and will often refuse to do anything or just act out because he now has nothing to lose. For example, I have seen many parents take away their son's video games, as well as TV and phone privileges, with no way to earn any of it back. We have to keep in mind that our sons with ADHD often experience many frustrations on a daily basis and can easily become demoralized. When it is necessary to remove privileges, it is better to have a plan in place for him to earn some of them back. Make sure that the goals you set for him are achievable.

Points to Consider

1. When deciding on treatment, do you have a good understanding of your son's strengths and weaknesses? This will be very important as treatment becomes more individualized.
2. Have you identified a professional(s) who can guide you in seeking the most appropriate treatment plan for your son?
3. Have you decided on a reliable way to keep abreast of changes and new approaches in treating ADHD?
4. What choices do you provide your son in his day-to-day life?
5. Could your son benefit from coaching or counseling?

Action Steps to Take Now

1. Write down your own plan to determine the best treatment or combination of treatments for your son.
2. Decide which professionals need to be involved in helping your son reach his full potential.
3. Determine which topics need to be the subject of further research for you.
4. Which one behavioral strategy can you apply or try again?

Chapter 3

Infancy and Preschool

Your bouncing young boy is wearing you to a frazzle. He is charming, yet he is constantly demanding adult attention, running from one activity to another, and having meltdowns at the slightest provocation. You may feel like he is running your life. You have stopped inviting friends and relatives to your home because you are embarrassed about his behavior. You are tired of being accused of being a bad parent.

Like most parents of boys, you knew to expect boundless energy and lots of activity. However, you are exhausted and are sure that your son's activity level is abnormally high. Perhaps you have already been told he has ADHD.

Remember that organization, thinking before acting, and being able to sustain attention are all developmental by nature, meaning that behaviors can occur within a range of ages and still be considered within the normal range. Parents often wonder how it is possible to distinguish typical behavior appropriate to the developmental stage from atypical ADHD behaviors and how long it should take their son to progress through developmental stages. As noted in Chapter 1, the intensity of the behavior, the frequency with which it occurs, and how long it lasts are important considerations. Dr. Russel Barkley (2020) reported that research has shown that a majority (57%) of 4-year-olds may be rated as inattentive and overactive by their parents. However, the majority of these children improve within 3–6 months. Even among those children who received a clinical diagnosis of ADHD, only half maintained that diagnosis through later childhood and adolescence. Barkley noted that when the "pattern of ADHD lasts for at least a year, ADHD will likely continue into later childhood" (p. 91). The lesson that we can take from this information is that the severity of ADHD symptoms and length of time they last predict which children will show a chronic course of ADHD.

Remember that organization, thinking before acting, and being able to sustain attention are all developmental by nature.

Although it is true that many preschool boys are highly active at times and have difficulty regulating their behavior and emotions from time to time, you don't want to stick your head in the sand and ignore problems in your son that may require support. The key will be to observe how your son's activity level and behavior impact his daily life, especially in comparison to boys very close in age because many of these things are developmental in nature. (For example, if your son has an August birthday, don't compare him to those with an October birth date, almost 9 months older than your son.) Questions you could ask yourself include:

▷ Could his behavior be caused by fatigue, hunger, boredom, overstimulation, stress, or anxiety?
▷ Do the behaviors occur primarily in one setting, like at home, at preschool, or in free play, or across all settings?

▷ Does his behavior cause significant disruption throughout his day on a regular basis?

When Is a Comprehensive Evaluation Warranted?

A preschooler who puts himself in danger by being overactive, distracted, or impulsive, and who has difficulty with daily activities—such as eating, playing with friends, attending preschool, and interacting in the community—merits comprehensive evaluation. The chances of a child like this growing out of this level of behavior without intervention are slim. The more knowledgeable you are about the disorder, the more you can help your son.

The moment he enters any room, 4-year-old Ian begins scanning the area. His eyes dart from one area to the next, and his body follows suit, as if he cannot fully take in one thing before his racing mind pulls him to the next. In fact, he has run into the street on several occasions and requires constant supervision. He talks nonstop in a shrill voice and has no idea about volume control. He is engaging and friendly with adults. In fact, he demands almost constant adult attention and interaction except when he is glued to the computer screen playing a game. He will not sit still for family meals and generally has his home in an uproar. He is no longer invited to some homes to play and has been asked to leave his first preschool. Ian is clearly a candidate for a comprehensive evaluation, including a thorough developmental history, reports and/or ratings of his behavior in different settings, and a neuropsychological and/or medical examination to rule out other conditions.

Awareness of developmental stages and early detection enable you to have a better understanding of your child's behaviors. The preschool years are an important window of time in development and provide opportunities to change behaviors before they become too ingrained. Your son will need you to be his advocate and safety net as he explores his world and adapts to the structure of a preschool setting.

> *The preschool years are an important window of time in development and provide opportunities to change behaviors before they become too ingrained.*

ADHD has been diagnosed in children as young as 2 in extreme cases and is the "most common mental health diagnosis for children ages 3 to 5," according to the *Harvard Mental Health Letter* (Harvard Health Publishing, 2007, para. 1). It is being recognized at earlier and earlier ages for several reasons. More is known about the condition, and boys are beginning "school readiness activities at earlier ages" in preschool programs (Wolraich, 2007, p. 9). These programs bring new demands in terms of compliance, attention and focus, and behavioral control. It can be a time of great stress for parents as they struggle to find answers and interventions for their son's behavior or find and locate an appropriate preschool, all while managing their own personal and professional lives. Parents often tell us that parenting preschoolers with ADHD has been one of their biggest challenges but also a time of great satisfaction as they watch their children mature. Remember, some days will be better than others!

Prenatal Issues

As noted in an earlier chapter, you must put aside any parental guilt if your son has ADHD and put all of your efforts into helping your child learn to manage his ADHD. Research reported in *The Lancet*, a British medical journal (Williams et al., 2010), showed that children with ADHD have a larger number of DNA segments that are either duplicated or missing, known as copy number variants. Genetically based neurological characteristics, including less activity in the frontal regions of the brain (especially those areas that inhibit behavior, resist distractions, and control activity level) and differences in the effectiveness of neurotransmitters, have been suggested. Although home environment plays a role in improving or worsening a child's temperament, it does not cause true ADHD. Because it is genetic, it is possible that you or your partner has ADHD or your child's biological parents have ADHD.

In addition to the genetic link, risk factors can be increased by (Barkley, 2020; Goldstein, 2011):

▷ prematurity and significantly low birth weight;
▷ prenatal exposure to alcohol, tobacco, and illegal drugs;
▷ complications of the fetus that interfere with normal brain development;
▷ excessively high lead levels; and
▷ postnatal injury to the prefrontal regions of the brain.

Many parents of boys with ADHD state unequivocally that they have known since before birth that their child had an abnormal activity level. A 4-year-old diagnosed with ADHD was described by his mother as a "kicking machine" in the womb. She said, "He was raring to go from the start."

Developmental Issues: Birth and Beyond

According to the Perinatal Collaborative Project (discussed in Barkley, 2020), some features in the early development of children predict a greater risk of development of ADHD, even though the risks are reported to be low. These risk factors include:

> ▷ smaller head size at birth,
> ▷ amniotic fluid stained by meconium (intestinal material from the fetus),
> ▷ signs of nerve damage and/or breathing problems after birth, and
> ▷ delays in motor development.

Developmental Sequences

Educating yourself about what to expect at different age levels is important for any parent, especially if you have a bouncing bundle of energy on your hands. These characteristics have been shown to be common in children later diagnosed with ADHD (Bailey, 2007):

Infancy (0–12 months):

> ▷ Very high activity level, constantly moving
> ▷ Little interest in cuddling
> ▷ Low frustration tolerance, impatient, and highly demanding of caretakers
> ▷ Intense reactions to stimulation
> ▷ Highly attention seeking

Toddler (1–3 years):

> ▷ Difficulty maintaining attention for even several minutes
> ▷ Distracted by noise or visual stimuli
> ▷ Poor eye contact
> ▷ Ability to pay attention to things he is really interested in, such as video games
> ▷ Excessively active
> ▷ Lack of interest in quiet activities
> ▷ Difficulty regaining control when excited
> ▷ Highly impulsive and risk-taking

▷ Accident prone

▷ Difficulty sleeping, either falling asleep and/or waking early

Preschool (3–5 years):

▷ Can't sit still

▷ Little interest in quiet activities, such as looking at books or listening to stories

▷ Limited task persistence, changing tasks every few minutes

▷ Inconsistent attention skills, especially between preferred and nonpreferred activities

▷ Weak social skills

▷ Behavioral problems, disobedience, and engaging in unsafe behaviors

▷ Very talkative

▷ Constant motion, such as running without looking

▷ Clumsy or poor coordination

▷ Difficulty waiting a turn

▷ Aggression, such as hitting other children or grabbing items from them

Consideration of Wide Variations in Normal Developmental Sequences

Developmentally, many children begin acquiring the ability to inhibit behavior at 3 years and can voluntarily direct their attention to a nonpreferred task at 4 years (Wendling, 2008). Developmental sequences can vary widely and still be considered to be within the normal range. Some 4-year-old girls can sit and color for 2 hours, while very few 4-year-old boys can sit for that long. Gender differences have been widely documented. For example, language seems to develop earlier in many girls compared to boys. Preschool girls are much more prone than boys to enjoy sedentary activities, such as coloring and looking at books. Any observer of preschool boys can attest to their boundless energy and rambunctious play.

Understand that attention and focus are developmental in nature and do not occur at the same time for all children. Developmental readiness determines what a child is able to do at any point in time. It cannot be rushed. Educate yourself about developmental stages and what you can realistically expect at various ages, taking into account gender and developmental differences.

Understand that attention and focus are developmental in nature and do not occur at the same time for all children.

Ruling Out Other Causes of Behavior

As a preschooler, your son will be very busy asserting his independence and will be exuberant as he explores his surroundings. A hallmark of the "terrible twos" is disruptive behavior, especially when overtired or overstimulated. These characteristics and a number of other issues make it difficult to diagnose in preschoolers. These include an overlap between symptoms of ADHD and other conditions, differences in parenting skills and childhood experiences that could exacerbate the condition, and especially the wide variation in normal developmental sequences. Parents of boys are acutely aware that boys often trail girls in meeting many developmental milestones, especially in language, fine motor skills, and the ability to sit and engage in quiet activities.

A cautionary factor for physicians and psychologists in diagnosing ADHD in preschoolers is that symptoms can mimic other conditions, such as anxiety, depression, behavioral disorders, hearing or vision problems, sensory issues, developmental delays, language processing problems, severe allergies, or lead exposure. Other factors should be ruled out, especially if that knowledge leads to effective interventions.

Jamie had fine motor delays resulting in difficulty cutting and coloring in a preschool setting. He quickly lost interest in activities that he could not complete successfully. When tasks were adjusted to his skill level, his willingness to engage increased. His lack of interest was related more to a mismatch between his skills and the task requirements than an attention problem.

A good clinician must look at the root cause of the behaviors and rule out other conditions. This is complicated when more than one disorder is present. Research suggests that up to 45% of children with ADHD have at least one other psychiatric disorder, such as Oppositional Defiant Disorder (ODD), bipolar disorder, anxiety, or an emerging Pervasive Developmental Disorder.

Five-year-old Donald was not following teacher directions and insisted on doing what he chose to do in the classroom. He was aggressive, had frequent outbursts and temper tantrums, and seemed to delight in antagonizing others. Teachers felt that he was the happiest when in the midst of a fight or argument. After a thorough investigation and months of child and family therapy, Donald was determined to have ODD in addition to ADHD.

Behaviors must be looked at carefully and thoroughly to determine their main causes. A neuropsychological evaluation by a neuropsychologist and/or a thorough evaluation by a developmental pediatrician or child psychiatrist may be necessary to rule out conditions whose symptoms might overlap with ADHD.

Joey had language delays and difficulty in processing auditory information. His preschool teachers complained that he did not follow directions but roamed around from place to place in his preschool classroom rather than working on the assigned task. A thorough language evaluation revealed that Joey did not process or understand many of the directions from his preschool teachers who gave only auditory directions. When auditory directions were paired with visuals, such as cue cards to remind him of expected behavior, and a visual schedule was implemented to structure to his day, his rate of on-task behavior increased significantly.

In addition to developmental differences and symptom overlap with other conditions, life experiences and parenting styles can also cloud the picture. This doesn't mean that parenting causes ADHD. Rather, chaotic conditions considered to be adverse childhood experiences can impact a child's behavior, causing him to have more disorganized behavior, mimicking ADHD. In addition to lack of a secure structured and consistent environment, studies have shown that the manner in which parents respond to a difficult child can impact the course of those behavior problems. A negative and critical style of management has been shown to predict the continuation of behavior problems into later years. Keep in mind that often young children have not yet acquired the skills they need to manage their behavior and benefit from supports to help them, like structure, clear expectations, visual cues, opportunities to try again, and having an adult model appropriate behavior.

Preschool Issues

Preschools are very different settings from home and from most daycares. They have much more structure and more demands. Placing your son with ADHD in a preschool setting could bring additional stress to both you and your child. It is commonplace for children with ADHD who are oppositional or aggressive to be kicked out of daycares and preschools because of their disruptive behaviors. When talking to preschools, be honest if your son has behavioral difficulties so that you can determine if the schools have had success in accommodating children like him. You don't want to set up negative expectations for him, but you also don't want to start him off in a setting where he cannot meet the expectations of the program and will likely be asked to leave.

> *Because our world is constantly changing, you want your son to value learning and see himself as a lifelong learner.*

Time spent researching the right fit between a preschool and your son could pay off and enhance his self-esteem. You want to avoid early experiences of failure because of the stress they bring to you and your child. He is building his sense of self-esteem as a capable learner and participant in the educational setting from these early ages. Because our world is constantly changing, you want your son to value learning and see himself as a lifelong learner. Your choices may be limited according to your geographical location, but it will be important to find the best fit that you can.

Helpful Questions in Your Preschool Search

Philosophy. What is the school's mission statement and philosophy? Your goal is to find a school that seeks to understand a child's strengths and build on those rather than focusing on the negative. Preschool is only the beginning of a long educational experience, so having it begin in as positive a way as possible is critical. Some questions to consider might be:

  ▷ What are the teacher's expectations for what your son should be doing at his age? How do those expectations match his skill set?
  ▷ Are expectations the same for boys and girls? What accommodations do they make for boys? How adaptable is the pro-

gram in accommodating individual needs? For example, if a child becomes too stimulated, is there a quiet space where the child can go and regroup but still be supervised?

▷ What rate of success has the school achieved in successfully engaging boys with ADHD? How parent-friendly is the school? Does the school allow parent volunteers in the classroom? How does the school communicate with parents and how often?

Physical Setup. Some questions to consider about the physical setup of the preschool include:

▷ Is the environment inviting, colorful, warm, and comfortable?
▷ Is it equipped with colorful materials to develop language skills, fine motor skills, early literacy, and math?
▷ What is the ratio of preschoolers to staff? Boys with ADHD function much better in small-group or individualized settings than in large-group activities.

Daily Routine. Some questions to consider about the preschool schedule and routine include:

▷ Do children follow a structured schedule that is consistent?
▷ Does the teacher explain and model each desired behavior and practice until all students know exactly what is expected from them, including how to walk from place to place in line, sit in circle time, and raise a quiet hand to get the teacher's attention? (Some of these may be long-term goals.)
▷ Is movement throughout the day a key feature?
▷ How long are children expected to sit still?

Curriculum. Some questions to consider about the curriculum at the preschool include:

▷ Does the school use theme-based units of study that focus on concepts (such as community helpers) as well as social skills? For example, the social skill of being a good friend could be taught through literature, songs, games, and role-playing.

▷ What kinds of continuing education do the teachers receive to enable them to keep up with trends and "what works" with children? For example, boys with ADHD typically do much better at the beginning of the school year, when things are new and fresh for them. They become easily bored, resulting in an increase of problem behaviors. A proactive preschool would be alert to those patterns and program activities to avoid boredom, such as bringing in exciting new educational materials periodically.

▷ Does the curriculum involve hands-on activities?

Behavior Management. Some questions to consider about the preschool's behavior management style include:

▷ What are some techniques the teacher will use to gain and keep attention? Does the teacher use frequent visual and verbal cues, maintain close proximity to active children so that they can intervene quickly, and provide frequent feedback (Rief, 2008)? Does the teacher try to discern what might be effective for individual children? For example, if your son can't sit still in circle or music time, could he be given an instrument to play while classmates are singing or a job to do, such as assisting the teacher in turning pages in a story, to redirect his attention in a positive way?

▷ What are the teacher's disciplinary techniques? Is time-out used, and how often? If time-out does not prove effective for your son, what alternatives will be considered? Remember, if your son is placed in time-out often, he will miss learning opportunities.

▷ How closely are children monitored for safety?

Importance of Structure

As in the home setting, consistency and structure are critical for your son's success. Your son should have an understanding of the expectations and boundaries for his behavior, consequences, and rewards. The preschool structure should allow for the teaching of good school-related habits, such as:

- ▷ staying in an assigned space,
- ▷ following a routine,
- ▷ organizing a workspace,
- ▷ following teacher directions,
- ▷ cooperating with classmates,
- ▷ waiting for a turn, and
- ▷ cleaning up after completing a task.

Jamari's son, Jackson, started out attending a Montessori preschool. Things seemed to go pretty well for about 3 months, and then the teachers started having conferences because Jackson was often "wandering about." He would go from area to area but not really complete any of the lessons, thus interfering with the other children's work. Jamari and his wife decided that the Montessori program was not structured enough so they moved Jackson to a preschool with a traditional schedule. This helped because the class's daily schedule was more structured with a series of short activities, as compared to the more open schedule of the Montessori school.

Jamari and his wife, Sylvia, structured their home routine to help Jackson when he was a preschooler, using a behavior and reward chart they found on Pinterest that had a place to write the expected behaviors and a spot to place either a happy, sad, or neutral face depending on his behavior. They explained the chart to him and reviewed it daily. For example, one rule was, "No screaming at Mom or Dad." Each day Jackson could earn a reward if he had a certain number of happy faces. This was a concrete way to teach Jackson responsibility and help him learn about the importance of self-control.

As in the home setting, consistency and structure are critical for your son's success. Remember that he is not yet able to provide structure for himself, so he needs boundaries for his behavior to help him stay in control. You must be very clear about expectations and boundaries for his behavior, consequences, and rewards. Remember that rewards and consequences for children at this age need to follow the behavior as soon as possible so that they can easily make the connection with the behavior. Use visuals, like a picture of a red stop sign or a child taking a deep breath, or frequent verbal reminders to prompt behaviors when necessary. Involve your son in picking out the pictures or thinking up a good verbal reminder. One final word is to make sure your expectations are always realistic and include things he is capable to doing. Engineering his environment for success is important.

> *Remember that rewards and consequences for children at this age need to follow the behavior as soon as possible so that they can easily make the connection with the behavior.*

Teacher Characteristics

A preschool teacher who is firm but loving is important for your son. Energy and creativity are important, as well as a love of children and knowledge of their developmental differences. A teacher who is highly organized, is intuitive about behavior, and has situational awareness will assist a boy with ADHD in acclimating to his new situation. The teacher should also be effective in communicating concerns and positive accomplishments with you so that you can work together as a team.

When Marsha's son, David, was in preschool, he was an active boy and enjoyed playing outside. One day during playground time, David decided it would be fun to climb over the chain link fence that bordered the playground. David made it to the top of the fence, and his teacher spotted him just as he was perched on the top with one foot dangling on either side of the fence. She calmly coached him down and helped him understand the importance of staying with the others. David's teacher foiled his getaway plan but used it as a teaching opportunity to help him understand the importance of staying with the class.

Think back to the questions you can ask when finding a preschool for your son. If you have the chance, talk to your son's potential teacher so that you can get a feel for their personality. You don't want a teacher whose personality is soft spoken and flat, because your son can take advantage of that. On the other hand, you don't want a teacher who is gruff and intolerant. It's best to try to observe the teacher in action even if it means scheduling a time to return another day.

Considering an Additional Year in Preschool

Sometimes preschool staff may recommend having a boy repeat a year of preschool. Before that decision is made, there are many factors to consider. These include birth date, physical size, social maturity, fine motor skills, and progress in his current setting. Many parents of boys who have August or early September birthdays decide that holding them back and having them repeat a year of preschool before entering kindergarten allows them to mature and be more ready for the academics presented in kindergarten. Fine motor skills and attention are two of the many skills that are developmental in nature, meaning they don't come online for children at the same time.

You should gather as much information as you can from his teacher and the school. If you are thinking about retention, important questions are:

> ▷ Would an additional year to mature make a significant difference in his performance?
> ▷ What would a repeated year in preschool look like for him in terms of curriculum?

Some parents who chose to hold their son back have him repeat in a different preschool, possibly one with a more academic curriculum or at least new activities so he won't be bored. I know this is hard, but try to project ahead and think about how this retention would impact him as an elementary school student, a teenager, and a college student.

If you are still not sure, take your son to a local clinical or school psychologist and have some educational testing done. For an investment of a few hundred dollars, a good psychologist can help you determine your son's readiness for elementary school. When I test preschool students for readiness, I use the Wechsler Preschool and Primary Scale of Intelligence IV, a preschool-age IQ test, and school readiness tests, such as subtests of the Woodcock-Johnson IV Tests of Achievement. With each year that passes, especially in elementary and middle school, it becomes harder to retain a student. My advice is that if you are in doubt, seek a psychologist's opinion.

When More Support Is Needed

As a parent, you can easily be in denial about problems and postpone action. Monitor your son's behavior and adjustment carefully. Early intervention services can be very valuable to your child, so you will want to keep your eyes open to his needs. You don't want him to go for years with untreated symptoms that may cause difficulty with learning and social relationships and result in low self-esteem.

When a significant level of support is needed, you should consider a preschool designed to handle developmental delays that interfere with a child's functioning in a typical preschool environment. These delays would cover a wide array of conditions, including behavioral, speech and language, gross and fine motor, and intellectual. These preschools are usually offered in conjunction with community agencies and the public school. Federal law requires that school districts provide early identification and intervention services for children with disabilities whose deficits are severe enough to impact their functioning. If you think that your child's symptoms are severe enough, contact your local school district to find out how to access an evaluation and possible specialized preschool services. There will usually be a screening evaluation and then a more in-depth evaluation (if needed) to determine if your son qualifies for these services. Infants and toddlers may qualify for Part H services, and preschoolers (ages 3–5) may qualify for Part B services through the Individuals With Disabilities Education Act (IDEA). My experience has been that a preschooler with a speech or language delay often qualifies for speech/language services, but behavior has to be obviously and significantly impacting the child in order for him to qualify for services in that area. If you are in doubt, check it out with your local school district. See Chapter 6 for more discussion of legislation governing disabilities.

Chad's parents were at their wit's end because he had been asked to leave two daycare centers. Complaints from preschool teachers included having tantrums, hitting other children, throwing classroom tools, and refusing to stay in his assigned area. His parents had tried reasoning with, rewarding, and punishing him—all to no avail. After a thorough evaluation, including a cognitive assessment and developmental history by a school psychologist, an in-depth speech-language evaluation by a speech language pathologist, and an assessment of his fine motor skills and sensory needs by an occupational therapist, Chad was determined to be eligible for a special needs preschool program that focused on behavioral goals along with emerging academic skills. The classroom had a low student-to-teacher ratio, additional assistance from a classroom aide, and a highly structured behavioral management program where behaviors were taught and reinforced. In addition, he had occupational therapy to help him improve his fine motor skills that were impacting his ability to hold a pencil, cut, and color. Chad had his ups and downs but eventually improved in his ability to follow directions, stay in his assigned area, and keep his hands and objects to himself. Without that early intervention, Chad would have encountered much more difficulty in elementary school.

As noted previously, an evaluation by a developmental-behavioral pediatrician, neurologist, child psychiatrist, school psychologist, clinical psychologist, or neuropsychologist might provide instructive information and give you more direction. For example, if a child was determined to have fine motor delays or sensory issues that impacted his performance, then occupational therapy might ameliorate some of his difficulties. If he had delays in pragmatic or social language that impacted his social skills, then language therapy and social skills groups might provide much-needed assistance. The value of early intervention should not be underestimated.

Medical Intervention With Young Boys

The challenges of managing a young boy in a structured, educational setting may prompt your son's preschool teacher to encourage you to try medication. The use of medication in young children with ADHD requires careful consideration of the severity of the behavior balanced with the side effects from medication. Most pediatricians recommend medication for young children only when behavioral interventions implemented with fidelity over time have proven to be ineffective or when the child is exhibiting dangerous behavior. There are studies on long-term effects of medication on preschool children's developing neurological structures but much fewer studies than those done on older children.

As reported in the *Brown University Child and Adolescent Behavior Letter* ("Pharmacological and behavioral," 2009), a review of 4 decades of research showed "that methylphenidate (Ritalin) has a greater evidence base than other medications, psychosocial interventions, and alternative treatments in the short-term treatment of ADHD in preschoolers" (p. 4). A National Institute of Mental Health study (Wolraich, 2007) found that the effectiveness of methylphenidate was more limited in preschoolers than in older children. Other studies have shown that preschool children can be more sensitive to side effects of medication, including irritability, insomnia, and weight loss (Bower, 2006).

However, the FDA only recommends amphetamines (e.g., Adderall and Dexedrine) for young children under the age of 6, according to Dr. Mark Wolraich (2007), professor of pediatrics at the University of Oklahoma. It is widely believed that the difference in the FDA recommendations for amphetamines versus methylphenidate "has more to do with the regulations that were in place when the FDA approved the medications than they do with how much evidence there is about how well amphetamines work or how safe they are in preschool-aged children" (Wolraich, 2007, para. 3). As noted in a personal communication, Dr. Michelle Chaney said, "Adderall and Dexedrine have FDA approval for ages 3 and up. Many practitioners still prefer a trial of methylphenidate over amphetamine for younger kids as it is often better tolerated." As cited in the *Brown University Child and Adolescent Behavior Letter*, doctors "have to balance exposing children's rapidly developing brains to psychopharmacological agents against the potentially damaging consequences of not treating the disorder" ("Pharmacological and behavioral," 2009, para. 3). It is very clear that if medication is used, then it should be closely monitored by medical personnel.

A review of the literature also indicates fewer studies on the effects of various treatment approaches for ADHD in young children compared to older children. There are even fewer studies comparing the effectiveness of alternative treatments to pharmacological treatments. The primary alternative treatments would be behavior therapy and parent training. Behavior therapy for preschoolers often takes the form of play therapy in which the therapist would use games, toys, and stories to help children develop coping skills. (See the resources for parent training in Chapter 2.)

Some studies indicate that elimination diets (e.g., additive-free, sugar-free, carbohydrate-free) have shown some promising results but not enough evidence to suggest they are a viable treatment. Some clinicians believe that diets higher in protein and lower in carbohydrates and sugars provide a more stable sugar level and prevent meltdowns based on metabolic problems, which might exacerbate ADHD.

A study of 135 preschoolers over a 5-year period released in 2007 and published in the *School Psychology Review* indicated that preschoolers with ADHD may require "more behavior therapies and less medication" (as cited in Breaden, 2007, p. 5). The September 2007 issue of the *Harvard Mental Health Letter* (Harvard Health Publishing) suggested that "parent training and specialized day care should be considered before resorting to stimulant medication" (p. 1).

Home/Community Issues: Being a Proactive Parent

You know your child better than anyone else. Educate yourself to have a thorough understanding of ADHD and how your child's daily interactions are affected. The diagnostic criteria are the same for young children as for older children. If your child is diagnosed with ADHD as a preschooler, you may want to get him reevaluated when he enters school. Observe your child's presentation of the following characteristics of ADHD at home and determine ways you can assist him with:

   ▷ excessive activity,
   ▷ poor attention to tasks,
   ▷ impaired impulse control and ability to delay gratification,

> ▷ deficits in memory or storing information to use in guiding behavior in the future,
> ▷ difficulties with regulating emotions and motivation,
> ▷ diminished problem-solving ability,
> ▷ delayed development of internal language, and
> ▷ more variability in quality of work.

Be a detective in determining ways your son's characteristics affect his daily functioning and try to provide supports when you can to help him work around and grow in his deficit areas. At all times, remember that some behaviors are not within your son's control. You don't want to hold him responsible for things he cannot yet do. For example, if he cannot manage his frustration when he can't do something, work with him to assist him in developing those skills. Often helping him identify and name the feeling is a helpful first step. For example, he can recognize and communicate that he is frustrated, sad, or angry. He can use his language to communicate his difficulty and seek help in managing it. Children are very individual in what helps them manage frustration, so work with him to figure out how to solve this problem. Some things children I have worked with have found helpful include:

> ▷ learning to take a break and come back to it later,
> ▷ holding or squeezing a sensory toy,
> ▷ taking deep breaths,
> ▷ coloring, and
> ▷ using visualization to take a quick mental break and think about something that brings them joy, like a pet or special place.

Be a detective in determining ways your son's characteristics affect his daily functioning and try to provide supports when you can to help him work around and grow in his deficit areas.

Remember that behavior is often the tip of the iceberg or what is visible to the eye. Much more lies beneath the surface, like feelings about previous experiences and relationships. In *The Essential Guide to Rising Complex Kids With ADHD, Anxiety, and More*, Elaine Taylor-Klaus (2020) encouraged parents to suspend judgment about behavior. She recommended "fully understanding and accepting the challenges for what they are" (p. 69). She suggested that parents should approach teaching self-management with patience, helping children learn it "slowly but surely, in developmentally appropriate ways" (p. 69). It can seem like a long haul, but just keep your eyes on prize of having a child who ultimately learns to control his behavior.

Whether your son has been diagnosed or is suspected of having ADHD, there are a number of things you can do to help manage his behaviors in the home and community.

Engineering Success

Understand the Symptoms of ADHD

Knowledge can be a very powerful ally. A few things I recommend you do to learn more about ADHD include:

▷ Seek out parent training or coaching in effective management and discipline. Contact your pediatrician, community agencies, or school district for information on resources. In some areas, CHADD has local chapters that hold monthly meetings with speakers and offer the chance to connect with other parents who have children with ADHD. You can access information online through groups like CHADD (https://chadd.org), ADDitude (https://www.additudemag.com), or other sources for parent training listed in Chapter 2.

▷ Learn what management tools are effective with your child. Distraction is often effective for some children when they start to get upset. Some benefit from reminders (either visual or verbal) to use coping strategies. Remember that boys with ADHD often have a low frustration tolerance, excitability, and impulsivity, and may overreact. Teaching them calm-down strategies, such as stopping and thinking before acting, deep breathing, mindfulness, or putting the situation into perspective, can be helpful. Other children become completely overwhelmed by too much stimulation and benefit from a quiet area to regroup. Behavior modification techniques, including immediate consequences, praise, ignoring negative behavior that is not dangerous, and teaching replacement behaviors, can be very effective.

▷ Be positive and focus on strength areas. If your son is innovative, provide items that will encourage that talent. If he enjoys helping others, try to engineer those opportunities. Try to praise your son several times a day for things he is doing correctly.

▷ Create an environment that promotes success. If your son is accident prone, put away items that can be easily broken. If he has trouble cleaning up toys, provide an organizational structure. Placing pictures on shelves or drawers to show where things go can help in cleanup. Remember that preschoolers cannot often break down tasks like being asked to clean up a room without help getting tasks into manageable steps. If he has trouble transitioning from one activity to another, use a kitchen timer or a visual timer like Time Timer (https://www.timetimer.com) to count down the time before he has to switch activities, or give verbal warnings.

Structuring His Day

▷ Provide a structured environment with adequate opportunities for activity and rest. Mealtimes, naptime, and bedtime should be consistent. Some children benefit from having a visual schedule that shows their daily routine or a visual cue card to prompt certain behaviors, like remembering to clear their plate from the table. If you enter "visual schedules for preschoolers" in a search engine, you will find many examples.

▷ Prepare your son in advance when a change in schedule is unavoidable.

▷ Provide plenty of time for physical release throughout the day, including playing outside or engaging in some energy-releasing activity. This can be especially helpful if you are taking him somewhere requiring him to be seated for a period of time.

▷ Keep your son busy in productive activities. Idle time may create problems.

▷ Make sure media and technology don't replace activities needed for growth and development, such as social interaction, physical activity, creative play, and tasks developing fine motor skills like cutting and coloring. Recommendations from the American Academy of Pediatrics (AAP, n.d.) reflect an understanding of the diverse needs of families and children rather than suggesting specific time limits on media use. Especially for children 18 to 24 months old, AAP recommends watching high-quality programming with your child if you choose to have them exposed to media, rather than the previous recommendation of no screen time. According to AAP, children under 2 benefit from adult interaction while using media because they are developing their cognitive, language, and social-emotional skills. Programs like *Daniel Tiger's Neighborhood, Sesame Street,* or *Dora the Explorer* depict prosocial interactions (sharing, turn-taking, cooperating, and empathizing) and can be helpful in developing social skills. AAP developed an excellent planning tool for families to create a media plan (available at https://www.healthychildren.org/English/media/Pages/default.aspx#planview).

▷ Plan ahead for times when long periods of sitting will be required, such as when traveling in a car. Bring snacks, games, books, and videos (if you choose) to keep your son occupied.

▷ Be prepared to remove your son from highly stimulating activities if he becomes easily overwhelmed. Children frequently cannot calm themselves down and need some quiet time to regroup.

Managing Behaviors

▷ Think ahead about what behavior you expect of your son in different situations. Discussing expected behavior beforehand is often helpful.

▷ Practice how you would like to respond in situations to avoid overreacting. Remember, you are only human so this won't always work.

▷ Be as consistent as possible. Follow through on directions and consequences. If not, you will likely pay for it later because your son will doubt that you mean what you say. Consistency enables your son to know exactly what you expect and to have a clear understanding of the rules. Behavior cues used consistently by parents and caregivers, as well as by teachers, can be critical. For example, if he gets too loud, get his attention and give him a visual cue like motioning with your hand to lower his volume.

▷ Monitor your son's activities closely for safety if he is impulsive. Cover electrical outlets and lock up cleaning products and other dangerous items. If your son is a climber who enjoys getting into kitchen cabinets, provide a cabinet at floor level just for him that contains items of interest.

▷ Some behavioral problems can be avoided by providing distractions if you see that your child is getting upset. Suggest a walk or sing a song (Alexander-Roberts, 2006).

▷ Help your son learn to label the feelings behind the behavior as soon as he is able. For example, if he is frustrated, help him figure out what that feels like and how to communicate it. The next step will be to help him figure out how to cope with those feelings. Language can be very powerful in helping him manage his behaviors.

▷ Use time-out judiciously. Some experts estimate that time-out should include 1 minute for each year up to 5 years of age. Time-out can often begin at 2 years of age (Alexander-Roberts, 2006). It seems to be most productive if it is framed as a calm-down spot where the child can regain control to continue enjoying his day rather than a punishment.

Teaching and Learning

▷ Keep eye contact with your son, especially when giving directions. If necessary, gently hold his chin so he is looking right at you to ensure he is listening. (Caveat: Be alert to situations where holding his chin could set up a power struggle. Sometimes it is better to avoid eye contact in dicey situations so as not to challenge or antagonize.)

▷ Keep directions clear and simple. Boys with ADHD are especially unreceptive to long directions or conversations. Keep directions to only one step until you are sure your child can handle two-step directions.

▷ Provide repeated practice for new skills, especially social skills like sharing a toy. Children with ADHD seem to learn through experience and practice rather than by observing social cues.

▷ Don't assume that your son understands cause and effect. Specific training in identifying cause-and-effect relationships in stories, movies, and real-life situations can be helpful.

▷ Ensure that the environment is free from distracting stimuli when engaging in a teaching activity. Boys with ADHD are less able to screen out competing stimuli than other children.

▷ Allow fidget toys or items that may help the child sit and focus—for instance, when a book is read. Effective fidget items are things that keep the child's hands busy or provide sensory input for his body, like sitting on a ball chair, bumpy cushion, or wearing a weighted vest. They serve to calm him but do not become a distraction. Handheld fidgets can be favorite toys, such as small cars, a stuffed animal, or a squishy, sensory toy, as long as they do not become distractions. Search online for "sensory fidgets" to see a variety of options.

▷ Use as many of your child's senses as possible when teaching a new skill. For example, when teaching the names of fruits, allow your son to draw them, touch them, smell them, and taste them. Interactive learning will be the most productive.

▷ Give him a head start on learning to focus and develop some internal limits on behavior. A kitchen timer or Time Timer (https://www.timetimer.com) can be used to help your son extend the time he can focus on one activity.

Support for Parents

There is no question that parents of boys with ADHD are under much more stress than parents of boys without ADHD. All of us have probably been impacted by the eye rolls when our son misbehaves. It is no wonder parents of boys with ADHD have self-doubt about their parenting skills and often lower self-esteem. If you have more than one child with ADHD, then of course your stress level will be even more elevated. Or if a global crisis of some sort interrupts your son's daily schedule, your challenges will be magnified. Even under the best of circumstances, your son's behavior is baffling and often disruptive to the entire family. You may feel you are constantly on guard and never have time to yourself. Even finding a babysitter who can handle your son effectively may be difficult.

Realize that time away from your son is important to allow you to regroup and keep a positive attitude. The search for a competent babysitter who understands your son will be well worth it. Find someone who is willing to be educated about ADHD. Oftentimes, your son will respond more positively to someone who is willing to engage in high-energy activities while keeping in mind the importance of safety. If money limits your ability to have a babysitter, try to exchange babysitting duties with another parent who understands ADHD and its management techniques. You want to avoid putting your son in situations that could be damaging to his self-esteem if he is made to feel like a bad boy rather than someone who needs additional time to master some skills.

Remember that you are human and will lose your patience from time to time. Build in little breaks that will make this less likely to happen. Finding a parent support group may be helpful if that group is positive and focused on sharing what works and new techniques and trends. A support group of parents of children who have ADHD can be aware of and share information on local resources and services. To find support groups, check online, local colleges or school systems, or with pediatricians or other health professionals. As noted previously, CHADD, an organization for children and adults with ADHD (https://www.chadd.org), has support groups in some areas. Parent training specific to children with ADHD is available through a number of organizations, including CHADD, ADDitude (https://www.additudemag.com), and Impact Parents (https://impactparents.com). More intense and specialized training, such as Parent Child Interaction Training (http://www.pcit.org), may be available in your community or virtually. Keeping up with the latest research can be helpful. Search online for "childhood ADHD" or "ADHD in preschool" to find the latest research findings. Try to use only trusted sources, as there is plenty of inaccurate information out there.

Don't be afraid to use the help of a psychologist, counselor, or coach to learn problem-solving approaches specific to your own family. Often family therapy can be helpful in establishing a cohesive family bond. Remember that the same parenting style that works for one child does not always work for another. Cindy and her partner took two parenting classes that were offered at a local preschool. One class was called Conscious Discipline (https://consciousdiscipline.com), and the other was Redirecting Children's Behavior (https://www.positiveparenting.com). In one class, Cindy learned a strategy to curb her tendency to overreact to her son's behavior—STAR, or taking time to Stop, Take a deep breath, And Relax. To remember to use the strategy, she placed paper stars at strategic places around the house.

> Remember that you are human and will lose
> your patience from time to time.

Assistance With Siblings

In addition to the challenges in preschool and in the community, your son with ADHD will, of course, bring his difficulties into the home. His high activity level, impulsivity, and difficulty in organizing his own behavior will inevitably create conflict with siblings. Brothers and sisters are often jealous of the additional time parents must spend with a child with ADHD. They may actually see the child with ADHD as lucky and envy him. You want to help other family members have some understanding of ADHD behavior with the goal of treating the child as a full and integral member of the family. I often think children with ADHD are highly perceptive about what others think and pick up quickly on those disapproving looks.

I often recommend books to help parents explain ADHD to siblings. Books often allow for an open discussion within a supportive context and enable children to identify with the issue or character. Some books are: *My Brother's a World Class Pain: A Sibling's Guide to ADHD/Hyperactivity*; *Learning to Slow Down and Pay Attention:*

A Book for Kids About ADHD; and *Cory Stories: A Kid's Book About Living With ADHD.*

Some More Tools for Your Toolbox

Remember that it is often very difficult for a boy with ADHD to hold his behavior together in school and community settings. His behavior may disintegrate in the home setting, where he feels safe. Providing a quiet place where he can regroup without trampling on the rights of other family members will be important. I have found it is important to encourage parents to physically get on their son's level when they are talking to him. When standing, parents tower above their son. When talking to, disciplining, or teaching him, parents should kneel, sit, or bend down to look him in the eye. This simple technique has an amazing effect in getting active boys to actually listen and understand.

A second technique I have found helpful is to lower one's voice as the boy's voice gets louder. Energetic preschool boys are often loud with their play and voices. An often-effective strategy is to talk softer and get down to a whisper as your son gets louder. Inevitably, your son will take your cue and start to whisper too.

A third strategy that often works well for preschool-age active boys is teaching parents and siblings to make a game of things. Boys usually enjoy games, and their competitive nature fits well with playing racing games. For example, when cleaning up toys, I would often race my son to see who could pick up the highest number of blocks the fastest. A family I worked with had an older daughter who often played the game of follow the leader to get her brother to go where she wanted to go or do what she wanted him to do.

These techniques won't always work, but having more strategies in your toolbox can sometimes make your life much easier. The challenge is remembering them in the heat of the moment when you need them the most!

Self-Esteem

Self-esteem is a collection of beliefs a person has about themselves. It begins developing in toddlerhood and continues throughout life. It fluctuates, because it is often based on interactions with others and opportunities for success. It can be defined as pride in one's self or self-respect.

If your son says negative comments about himself, give him a hug and reassure him that you love him just the way he is.

Self-esteem in preschoolers is in its early, developmental stages. The preschool boy with ADHD has probably heard hundreds, if not thousands, of redirections from his parents, teachers, caregivers, and classmates. He is likely bombarded with many more negative than positive comments. All of these redirections and negative comments can take a toll on your young son's self-esteem.

Preschool-age boys with low self-esteem may say things like "I'm a bad boy" or "Stop it, me. Be quiet." They may hear this from their classmates and even some teachers and parents. You may even overhear your young son say these things when he is angry or frustrated at himself. If your son says negative comments about himself, give him a hug and reassure him that you love him just the way he is. You can admit that his behavior sometimes frustrates you but that you still love him very much and are working very hard to help him. Tell him that there is nothing he can do to make you stop loving him. Each night when you tuck him into bed, make it a nightly ritual to tell him how much you love him.

Strategies to Increase Self-Esteem

Helping your son develop a can-do attitude must be based on opportunities to accomplish realistic tasks. Don't expect more from him than he is capable of giving. His frustration tolerance may be limited, so patience will be required.

Giving honest, accurate feedback will help him as he develops his view of himself. Focus on what he has done right, perhaps the effort he has put into something, and identify what you are continuing to work on with him to make his life easier. Do not compare him to other children, especially siblings. More than likely, he will be making his own comparisons.

Providing a safe, secure environment for him, both at home and at school, will enable him to be able to take risks as he strives to accomplish tasks. Give him chances to make some of his own decisions and help him learn to solve problems.

> *Helping your son develop a can-do attitude must be based on opportunities to accomplish realistic tasks.*

Most preschool-age boys with ADHD love it when adults read out loud to them. Books are a great resource to help build the self-esteem of preschool boys. A few books I recommend to clients with preschool-age boys include *No David!*; *Alexander and the Terrible, Horrible, No Good, Very Bad Day*; *I'm Gonna Like Me: Letting Off a Little Self-Esteem*; *Have I Ever Told You?*; and *Love You Forever*. Reading books like these with your son helps him identify with the character, learn how the character solves a problem or learns a new behavior, and then apply that solution to his life. Books provide a nonthreatening and peaceful way to teach your child and build his self-esteem.

Begin by asking your son to sit on your lap or right next to you so you can both see the pictures. As you read the book aloud, use an animated voice. Help your son identify with the character by pointing out similarities between him and the character. Look for positive things that are related to the character and your son in addition to troublesome behaviors.

For example, in *No, David!* by David Shannon, the character likes chicken but forgets to chew with his mouth closed at the dinner table. If this happens to your son, mention that the boy in the book forgets to chew with his mouth closed too and talk about what his mom says. Discuss how you tell your son to chew with his mouth closed, and then mention that it's an important manner to learn. At the end of the book, reinforce how much David's mom loves him and how much you love your son too. Most boys enjoy having the same book read to them multiple times, so each time you reread the book, you should emphasize different points to help your son.

There are additional activities you and your preschool son can do to help build self-esteem. One way is to provide your young son with an age-appropriate journal. Dr. Janet Mentore Lee wrote a kid's journal called *The Daily Doodle: A Journal for Children Ages 4–7* as a way to help kids feel reassured, validated, and supported. Each page of the activity book is a writing, scribbling, or doodling prompt that will help your child express his inner thoughts, feelings, and coping skills. Depending on his developmental level, you can help him write words or letters. *The Daily Doodle* provides prompts and is a great way to collaborate, create, and connect with your child, critical components to a parent-child relationship and building self-esteem.

Another activity you can do with your preschool son is to help him create a self-portrait. A large piece of butcher paper or many sheets of paper taped together work well. Place the paper on the floor and ask your son to lie on top of it. Use a pencil or marker and then trace the outline of his body. Tell him you'd like to work with him to make a self-portrait. Use his favorite art supplies, which could include crayons, paint, ink, chalk, and so forth. Place a small mirror within reach and encourage him to look at it frequently. Help him by drawing in his ears, eyes, and mouth, and allow him to color his features. Comment about his beautifully colored eyes, nice hair, wide smile, or strong arms. When the project is completed, hang it up in his room. You could even take his picture next to it and tell him you are going to email it to relatives, share it with friends, and brag about how cool he and his portrait look. An alternative to the life-size portrait is just to draw the shape of your son's head on paper and then allow him to color in his facial features.

Regardless of the activity you complete with your son, reinforce how much you love him and enjoy being with him. Don't stress too much if he is wiggly while you read or squirms as you trace his outline. Try to have fun with him and reinforce his positive qualities. One wise parent of a preschooler with ADHD that I have worked with always tried to strive for a ratio of five positive comments to one negative comment. He sadly realized that he rarely achieved it. To encourage himself he even bought a small counter to keep in his hand and click as he said positive comments. This helped for a while, as he tried to change his mindset toward saying more positive comments.

When it is all said and done, having a positive and close relationship with your son will be invaluable as you and he tackle any obstacles ADHD might bring. Many successful people with ADHD point to their mother or father who was always there for them and never stopped believing in them. You can be that person for your son.

Points to Consider

1. Remember that organization, thinking before acting, and being able to sustain attention are all developmental by nature, meaning that behaviors can occur within a range of ages and still be considered within the normal range.
2. Time spent in researching the right fit between a preschool and your son could pay off and enhance his self-esteem.
3. As a parent, you can easily be in denial about problems and postpone action. Be proactive.
4. You will walk a fine line in helping other family members have some understanding of ADHD behavior while treating your son as a full and integral member of the family.

Action Steps to Take Now

1. Develop a stronger relationship with your son's preschool and do your best to ensure that his needs are being addressed. Use the questions in this chapter if you interview prospective preschools for your son.
2. Be a detective in determining ways your son's characteristics affect his daily functioning, and try to provide supports when you can to help him work around those and grow in his deficit areas.
3. Recognize your child's temperament or patterns of personality characteristics. Structure his environment to enhance chances of good behavior.
4. Seek out parent training in effective management and discipline.
5. Try some of the tools suggested in this chapter, such as using books to illustrate good behavior, changing tasks into games, or getting down to your son's level when you talk.
6. Be positive and focus on your child's strengths.

Chapter 4

The Elementary Years

Most ADHD diagnoses come during a child's elementary school years. So if you've skipped Chapters 1–3 and turned directly to this page, you wouldn't be alone. (I just hope that when things settle down—as much as they ever do with an elementary-age son with ADHD—you'll start again from the beginning.)

Here's what's happening: Your son's emotions are still developing, but he's probably way behind the curve of other kids his age. He may look like a little man, but he's really a bundle of raw emotions and feelings strung together in an almost primal way. You need to spend extra time teaching him how to stop and think, rather than just react because it will not come naturally to him. And you'll need a ton of patience, because those times you'll need to do the teaching will be exactly the times you'll be most challenged by his behavior.

Your son is in school full-time now, and he'll likely be expected to master the same curriculum as all of the students around him. Both of you will need plenty of tools to meet this goal without lowering the bar for his academic success, so I'll spend a lot of time in this chapter sharing strategies that will help your son succeed in the classroom. Your son's teachers will be a critical part of his success, and I'll help you identify some of the characteristics of school settings where a boy with ADHD can flourish.

These are the years when your son is learning basic skills and work habits he'll use for the rest of his life, as well as his identity as a learner. I'm not going to sugarcoat it—these years can be tough. But there is tremendous satisfaction in knowing that all of the hard work, patience, and consistency you invest now will establish a firm foundation for your son.

I have been in the trenches with many families, and I know that sometimes it seems like the struggles are never going to end. But take my word for it. One day, you're going to look back and say, "Wow, those years went by fast."

Going to School

Your son's elementary school career will be full of ups and downs. Each year, he will face new challenges and expectations. His behavior and adjustment to school will be related to how well he can handle the increased demands on his organizational skills and coping mechanisms. ADHD impacts not only his focus, but also his ability to inhibit behavior and his executive functioning skills (e.g., planning, remembering, and organizing). If your child responds impulsively, he does not have the luxury of planning ahead, thinking about what he has learned in the past, or delaying gratification (Barkley, 2000). As boys move from preschool to elementary school, they will be called upon to be more independent, organized, and goal-directed—areas that are weaknesses for most boys with ADHD. Barkley (2000) stated, "The solution . . . is not to carp at those with ADHD to simply try harder," but to provide "the sorts of cues, prompts, physical reminders and other captivating information that will guide behavior toward the intended goal" (p. 33).

One mother told me that her son, Lionel, was a mess. His teacher told her Lionel always had papers everywhere—crumpled ones in his desk, several scattered on the floor around his desk, and others pouring out of folders where they had been hastily shoved. None of the children wanted to sit at his table because he was always bothering them to ask what he should do next. Furthermore, the class received rewards based on their table's performance, and all of the children knew Lionel would lose points for his table. His inability to be accepted by his classmates didn't stop there. At recess, none of the children wanted to play with Lionel because he was so rough and often hurt them, even though he always apologized without being prompted, and said he didn't mean to hurt anyone.

Academically, Lionel was falling behind in all subjects, especially reading comprehension and math problem solving—two of the areas that required the most concentration and memory. His parents didn't know how to help him when he got home, because they could not read the scribble in his agenda planner, and Lionel never knew what he was supposed to do. They actually dreaded picking him up from school, because he often had meltdowns in the car based on how his school day had gone. He would cry because none of his classmates picked him for their team. Lionel often said the very words that tear at a parent's heart: "Everybody hates me!" The saddest part was that they knew he was not exaggerating, because he was rarely invited to any birthday parties or to play at anyone's house. They had always known he wasn't the perfect, well-behaved child, but he had managed to fit in much better in kindergarten, first grade, and second grade than he had in third grade. It seemed that the other boys were maturing and leaving Lionel in the dust.

They immediately set up a meeting with Lionel's teacher, who fortunately had a real heart for children with ADHD. She had a good perspective on Lionel's areas of greatest difficulty. She identified he was below grade level in reading and was able to refer him for additional reading instruction while at school in addition to providing his parents with materials they could use at home to support what they would be studying in class. She moved Lionel's group closer to her table, so she could more easily keep an eye on him and support him when he appeared lost. She used more visuals so that he could see what the finished product should look like and always checked on him after he had started the assignment to answer any questions he might have. She stopped letting children pick their own teams and assigned them instead. She often joined Lionel's team to encourage his participation as well as his inclusion by other team members. As Lionel's confidence grew and his despair lessened, he began to feel like he fit in with his class. His teacher began to think what had seemed like poor attention and performance was more linked to his anxiety and being overwhelmed by the demands.

Problem-Solving Perspective Required

If you are like most parents of boys with ADHD, you will find that your son's elementary years will be filled with learning and new challenges for you as well. There will be little room for complacency. Just when you think you've figured out how to handle your son's difficulties and are experiencing a period of smooth sailing, a new problem will pop up. If a boy with ADHD is anything during these years, he is consistently inconsistent. In talking about kids with ADHD, Dr.

Sam Goldstein (n.d.) said, "They know what to do, but do not consistently, predictably, or for that matter, independently do what they know" (para. 3).

> *If a boy with ADHD is anything during these years, he is consistently inconsistent.*

I recommend that you adopt this stance: Look at every situation that arises as simply another puzzle with a solution. You and your son will fare much better if you and he keep that problem-solving perspective, because you never know when you will need it. Even when challenges come at you fast and furiously—and I know they will, especially during the elementary years—I encourage you not to feel defeated by problems as they arise. Don't let your son feel beaten either. Instead, make sure he knows that together you're going to look at your resources, as well as his strengths and capabilities, and work to make things better. As his world has gotten bigger, your team can also grow. You can turn to his teacher, his principal, his school guidance counselor or psychologist, his doctor, and trusted friends for help and support. Yes, don't be reluctant to approach the principal when you need assistance, especially if they are very student-centered and involved with students. An important part of the problem-solving mentality is to remember that you don't have to have all of the answers yourself.

Elementary schools are not the same as when you were a student. Your son may be faced with high-stakes testing, mandatory retention, a curriculum that doesn't account for differing developmental levels, reduced opportunities for recess, virtual learning demands, and a complex social milieu. But don't despair. Some positive changes may actually make your son's life easier. Schools and teachers are generally much more knowledgeable about ADHD and how to effectively serve those students. Increased use of technology in the classroom is also a plus for most boys with ADHD.

Your goal is to help him be as independent as possible while providing enough support to enable him to view himself as a capable learner.

When you factor in his ADHD and the likelihood that your son may also have academic deficits, he is definitely going to need your involvement and support if he is to develop and maintain a positive attitude toward learning. That doesn't mean you have to sit with him for the duration of his homework time and or that you are going to be doing any of his work for him. It means you might have to help him get started on his work, ensure that he understands what he is supposed to be doing, help him break the assignment down into manageable chunks or help him figure out how to make study aids like flash cards. It is well-documented that children diagnosed with ADHD often have learning disabilities and lower performance on standardized testing. There will be increased demands on his organizational skills and his persistence, often exceeding his capability. These are critical years for him when he is cementing his view of himself. Your goal is to help him be as independent as possible while providing enough support to enable him to view himself as a capable learner. Educate yourself so that you can make the best possible choices for him.

Emotional/Behavioral Developmental Milestones

Along the way, your son is maturing a little bit every day, albeit more slowly than children without ADHD. Elementary-age boys with ADHD often have great difficulty with regulating emotions and with self-control. To keep tabs on your son's progress, try to have some awareness of when these developments occur in the general population with the understanding that they may be more delayed in your son and may impact his school experience. Based on research and child development theory, consider the following stages and range of normal development (Teeter, 1998):

> ▷ **Ages 6–9:** Self-control improves and more internal thinking develops.
> ▷ **Middle childhood:** Children are influenced by and use standards set by parents.
> ▷ **Ages 7 and up:** Self-talk guides behavior and enables children to take the perspective of others.
> ▷ **Ages 6–12:** Children become more adept at regulating emotional reactions to situations.
> ▷ **Ages 10–12:** Children are better able to control negative feelings and separate actions from feelings.

School Choices

Your choice of schools (and whether you have a choice at all) will depend upon where you live, your financial situation, and whether your local school district allows freedom to move from one school to another. In some cases, your local public elementary school may be your one and only option. If that's your family's situation, I encourage you to keep reading; what you learn here may enable you to help your school become a more welcoming place for all children with ADHD, including your own son.

However, under normal circumstances, many communities offer a variety of choices—public schools, charter schools, and private schools. Many school districts have virtual schools where students complete class work via the computer. Demand for pod schools and microschools grew during the COVID-19 pandemic, whereby parents hire a tutor or teacher for all or part of the day to work with a small group of children. Homeschooling is another option discussed in Chapter 6.

Select the type of environment that will provide the best learning opportunities for your son and one that will not overload you with stress. Time spent researching your options will likely pay off and will certainly give you peace of mind that you did the best that you could.

Consider the overall philosophy of the school. Boys with ADHD do better in schools with structure, good communication with parents, solid curriculum that matches instruction to their abilities, energetic teachers who utilize experiential learning and a variety of instructional techniques, high expectations for learners, and reasonable class sizes. The staff must have an understanding of ADHD as a neurobiological condition with deficits in impulse control and executive functioning so that they don't immediately attribute a boy's problems to laziness and lack of motivation. When you're evaluating a school, consider asking the following questions:

- ▷ Does the curriculum match state guidelines? In most states, you can go to your state department of education's website and access the curriculum for various grades.
- ▷ What is the average class size? Smaller is often better; 20 students or fewer is optimal.
- ▷ Does it appear to be a highly organized and structured environment?
- ▷ Do the students sit in desks or at tables? A highly distractible child usually does better at a desk.
- ▷ Does the school provide opportunities, such as tutoring, for extra help if a child lags behind academically?
- ▷ What kind of success rate has the school had for boys with ADHD?
- ▷ Is close supervision provided at all times, especially during transitions?
- ▷ What is the school's communication policy with parents?
- ▷ Is the school willing to accommodate your son's needs with strategies such as preferential seating, frequent cueing to task, a behavior plan, or allowing movement as long as it does not disturb others?
- ▷ What is the behavior management plan? Is it proactive and designed to eliminate chances misbehavior will occur? Children with ADHD benefit from close supervision, struc-

ture, clearly defined rules, positive reinforcement, contingency management that uses motivational incentives, and being held accountable for their behavior.

▷ Does the staff make organization a priority and assist students in developing organization skills?

Teacher/Classroom Match Is Important

Once you have selected a school, a good plan of action may be to have a conversation with the principal and provide some information about your son to help the school make a good teacher match for him. Some teachers are much more effective than others in dealing with boys with ADHD. The ultimate decision will be up to the principal, who has to consider many factors. Teachers who are patient, have high energy, are structured and loving but firm are usually most effective with boys with ADHD. One confounding factor about these children is that their focus is often governed by their motivation, so it is key to have a teacher who tries to make learning interesting and establish a relationship with them. Some families have the good fortune to find a teacher who is flexible enough to work with their son's built-in restlessness. Those teachers allow children to move about after tasks are complete or even during a task, as long as it does not bother other students. Or they might allow a boy to stand beside his desk and work. Having a teacher who can appreciate your son for his strengths and not become too annoyed with his impulsivity and activity level will be invaluable.

Will was cruising along in kindergarten and first grade. He seemed to be able to hold it together during sedentary classroom time until recess, when teachers commented that he became a "wild man," totally different than he was in the classroom. At the end of first grade, his best friend (who also happened to be one of the most popular kids in the class) deserted him. Will liked to direct what they would play, which had become tiresome for his friend. His ability or willingness to take the perspective of others had not yet developed.

In second grade Will found himself without a best friend and in a class with a teacher who was very rigid, cold, and boring. Will was advanced academically. When he completed his work before everyone else, his teacher made him sit silently and would not allow him to work on anything else. One day, while his mother was presenting a program to Will's class, she realized just how sad her son had become while at school. He had stopped participating in class and lost his spark. Will began to balk at going to school and became depressed. He often had to be carried to the car, kicking and screaming, because his mother knew that allowing him to miss school because of a tantrum and reluctance to go would only make the problem worse. After many conferences and much insistence from his parents, the school transferred him to another second-grade classroom, where the teacher immediately recognized Will's need for permissible movement, stimulating activities when he finished his work, assistance in developing his social skills, and boosting his self-esteem. She lovingly said, "He needs fluffing up." Even though the change was positive, it took time for Will to make the adjustment. His parents had to continue trying to provide opportunities to make social connections and to help him regain his interest in school. It finally happened but was years in the making.

Information for Your Teammates

Your Son's Teachers

The quality of your young son's education can have a direct relationship to his adult life. In my practice, I have observed excellent teachers who know exactly what strategies work with boys with ADHD. As your son's most powerful advocate, you should have a solid understanding of instructional techniques that might help your son and share them with his teachers if they are open to it. More than likely, many of his teachers will already be implementing many of these strategies. You can develop your own personalized list of interventions that seem to help your son and share them with new teachers when appropriate. Your goal is always to establish a collaborative relationship, not to tell the teacher how to run their classroom. You might even want to incorporate some of these techniques during homework time.

Classroom Organization/Management

In an ideal world, your son's educational environment will include the following:

- A positive classroom environment is necessary, especially one in which the teacher has an understanding of ADHD and is familiar with strategies to prompt your son to become an active participant in the learning process.
- Specific classroom procedures should be established and practiced consistently. In kindergarten, children may need practice to understand how to stand in line, take turns, raise their hands, and wait to be called on before speaking.
- Organizational skills should be taught and modeled throughout the school day, with assistance where necessary. Use of color-coded folders for each subject and a separate folder for homework can be very helpful.

- Seating should be available to your son in a distraction-free area, close to the point of instruction but as far away as possible from air conditioners, high-traffic areas, bathroom access, and other active students.
- A study carrel or separate area of the classroom should be provided where a child can choose to go and work when distractions become too great. In some cases, students have referred to these areas as their office rather than as a punishment.
- Work areas should be kept neat and free of distractions.
- Students with ADHD should be placed near positive role models.
- When possible, core classes should be scheduled early in the day. An optimal schedule for a boy with ADHD is to have lunch and physical education or recess at intervals that break up the day.
- Achievement motivators that stress effort and persistence should be provided. In other words, the child is rewarded for doing his very best, not only for producing an "A" result.
- The concept of time-out should be used as a chance to regain control and get back into a "learning frame of mind" rather than as a punishment.
- Supervision should be provided, especially during transition times. Boys with ADHD are more likely to get in trouble while moving from one area to another.
- Movement should be allowed as long as other students aren't disturbed. For example, the boy with ADHD may be allowed to get out of his desk to retrieve something, walk around the classroom, go to the restroom, or get a drink of water as long as he doesn't take advantage of the situation. Work by Rapport and colleagues (2008) suggested that activity may serve a purpose in helping students with ADHD to process information.
- Acceptable substitutes for motor behavior should be provided, such as allowing the student to squeeze stress balls, sit

on a ball chair or bumpy cushion, or chew gum if permitted by the school.

Behavior: Rewards and Consequences

Children with ADHD may require more relevant rewards and consistent consequences closely following the behavior than other children. An individualized behavior plan using tangible rewards is sometimes necessary and can be developed by the teacher, a school psychologist, or a behavior specialist. Stickers, happy faces, or check marks can be redeemed for opportunities for extra computer time, to mentor another student, to be a teacher's helper, or to have lunch with a special teacher or administrator. Sometimes a response/cost plan, whereby a student can also lose something for poor behavior, works for some students and may be necessary for serious behavior. For example, if a student hits someone, he might lose all of his points for the day or lose one of the privileges he had already earned. (A caveat is that some students react very badly to losing all privileges and having nothing else left to work toward, which makes their behavior more difficult to manage the rest of the day.) As noted previously, it is critical for rewards or consequences to be delivered as close to the behavior as possible. The following are also important for boys with ADHD:

- Sincere verbal praise for specific behavior is invaluable as a tool for reinforcing the desired behavior. Make sure to "catch him being good."
- Students should be taught how to become independent learners and how to self-monitor their own behavior, especially catching themselves daydreaming and then refocusing.
- Frequent visual cues between student and teacher help maintain optimal attention and control behavior. A cue could be a special sign that only the boy with ADHD and his teacher know. This is a great proactive way to help a child.

Lesson Presentation

Teaching boys with ADHD sometimes requires a little bit more ingenuity (and a lot more patience). Ask your son's teacher to think of this list as extra tools for their toolbox that research has shown can be very effective:

- Give directions in short sentences, accompanied with visuals when possible. In the upper elementary grades, it is often helpful for a child to see what the finished product should look like.
- Offer assistance breaking down longer assignments into manageable chunks. Some children are overwhelmed by the amount of information on a page and benefit from covering part of the page with a blank sheet of paper. When a child is overwhelmed, he often shuts down rather than attempting to start on a project.
- Establish eye contact with a child with ADHD before delivering key points of instruction. Watch for signs that indicate lack of comprehension, especially daydreaming.
- Provide frequent review and repetition of previously learned material.
- Understand the child's capability and provide lessons that are challenging without being frustrating.
- Hands-on, experiential learning is a favorite for boys with ADHD. Their attention to task increases significantly when it is of high interest and they have something to manipulate.
- Ignore minor inappropriate behavior (Parker, n.d.).
- Provide warnings before transitions (e.g., "Five more minutes before science").
- Demonstrate proper behavior. Helping a boy compensate for social skills deficits can be very beneficial, especially in younger grades. Sharing and turn-taking can be especially difficult for young children with ADHD. Teachers can model behavior, reinforce appropriate behavior, and help the child initiate interactions.

- ▶ Use of computerized instruction as part of the curriculum is a positive way for most boys with ADHD to learn, because it is stimulating, fast-paced, and interactive.
- ▶ Target his learning style. Because boys with ADHD can be incredibly focused on topics or activities of their choice, an effective motivator can be to allow them extra credit on selected topics with the project to be matched to their learning style. If a boy is talented verbally, then he might research something and present to the class. If he's good with his hands, he might build a project instead.

Your Son's Peers

Outside of your family, your son's school offers the most important opportunities for his socialization, and elementary school is when your son should be making great strides in learning how to appropriately interact with others. During this time it is common for boys with ADHD to have one of two problems:

- ▷ They may lack social skills appropriate for their age.
- ▷ They may have the skills but may not stop and think before they act.

If your son is having problems with his peer group at school, you need to understand the root of the problem. More than likely, his teacher can share information about his functioning in the classroom, and you can make observations on your own at birthday parties or other social outings. Often, he has not yet developed the necessary social skills and may need more assistance.

Dr. John Taylor (2001), a clinical family psychologist, classified children and adolescents with ADHD as having difficulty in many of the following areas:

- ▷ turn-taking in games and conversation,
- ▷ accepting criticism,
- ▷ losing in games or competitions,

> ▷ understanding and following instructions,
> ▷ honoring other people's "personal space,"
> ▷ resisting peer pressure,
> ▷ disagreeing with others in inappropriate ways, and
> ▷ having difficulty solving problems.

If you have pinpointed some problem areas for your son in this list, it is very important not to just ignore them. Instead, go about helping him acquire those skills in a number of ways.

> ▷ Communicate with his teacher and solicit their help. Sometimes children need to be explicitly taught social skills; they don't acquire them by osmosis. Some schools have social groups run by a guidance counselor or school psychologist where children are taught skills and have the opportunity to practice them using role-playing. Some classroom teachers are excellent at weaving social expectations into their daily curriculum and setting up opportunities where children can interact successfully.
> ▷ Make sure he has playdates or opportunities to practice those skills outside of school. Children who struggle with social skills usually do better initially when activities are highly structured, such as making a craft, bowling, or swimming, and involve only one other child.
> ▷ Use literature that highlights social skills through stories that you can read and discuss with your son. This notion is called bibliotherapy. *Teaching Problem Solving Through Children's Literature* contains book titles and specific lesson plans for each book that teachers or parents can use to help kids increase their social skills.
> ▷ Consult Social Thinking (https://www.social thinking.com), which has a wealth of material for teaching and encouraging good social skills, including a free newsletter, webinars, worksheets, and articles as well as a number of books for sale, including *Superflex . . . A Superhero Social Thinking Curriculum* (ages 7–10) and *Superflex Kool Q. Cumber to the*

Rescue, Superflex Takes on Brain Eater, and *Focus Tron Bundle* (ages 8–13). There are also games, such as *Do Watch Listen Say* by Quill, and books, such *You Are a Social Detective* (ages 4–13) by Michelle Garcia Winner, that can be used to teach social skills.

Quavon was a fifth grader who had previously been diagnosed with ADHD, Inattentive presentation. He was very timid and did not know how to initiate interactions with his classmates. One day he complained to his teacher on the basketball court at recess that no one would play with him. She grabbed the ball and said, "Quavon, you and I will make a great team," and they began to play. Within 5 minutes, a number of other boys had joined the game. The fact that the teacher whom the kids admired chose to play with Quavon elevated his status in his peers' eyes. The teacher continued to set up situations where Quavon could interact comfortably, and little by little, his skills began to grow.

A Quick Look at Behavioral Difficulties: Causes, Presentations, and Possible Solutions

As we have stressed throughout the book, no two boys with ADHD will be alike. Your son's ADHD may manifest itself in very different ways than another boy's. Scan Table 3 to see if you recognize any familiar behaviors. If you do, it will help you understand not only the likely causes, but also ways you might work with your son to overcome the challenge(s).

One student, Cody, reached all of his developmental milestones early and appeared to be a very bright child in many ways. However,

Table 3
Causes, Presentations, and Solutions
for ADHD-Related Behaviors

Cause	Presentation	Possible Solutions
Faulty sense of time	▸ Always late and behind schedule ▸ Doesn't get started on tasks ▸ Misses deadlines ▸ Poor planning	▸ Use agenda to record assignments ▸ Break tasks down into units ▸ Use a planner or calendar ▸ Maintain a schedule
Impulsivity	▸ Limited self-control ▸ Doesn't listen to others ▸ Jumps from one task to another ▸ Blurts out in class ▸ Acts before thinking ▸ Gets in trouble in class and home ▸ Doesn't consider consequences	▸ Provide structure ▸ Conduct role-playing to reinforce listening and stopping and thinking ▸ Track unfinished tasks via checklist ▸ Share stop/think strategies ▸ Use a behavior plan ▸ Teach use of internal language—thinking through a situation in his head—especially consequences
Inflexibility	▸ Trouble with transitions ▸ Easily agitated ▸ Uncooperative	▸ Give prior notice for change ▸ Teach coping skills ▸ Practice change in plans

Table 3, *continued*

Cause	Presentation	Possible Solutions
Overarousal	▶ Fidgeting ▶ Excessive talking ▶ Constant movement ▶ Easily stimulated	▶ Allow permissible movement ▶ Use fidget items ▶ Ignore low-level behaviors ▶ Provide a calm-down area
Disorganization	▶ Loses papers and materials ▶ Can't find household items ▶ Doesn't show up with what he needs	▶ Help create a workable filing system ▶ Create a designated place for items ▶ Have him put things at the door needed for an activity
Inattention	▶ Thinks of many things rather than focusing on task at hand ▶ Misses key information ▶ Forgets information	▶ Help him learn to catch himself drifting off and refocus ▶ Establish eye contact ▶ Help determine effective memory strategies

since early childhood, Cody had shown real difficulty tearing himself away from things he enjoyed, especially outside play, playdates, computer or video games, and television. He was very unorganized. He was always forgetting something, and his backpack was a mess. No previous attempts at organization seemed to have helped. Despite his disorganization, Cody sailed through school until third grade, where he was having some difficulty with reading comprehension and writing assignments. He'd never been an avid reader and never wanted to complete a book. When reading aloud, he omitted or incorrectly read words, which impacted his comprehension. He had difficulty summarizing a story and answering higher order thinking questions about a story, especially if it was about a topic in which he had limited interest. His teachers noted inconsistency in his writing. Some of his writing was targeted to the topic and followed rules of grammar and punctuation, but other times it was full of run-together sentences and disorganized ramblings. Cody excelled in math and could solve multistep problems in his head. But he had difficulty with multiplication facts and showing his work on multistep problems.

Luckily for Cody, he was already in a structured, predictable classroom setting with an enthusiastic teacher who was determined to develop strategies to help him be successful. Some of the strategies that proved effective included:

- ▷ His teacher initiated weekly communication with parents about his progress in class.
- ▷ Parents agreed to have Cody empty his backpack every night and get all of the papers in their proper places.
- ▷ Parents helped him establish a designated place by the door where he could put all of his school items for the next day.
- ▷ Cody earned video game time at home based on the number of minutes of independent reading he did.
- ▷ His teacher developed a monitoring checklist (see Table 4) broken down by subject. He was placed on a reward system and was able to select his reward from a menu of reinforcers that he could earn dependent on his total number of points, which included additional time on the computer, opportunities to assist his teacher, and homework passes. He was required to self-monitor on the items shown in Table 4 with teacher oversight.

In my work as a school psychologist in the public school system, individualized behavior and/or self-monitoring plans are often developed for students. Cody's plan had its ups and downs, but his teacher was able to establish that he did not have academic skill deficits but rather performance deficits. Everyone was motivated by his progress—his teacher, his parents, and most importantly, Cody. His situation shows that interventions in the classroom and at home are

Table 4
Self-Monitoring Chart

	Good (2)	Fair (1)	Needs Work (0)
All Subjects			
Did I have all materials ready and available?			
Did I catch myself daydreaming and refocus on work?			
Reading			
Did I use comprehension strategies when reading?			
Did I reread if the sentence did not make sense?			
Writing			
Did I complete a brief diagram to organize my writing?			
Did I proofread all of my writing for complete sentences, punctuation, and capitalization?			
Math			
Did I follow my teacher's plan to solve word problems?			
Opportunity for Parents to Add Bonus Points			
Bonus points for kind deeds, extra work, or exceptional behavior:			
Total:			

often multifaceted and require commitment from all involved parties, especially the child, in order to be successful.

Consistent Expectations Between Home and School

Home plays a far more important role than just a place to do homework (which I'll cover in the next section). In fact, the expectations you set for your son at home are just as important to his success as anything that happens in his classroom.

Remember that boys with ADHD often have difficulty imposing structure on themselves and need it provided externally.

I recommend that you extend some of the concepts of structure, activity, and discipline used at school into your home. Your son should understand that school is not the only place he needs to maintain self-control, nor is it the only place where he can depend on a certain amount of structure and sameness. Remember that boys with ADHD often have difficulty imposing structure on themselves and need it provided externally. Some things to try include the following:

▷ Provide a structured home setting. Have a predictable schedule and try to stick to it.

▷ Try to avoid sending your son to school tired. He will have to expend so much energy to battle his ADHD during the day and will need some reserves.

▷ Help him establish some order in his room, especially for important things. He should have a specific place to keep his backpack, lunch box, or anything traveling with him daily to school.

▷ Until he consistently is able to keep order to his backpack, have him empty it every night and put all of the papers in their proper places.

▷ Provide a quiet, uncluttered homework center. Eliciting his help in selecting and creating the space might result in more compliant use.

▷ Try to feed him a healthy, balanced diet that is not loaded with processed food.

Your son likely looks forward to recess or physical education because they allow him to blow off steam and release some of the excess energy that can build up. It's no different when he's at home, where you might try the following:

▷ Make sure that he has ample opportunity for activity. If he tends to be sedentary, don't give up until you find an active outlet that he enjoys. Some parents find that children benefit from running or riding their bike before going to school in the mornings.

▷ Make sure your son is not overscheduled so that he has ample opportunity for breaks, activity, and sleep. You want to strive for a balance—enough activities for exposure but not an overload.

▷ Try to avoid placing him in situations where the problems associated with his ADHD will be aggravated. Think ahead. For example, if he seems to have trouble with auditory processing and sitting still, he may not be ready for music lessons.

Never presume that because your son is in school, it's now his teacher's responsibility to see that he behaves properly. That job is yours as well. If your son is having difficulty at school, I recommend that you establish a system for communicating with his teacher (whether it is via email, notes in the agenda planner, or on a daily behavior log). That way you can work as a team to steadily improve your son's behavior and self-discipline. At home, try to put these practices in place:

▷ Work to understand the difference between willful acts of disobedience and behaviors that are the result of his ADHD and may not be under his control. Deal with them accordingly, because open defiance should have definite consequences. Impulsive behaviors may provide teachable moments when you can help your son develop strategies for dealing with his ADHD. Each day is an opportunity to try again.

▷ Give directions in short, concise sentences, using prompts or visual reminders if memory seems to be an issue. Make sure you have eye contact before giving the direction.

▷ Make sure that your son is fully capable of doing what you expect him to do. If you ask him to clean his room, he may have no idea where to start and be overwhelmed. If so, break the task down into manageable parts. Ask him to pick up all of his clothes from the floor and put them in the dirty clothes hamper. When finished, ask him to make his bed or clean off his desk. It is frustrating, but he may eventually get the complete job done. Work with him on how to break big jobs down so he learns to do them for himself.

▷ Sometimes a written or pictorial checklist can be helpful.

▷ Provide plenty of positive reinforcement and limit the negatives to the really important things. Definitely choose your battles wisely. Remember, your son probably gets plenty of negative feedback outside the home. There is a difference between being firm and being overly critical.

▷ Give consequences within short order of the offending act. Providing them consistently is also key. Children with ADHD need consequences to follow the misbehavior as soon as possible to have maximum effect.

Homework

Be honest. You'd rather walk over hot coals than try to get your son to do his homework, wouldn't you? It's daunting for so many reasons. He probably had a frustrating day at school and doesn't look forward to sitting down at a desk again. Frequently boys with ADHD have weaker executive functioning skills and have great difficulty initiating activity, planning, and organizing. They honestly may not even remember what the teacher wants them to do. My son never liked to settle down to do homework and usually waited until the last minute. In high school, he always put off planning for large projects, especially term papers and science projects.

For many parents homework is a nightly battle. Unfortunately, this is classic ADHD behavior. Homework requires sustained mental effort—and that's difficult for boys with ADHD. Barry and Cecelia found that applying Grandma's Rule worked for their son, Joel. Grandma's Rule means that you have to eat your veggies before you can have dessert. In other words, work comes before play. Thus, Barry's son had to complete his homework before he could play any video games, one of his preferred activities. Joel's 504 plan also included a reduction in his homework load and receiving his homework early, so he could get started over the weekend. These accommodations helped reduce frustrations.

Homework can be very stressful. The following guidelines have worked for many families:

▷ Establish ground rules and stick to them. For example, turn off the television and loud music, and don't permit your child to receive phone calls or text messages during study time.

▷ Figure out the optimal time for homework in your household. Some children need a break after school, and others cannot be corralled after playing outside.

▷ Determine how long your son can work without becoming frustrated. Provide frequent activity breaks and/or snacks. Your son needs to be willing to return to work after the break is over.

▷ Remember that he may have difficulty determining where to start and how to approach different tasks. Help him to learn to prioritize tasks so the most difficult and important ones are done first. Guide him in making a plan and taking one task at a time. You may need to cut assignments into parts so he doesn't feel overwhelmed.

- ▷ Provide help when needed, but do not become so involved that your son is not independent—a fine and tricky balance. He is not developing his skills if you are doing the work for him.
- ▷ Allow him to use the computer or tablet (with teacher permission) for producing written work.
- ▷ If homework time produces too much conflict that cannot be resolved, then consider the services of a tutor or even a high school student (if you can afford it).

High-Stakes Testing

In most states, standardized testing plays a role in a school's evaluation and sometimes in whether a student is promoted. These tests are usually 45–90 minutes long, often have a great deal of information on a page, and can be very tedious and boring—clearly not optimal for boys with ADHD. Accountability is critical for schools, so help your son make the best of the situation. Many school districts have practice tests on the computer, an effective way for a boy with ADHD to learn. Take advantage of opportunities for your son to practice if they are available.

Work to learn more about what is covered on the test and try to incorporate some of those skills into your daily interactions with your son. For example, if fractions are on the test, involve him in measuring when cooking or when building a project. If he might be asked to make a prediction about what he thinks may happen in a story, then ask him to make a prediction when you are watching a television program or reading a story together.

From time to time, a boy with ADHD has heightened anxiety because he recognizes that he has performance deficits. Try to be sensitive to that possibility and help him figure out coping strategies to use when he is anxious, such as breathing deeply or visualizing himself in a peaceful place. Learning to control his anxiety could be key to optimal performance. We probably all remember drawing a blank on an exam, a common result of anxiety. You and his teacher will walk a fine line between motivating him to do his best and putting too much pressure on him. Remember to focus on the effort he puts in and not the results. If he has tried his hardest, what more can you ask? If your son needs extended time or other accommodations related to his ADHD, a 504 plan or IEP can be considered (see Chapter 6).

Retention

Most studies have not shown benefits to retention. However, it is a decision that must be made based on individual circumstances, your knowledge about your son, the educational environment, and advice from educators and others involved with your son. Currently most school districts are very reluctant to retain a student based on the research, which doesn't support retention's effectiveness. Some questions to ask are:

▷ Does your son's birthday make him one of the youngest or oldest children in the class?

▷ Would the retention be likely to produce long-term benefits? Surely the retention year would be easier for him, but what about subsequent years?

▷ Is he delayed in areas other than academics? What are his social skills like? What about his physical size?

▷ If he has siblings, how would that impact retention? If he would end up in the same grade as a sibling, sometimes that can cause conflict.

▷ What is the school's recommendation?

▷ If retention seems to be the best option, can you frame it in a positive way to your son?

My experience has been that retention is easier on children than their parents. However, it is a complex decision that must not be taken lightly. Consideration should be given to repercussions for the retention year as well as its impact on the remainder of your son's school career.

Jason was a young man who seemed to be constantly in trouble with his teacher as well as his classmates. He seemed to have no patience with his work, throwing down his pencil or balling up his papers when he made mistakes. He had been able to keep up academically until third grade, when the reading required more concentration and the math involved more steps. He was in danger of retention, and he knew it. That seemed to fuel his anger and anxiety. He got into trouble every day. His parents were upset that recess was being withheld from Jason because he had not completed his work. They felt, and rightly so, that he needed an outlet for his energy. He started lying about his homework, fighting with his siblings, and ruining most of the family's plans.

His family consulted with Jason's psychiatrist, who advised against any change in medication but did strongly recommend private behavioral therapy and an evaluation through the school district to determine if Jason also had a learning disability. The results of the evaluation indicated that he had difficulty with higher order thinking and was very concrete in his thinking. All of his academic skills were significantly below grade level, and his class work was at his frustration level. Jason subsequently qualified for services for a learning disability and received some of his academic instruction in a smaller classroom setting at his grade level. His parents reluctantly committed to private behavior therapy, which systematically targeted social skills and provided Jason with tools to use when confronted with difficult situations with his peers. Progress was slow and inconsistent, but Jason's parents could see that he was doing better. Without that significant intervention, Jason might have been retained and his interest in school and his academic skills might also have continued their decline.

What to Do When There's No Progress

Even after diligent research, excellent communication, and support at home, your son may be struggling too hard in his current setting. If you feel he is not learning and/or is miserable, be proactive. Schedule a conference with the teacher and ask for their honest assessment of the situation. Together, brainstorm additional strategies or accommodations that could work. If your son is on medication, consult with the prescribing doctor to see if adjustments are in order. If a change is made in medication, sign a release for the teacher to communicate directly with the doctor to provide firsthand information about the effects of the medication during the school day.

Inquire if the school has any additional resources that can be tapped. Is there a guidance counselor or school psychologist who could observe your son and provide feedback? Sometimes fresh eyes may look at a problem from a different perspective and come up with solutions. Consult with the principal because they are the instructional leader of the school. Changing teachers or classrooms is usually not an option but could be explored.

If no workable solutions are forthcoming, you could explore the advisability of changing schools. This should not be entered into lightly because stability is important. However, sometimes the school/student match just doesn't produce the desired results and could end up damaging a student's attitude toward learning.

Time to Change Schools

How do you know when it's time to move your son to a different school? I know boys with ADHD have their ups and downs, but sometimes the bad times far outnumber the good ones. When this occurs, it may be a sign that it's time to change to a different school. In some cases, your son may be asked to leave, especially if he is disruptive in a private school. If your son had a rough start in preschool, you may have been hoping that things would be different in elementary school because your son is slightly older and should have matured. This would be a welcome change, but your son's school troubles usually do not spontaneously disappear during elementary school. Remember, his ADHD is a condition that may be with him all of his life. It takes time and patience for him to learn to manage it.

If your son is attending a private elementary school, there is always the chance that he may not be asked back for another school year. It can throw you into a tailspin when your son's private school informs you that he can't return. You may feel panicked, disappointed in your son or yourself, or discouraged that you must search for another school. If this happens to you, and even if it appears to be your son's fault, don't blame him. It won't help the situation and will certainly hurt his feelings, reinforce that he failed again, and decrease his self-esteem. Yes, you want to have a straightforward conversation about his work habits, effort, and behavior, but rarely is it 100% your son's responsibility. Emphasize to your son that when a private school placement—or any school placement, for that matter—does not work out, it is always a combination of factors. Help your son recognize any important lessons from this experience so you can avoid a repeat experience.

Sometimes leaving private school is a mutual decision between parents and the school, and other times it is your decision not to return. Some parents find a private education more limiting for their sons with ADHD, because private schools are not required to make as many accommodations as public schools and may have fewer resources. Although many private schools do make accommodations, it can vary widely by school. One client believed her son's private school was not doing enough and told me, "It was heart-wrenching to watch Joey struggle. He was aware he was considered different, and it broke my heart! I knew it was time for a move." Do you feel like your son is a square peg being made to fit into a round opening? It's time for a change if the match between your son and his private school is not correct.

In a public school, your son's ADHD may be tolerated more than in private school—exactly how much will likely depend on his individual teacher. Some teachers have better classroom management skills and can handle your son calling out answers, squirming while seated, picking away at his eraser, or jumping up for frequent trips to the pencil sharpener. Having a teacher who understands your son and appreciates the strengths he brings to the classroom makes life better for everyone.

However, some teachers may not understand boys with ADHD. Try to help educate the teacher about your son and what helps him to be successful if the teacher is open to it. Many teachers are willing to learn more about ADHD and techniques that they can use to help your son and to make their classrooms run more smoothly. See the Information for Your Teammates: Your Son's Teachers section included on pages 141–145 and decide if that would be helpful for your son's teacher in working with him and others with ADHD. Other fact sheets are available on websites, such as https://chadd.org or other parent support websites.

> *Emphasize your son's strengths, needs, and the type of teaching style you believe works best for him.*

Occasionally the match between the teacher and your child is just not a good one. Many principals are very reluctant to change children's classrooms in the middle of the year, but others will with good cause. It can be quite a juggling act to advocate for your son while maintaining a working relationship with teachers and staff.

The student-teacher match is so important that I recommend parents talk to the principal to gain their support for making next year's teacher a good fit for your son. Emphasize your son's strengths, needs, and the type of teaching style you believe works best for him. Although most principals cannot honor every parent request, many will listen carefully to what you have to say, especially about a child with a disability. It is often helpful to have another person with you when meeting with the principal or school staff. Bring along your spouse, a friend, or even an advocate. Make sure you keep notes of the exchange and follow up with a letter thanking the principal for their time and document decisions or commitments made.

Although your son's ADHD behaviors can't get him totally kicked out of the public school system unless he engages in some very serious behaviors, he can be placed in a special education self-contained classroom focusing on behavior or sent to an alternative school. We discuss these types of placement in greater detail in Chapter 6. For now, just remember that the school staff must have your permission in order to place your son in a special education classroom or alternative school.

Sometimes things do not go well in the classroom for your son, despite your best efforts. If you've failed in numerous attempts to work with your son's teacher and engaged the principal, school psychologist, and/or guidance counselor to explore all options, and you still sense a growing despair for your son, then it may be in his best interest to research other school choices that might be open to him.

When considering a change, ask yourself these questions:

▷ Am I receiving daily (or almost daily) phone calls about my son's school behavior?

▷ Is the majority of feedback I receive from my son's teacher or school negative?

▷ Has my son been suspended from school?

▷ On multiple occasions, have I been asked to come pick my son up early from school because of his behavior?

▷ Does my son say he hates school, or does he feel sick each morning when it's time for school?

▷ Does my son's self-esteem seem low? Does he make statements such as, "I'm dumb. I'm going to drop out of school. My teacher doesn't like me. No one likes me."?

▷ Does my gut feeling or intuition tell me it's time for a change?

If you answered yes to the majority of these questions, it could be time for a change. If so, the next question is, "Where?" There are positives and negatives to any educational setting. Can you afford to send him to a private school? Does he need a special type of school? Are there charter schools in your area that have good reputations? Should you homeschool or consider a virtual school? Often the answer is not obvious or easy.

Barbara's son, Tom, attended public school from kindergarten through second grade, and it was generally a good experience. At the end of Tom's kindergarten year, the school wrote a 504 plan, which allowed reasonable accommodations for his ADHD. This plan was helpful because it allowed Tom to stand up and complete his work, be sent on an errand if he appeared to need movement, not have all of his recess taken away if he failed to complete his class work, and receive a reduced homework load. Tom's second-grade teacher understood that boys with ADHD required movement, and she allowed Tom to have a two-seat option. He was able to work either at his desk or at the table in the back of the room. He enjoyed this option because it provided choice, and at times one seat felt better than the other one.

At the end of second grade, Barbara and her husband, Brent, decided to move Tom to a private school. Although the public school's third grade had a good reputation, they were very concerned about the mandatory third-grade retention if Tom didn't pass the high-stakes state test. At this age, Tom rushed through his work and gave up quickly if the work became too challenging. Barbara believed Tom would rush through the state test, possibly facing mandatory retention if he did poorly.

When considering the move from public to private school, Barbara and Brent weighed the pros and cons. Some aspects in favor of a private school they were considering included:

- no mandatory third-grade retention,
- smaller class size,
- a more accepting environment with less stress,
- daily recess,
- lots of parent involvement, and
- manageable amounts of homework.

For their family, the only drawbacks were paying tuition and providing transportation.

The first private school they visited wasn't a good fit. After Tom took the admissions test, the principal told Barbara and Brent that the school couldn't meet Tom's needs. Although they were disappointed, Barbara and Brent kept the positive perspective that they would find the right place for Tom. As it turned out, they located a faith-based private school that offered small classes, structure, and a supportive learning environment. The principal openly accepted Tom and his ADHD and willingly honored the 504 plan that was already in place, allowing a smooth transition between schools. Tom successfully attended this elementary school from third through fifth grades.

Home and Community Issues

You know by now that your son doesn't leave his ADHD at school. He faces challenges at home, around the neighborhood, and in any activity he pursues, because ADHD permeates all areas of a boy's life. It is also common for boys with ADHD to have difficulties when interacting with their siblings and peers.

Siblings

If your son with ADHD has brothers and sisters, you understand there are times they fight like cats and dogs and other times they laugh like best friends. The sibling relationship is important for boys with ADHD because it helps them learn to form appropriate interpersonal relationships. Home is usually where boys with ADHD feel safest because of the unconditional love within a family. Therefore home is a great place to start teaching your son with ADHD how to appropriately interact with his siblings and others.

Most boys with ADHD require your specific advice and instruction to learn how to get along with their siblings. Forming solid, civil relationships does not come easily to most boys with ADHD, and siblings often find their brothers with ADHD annoying, interfering, and difficult. Sure, a lot of brothers and sisters find each other annoying, but boys with ADHD can seem off the charts. You must make it a priority to teach your son courteous and friendly behavior and provide him with opportunities to apply what he's learned with his siblings.

Home is usually where boys with ADHD feel safest because of the unconditional love within a family.

Consider establishing this primary family rule: "Treat others with respect." This directive must come from parents; after all, you are the head of the family. Your message must be, "We are a family. We treat each other nicely, and we support each other." Teaching mutual respect starts with you. Model it and live it—and that means treating your children with respect and requiring that they treat you and one another with respect as well. Establish it as a theme in every family talk, especially when that discussion involves conflict. If this message isn't firmly established during the elementary years, adolescence can be very difficult. If you expect your son with ADHD to respect you and the other family members, then you must first show that same respect to him. He has to know what it looks like.

I understand that this can be so hard to do. Boys with ADHD sure know how to push your buttons, don't they? Young boys with ADHD often react with noises (including body noises) rather than words because they feel emotions much faster than they can label and speak them as words. I've known boys who, when reprimanded for behavior, will do things like stick out their tongues, make a "raspberry" sound, say "la la la la la," or sing song lyrics. If your son does this to you, try to remember how primal his first reaction can be. When you ask him to stop the unwanted behavior, follow it up by saying, "Please use words instead of noises."

Name-Calling

When you establish the family rule "treat others with respect," you take an important step toward creating family peace. Name-calling falls in the category of disrespectful behavior you're likely to have to address with all of your children, but your son with ADHD may need extra patience in learning that ugly names are absolutely not part of your family's vocabulary. This means you don't ever call your son an unkind name, and he never calls you or any of his siblings a mean or profane name. Of course there will be slip ups. Agree on consequences and enforce them. One family I worked with made each child pay a dollar any time there was name-calling. It simply wasn't tolerated, and this consequence really made the "treat each other with respect" rule hit home.

Counseling

Occasionally, sibling disagreements become so intense that the situation requires the help of a mental health counselor, family therapist, or psychologist. Family discord often makes everyone feel miserable, and this feeling spills over into your son's life at school, at his friends' homes, and everywhere he goes. Often within a half-dozen or so sessions, a well-trained counselor can help turn around family problems. In my experience the time and money you spend working with a professional is time and money invested in family harmony.

Friendships

Some boys with ADHD are gifted communicators. If your son has this talent, continue to develop it, because it will carry him far in life. Others boys have communication and social difficulties because they speak before they think—which tends to get them in hot water. Other boys with ADHD seem to have difficulty processing language, which impacts their social skills. Many boys with ADHD don't think of others or about the way others perceive them. Sometimes, boys with ADHD will pass gas as I'm testing or talking with them. It just happens. A colleague who is bald was evaluating a boy with ADHD who commented, "I like your head. How'd you get it so shiny?" Another little boy asked me, "How did you get so old?" Often, whatever's on their mind or in their body just comes out. This is part of what gets them into trouble. Professionals call this "lack of inhibition," because boys with ADHD often don't have the little voice in their minds that says, "Don't do that because it could get you in trouble," or "Don't say that because it could hurt someone's feelings." They don't hold back their automatic thoughts. The words or actions just happen. So the next time he gets into trouble and you ask, "Why did you do that?" and hear him reply, "I don't know," he's probably telling you the truth. It just happened.

This brings us to another point: Asking your son the question, "Why did you do that?" is rarely helpful. I like the advice from Pete Wright (2009), an attorney and parent of two successful boys with ADHD and learning disabilities. He wrote:

> When my children misbehaved or messed up, I never asked them, "*Why* did you . . ." When the parent asks a child "why," the child learns to create good excuses, shifts blame onto others, views himself or herself as a "victim of circumstances"—and does not learn to take responsibility for his or her behavior.
>
> Talking about why the child misbehaved will not teach the child that he has control over himself, his environment, and his future. This will not teach him to take responsibility for his actions. When you ask "why," it's easy to slip in some guilt—"Why did you do this? You upset me so much. You made me feel terrible." Ask these four questions instead:
> - What did you do?
> - What are you going to do about it?
> - To ensure that this does not happen again, what should we do to you now?
> - If this does happen again, despite your good intentions now, how much more severe shall the punishment be next time? (para. 7)

If your son's ADHD is on the severe side, you may find that he's excluded from birthday parties and other social events. Some boys with ADHD have such aggressive behaviors that other kids become fearful of their impulsive behaviors. This is so painful to us as parents, right? This happened to Javery when he was 6 and 7 years old.

Unbeknownst to his father, Tavares, Javery was reacting impulsively by punching kids instead of telling them to stop teasing him. It escalated to the point that Javery was excluded from a few playdates and gatherings. When Tavares asked one of the dads about it, the father explained that the other kids were concerned about Javery's impulsive behavior, and they never knew if he was going to haul off and hit them. Tavares and Bethany, his wife, learned that allowing Javery to play with one child at a time worked out much better than playing with a group, because there was less conflict. For quite a while, they structured Javery's social life so they were there to watch him play outside the home or only allowed him to play at his own home with one child at a time. Soon Javery matured and outgrew the hitting phase. My son wasn't aggressive to others but benefited from structured playdates organized around common interests.

Whenever conflicts with other children arise, you need to listen to your son with ADHD. He is often telling you the truth, at least from his perspective. Of course, it is always helpful to get both sides of the story, but that is not always possible. Over time you can learn to recognize when your son is being honest. I have found many parents seem to have some type of "truth radar" and can usually identify when their son is telling the truth, because he becomes very emotional and insistent. Perhaps you recognize these signals from your son. Does he have certain behaviors that indicate he's being sincere? As a parent, watch your son for nonverbal cues and pay attention to his actions as well as his words.

> *Guide your son to be accountable for his actions, but if he is impulsive, help him understand that sometimes things happen that he didn't intend.*

On lying and ADHD, often children with ADHD can't believe they have actually done what they are being accused of because they certainly didn't intend to do it. Other times, they are too embarrassed to own up to it because it doesn't fit with who they try to be. Or they may be too frightened of the consequences to come clean about it. Guide your son to be accountable for his actions, but if he is impulsive, help him understand that sometimes things happen that he didn't intend. The only thing to do then is apologize and problem solve, perhaps with you, how he can avoid a similar situation in the future. We all make mistakes and try to learn to do better next time. If your son seems to make more than his share, spend time processing the situations with him and helping him come up with alternative solutions. A game called Angry Animals has characters with funny animal names, like Mad Meerkat, and has the players select cards with scenarios on them and choices for how to handle the situation. Boys enjoy this game and learn that there are different options for responding to every situation.

If you feel your son has deficits in social skills that are affecting him in the community, review the resources for improving social skills mentioned earlier in this chapter under the section entitled Your Son's Peers on page 145.

Sports

Many boys with ADHD are naturally athletic and excel in physical activities and sports. It becomes a natural outlet where they can showcase their talents. Competing in sports may help your son build a sense of accomplishment that could be missing from the academic areas of his life. Sports provide your son with focus, structure, and discipline. One of my colleague's young clients struggled academically throughout elementary and middle school but always excelled in sports. During high school, he was so accomplished that he was the top player on his football team and landed a college scholarship playing football. This young man's motivation to play football was the driving force behind maintaining his grade point average for athletic eligibility. The demands of football practice helped him develop time management skills as well.

From a very young age, Sharon's son, Juan, had amazing agility and could climb anything, especially trees and playground equipment. At the park, Juan would climb to the top of the monkey bars, stand up, and walk across them as if he were on a high wire. Other playground moms would comment, "Look at that boy. That's so dangerous." Sharon knew Juan would not fall—and he didn't. As Juan grew older, this agility helped him excel in skateboarding. My son was an outstanding athlete. Sports were an important outlet for his excess energy, provided a vehicle for making friends, and kept him interested in school. He knew he didn't like sitting at a desk in class, but his love for recess and physical education made the school day worthwhile in his eyes.

I believe one secret to parenting boys with ADHD is determining if your son has a passion for sports. Expose him to different sports opportunities from a young age. As soon as he is eligible, enroll him in organized youth sports. There are so many to choose from—T-ball, basketball, golf, tennis, roller or ice hockey, football, skateboarding, swimming, running, or martial arts. Pick carefully so you don't overload his schedule. Once you find a sport where he has an interest and natural talent, build upon it. It does not matter whether it is a group or individual sport. Many boys I have worked with have been helped tremendously by karate, which stresses listening, discipline, respect, and following directions. In addition to the comradery it provides, sports also is an excellent outlet for excess energy!

Compliment your son's athletic ability in front of others. Remember to tell him you are proud of him, and encourage him to stick with it and practice. Gary's son, Jamal, enjoyed playing baseball; starting at age 4, he played for eight seasons. Together they spent hours in the backyard throwing, catching, and hitting. During Jamal's first season of kid-pitch baseball, he hit a homerun. Gary was so proud of Jamal that he ordered a trophy topped with a baseball player and engraved with "My First Homerun" and the date. Jamal was so proud of himself and the trophy that for a while, it became a kitchen centerpiece. Although the trophy was nice, the recognition was the most important part of this experience and helped him start to learn that hard work and dedication pay dividends.

Many boys with ADHD jump from sport to sport because having a short attention span is part of their disorder. They find a sport and become passionate about it but lose the passion just as quickly. You can be the one to help your son persevere. Most importantly, if your son starts a sport, do not allow him to quit until the season is over. Although quitting is often the easy way out, it does not build his character. Even if your son believes he is the worst player on the team, don't let him bail on his team. Let your son earn the feeling of accomplishment and satisfaction that comes from sticking it out until the end. Teach him to push through when things get tough. Pushing through tough times goes against everything he naturally wants to do, but he needs to develop this ability for success in school and sports. My son enrolled in competitive swimming because of how much he enjoyed recreational swimming. However, he hated the rigor of the swim practices, even though he was a natural at backstroke. As a young child, he would cry about going to practice but was encouraged to stick it out until the session was over. He learned that once you commit to something, you have to see it through.

Remember, it is also okay if your son does not like sports. It may be hard for a dad to accept that his son is not going to have the same sports passion that he had as a youngster, but that may be the reality. Not every boy with ADHD is going to become a sports fanatic. If your son has tried group and individual sports but still does not have the knack for any of them, then you know more about his gifts and personality and can nurture his other talents.

Camps

Attending a day or sleepaway camp can build your son's confidence if it is the right setting. My son attended recreational, Boy Scout, and church camps—all of which provided good lessons in being organized and keeping up with his belongings. If you think your son isn't ready for a sleepaway camp, start with a day camp during the summer if you find one where you feel he can be successful and have a good time. Many boys with ADHD enjoy camps that offer outdoor or hands-on activities. Some favorites in my area are fishing, surfing, and baseball camps. You know your son best and understand the type of camp he'd enjoy most. However, it takes due diligence on your part to locate just the right type of camp for your son.

Sure, any parent can sign their son up for a camp and send him off, but it's different for boys with ADHD. You know his camp must be just the right fit, have the right type of activities, number of children, staff personality, and structure—or it could be a disaster. He'll come home early, say he hates camp, won't want to return, and give you a hard time. You know that if he feels miserable, some of it is going to rub off on you too.

In addition to more typical summer camps, some locations offer therapeutic camps for boys with ADHD. Dr. Bob Field operates the California-based, multisite Quest Therapeutic Camps for children with ADHD and other associated disorders as a day camp. If your son needs a therapeutic camp, a process similar to what Dr. Field describes below may be helpful.

In a personal correspondence, Dr. Field explained that his Quest camps are fun for kids and based on parental input and an individual screening assessment. Each camper receives an individualized treatment plan that helps address their most consequential problematic behaviors. The campers identify and understand specific behavioral goals. Using camp activities, therapy staff is able to observe difficulties as they occur and provide interventions right then and there. Counselors are advanced college or graduate students trained to help campers gain awareness as behaviors occur. In addition, during each hour of the day, campers receive specific staff feedback about the positive and negative aspects of their behavior. Campers are awarded points each hour based on their effort. As a camper progresses, higher points require increased effort, developing greater success. Combining a cognitive behavioral therapy approach and specially developed neurocognitive strategies, Quest's small-group therapy sessions facilitate the individualized goals of each camper. This model has been proven to successfully address problematic behaviors and help campers develop appropriate social skills.

Before you send your son to either a day or sleepaway camp, you need to think about a few important considerations:

▷ Can you handle the stress of sending him off on his own?
▷ Is he mentally prepared for camp?
▷ What is the camper-to-counselor ratio?
▷ What experience do the counselors have working with boys with ADHD?
▷ How is discipline handled?

If your son is attending a sleepaway camp, you may want to ask the camp staff questions like:

▷ How do you handle bullying?
▷ What happens if my son wets the bed?
▷ Who keeps and administers his medication?
▷ What happens if there is a medical emergency?
▷ Are electronics allowed?
▷ How can I communicate with my son?
▷ What efforts are made to help children make friends?
▷ What if he wants to come home early?
▷ What strategies are in place to help develop boys' self-esteem?

In addition to thoroughly researching and selecting the best choice for your son, mentally and emotionally prepare him for the experience. As mentioned previously, boys with ADHD do not tend to like unexpected change. Explain what a typical day at camp is like. If the facility is located close to your home, stop by and introduce your son to the director. Try to anticipate his feelings the first day of camp and give him words of encouragement that he can replay in his mind through the day. If your son is nervous about new situations and does not know any other campers, you might say something like, "On the first day of camp, a lot of kids won't know anyone. They may not look nervous on the outside, but I'll bet they feel nervous inside.

Remember that and talk to lots of kids, because they are hoping they meet a good friend like you." These types of simple steps set your son up for a successful camp experience.

Video Games

If you have a son with ADHD who doesn't love video games, he may be one of the few. Video games are a part of life for most boys with ADHD because games often provide them feelings of control and success. The fast pace and stimulation produced feel great to a kid with ADHD. Quite frequently I am asked my opinion on whether boys with ADHD should be allowed to play video games at all. Parents worry, "Are video games bad? Should we limit his video game time? Should we ban war types of video games?"

> *Video games are a part of life for most boys with ADHD because games often provide them feelings of control and success.*

For many people it comes down to personal belief. I know that some parents ban their sons from playing all games except those with an "E" rating for "Everyone." Other parents only allow video games on the weekend if their son had a good week in school. Others allow their son 30 minutes each day once his homework is complete. Some allow unlimited play because it occupies his time and gives them some respite. As one mom stated, "I was never into video games, so I don't understand the big obsession with them, but it gives him an outlet where he can chill. Actually, it helps him decompress from a hard day at school."

How you use video games is personal preference. Because the research is mixed on boys with video games, a good rule of thumb is to allow boys with ADHD some time to play video games because they can be a great reinforcement for good behavior. There are count-

Figure 6
Pros and Cons of Video Games

Pros	Cons
Can be used as a reinforcement tool	May cause kids to hyperfocus on the game
Some promote physical or mental exercise	Many are excessively violent
Can develop hand-eye coordination	May cause kids to be emotional or defiant when time to stop
May be a hobby leading to employment	Can be expensive
May build focus and concentration	May cause kids to spend too much time gaming
May build feelings of success	May cause kids to engage in less physical activity and have fewer opportunities for socialization
Can provide a way to socially connect with others by having knowledge about components of the various games	Can allow kids to connect with questionable people online

less times I have heard parents say to their son, "If you want to play your game, then I need your help doing so-and-so," or, "If you finish your homework without arguing, then you can play your game for 30 minutes." Nevertheless, I strongly recommend that parents use discretion with the amount of time they allow their sons to play. As I outline in Figure 6, video games have pros and cons, but too much video gaming is not a good thing and can lead to addiction. I do not endorse allowing boys to play without limits or play without some supervision. In this day and time, it is important for you to know what your son is playing and with whom he is interacting. Remember that impulsivity can lead to bad choices.

One mother called me out of desperation at trying to manage her 12-year-old son. His bedroom was in the basement of their home and they had allowed him to have his computer there. Whenever she entered his room, he quickly changed screens or interrupted his play. She had also noticed his language had become more aggressive and surly. His dad asked if he could play one of the games with their son; of course, he refused. They didn't like what they were seeing and decided to set some strong rules on video gaming. Luckily, their son was still young enough that they had the control to make these changes. He was invited to participate in setting the guidelines but did so very grudgingly. When he realized they were very serious about moving his computer from the basement to the first floor family living area, he finally agreed to participate in helping select and set up an area for his computer. Parents established parental controls on all of his games. He was allowed access to only some online games, which parents were able to view at any time. They helped him understand good online safety rules and limited his play to when homework was done with longer playing times on the weekend. It was a painful process, but they were glad they caught the situation early enough to do something about it.

Boys with ADHD are stimulated by the games' visual effects, real-life graphics, and intense action. Over and over I've heard a parent tell how their son becomes so hyperfocused on his game that he doesn't respond when called for dinner, he ignores his friends, or he doesn't notice when the phone rings. Does this sound familiar? When you tell him to stop gaming, he becomes agitated or irritable and begs for 5 more minutes. When you return, he becomes more defiant, and you become so provoked that you just reach over and pull the plug. He yells because you made him lose his save. Clearly defining the amount of game time, rules for stopping, and consequences for arguing help prevent this type of scenario. Boys with ADHD don't like new rules or things sprung on them, so with video games, and in everything you do, try to establish guidelines and procedures beforehand.

Self-Esteem

Think about your son's self-esteem. Does he appear to feel good about himself, or is he down in the dumps? Some psychologists see self-esteem as inconsequential, but I believe that if a boy has low self-esteem, then it permeates all areas of his life. If you work with a psychologist or therapist, my recommendation is to choose one who will assess your son's self-esteem. There are self-esteem measures that boys complete independently, which can then be discussed in a session.

If your son's self-esteem appears solid, you are fortunate. His self-esteem will help provide him with the confidence he needs to navigate life. Continue to nurture his self-esteem, because it can give him a sense of resiliency, which he'll need for bouncing back when he has a setback or challenge. It will allow him to stand up, brush himself off, and try again. This is an invaluable quality to develop. If you want to learn more about instilling this sense of resiliency in your son, I recommend *Raising Resilient Children: Fostering Strength, Hope, and Optimism in Your Child* by Drs. Robert Brooks and Sam Goldstein, because it is full of ideas for developing resiliency and self-esteem.

The self-esteem of many boys with ADHD is low. It can have been impacted by repeated failures, constant reprimands from adults, teasing from peers, or just because of the way he is wired. Your son's behavior, level of anxiety, popularity, physical appearance, and general satisfaction with life may impact his self-esteem. You may find your son's self-esteem is high in one area and lower in other areas. In my experience, boys with ADHD often have low self-esteem when it comes to behavior because they know that they frequently get in trouble. I also find that many boys with ADHD have anxiety, especially about school-related tasks, such as taking a test or being called on by the teacher. They may act up in school and become class clowns to try to build confidence by making people laugh.

Your son's low self-esteem stifles his decision-making ability. Some boys with ADHD can't make even the simplest decisions. If your son thinks poorly of himself, then over time he may become anxious, frustrated, or depressed. These depressed thoughts can limit his energy to get things done and lead to poor performance. Unchecked, it can become a difficult cycle to end.

If your son has low self-esteem, his automatic reaction to a new task that appears challenging is probably, "I can't." For many boys with ADHD, this "I can't" attitude can turn into what professionals call "learned helplessness." Your son learns that it benefits him to become helpless. This develops over a period of time, because when your son automatically says, "I can't," many parents and teachers spring to complete the task for him. What you must do is determine if your son's problem is an "I can't" or an "I won't" type of problem. This allows you to decide how quickly you should step in to help. If it is an "I won't" problem, then you need to wait and let him try to work through it on his own. If the problem is "I can't," then you should step in, provide instruction, and step away to let him try. When you do things for your son that he can do for himself, you can lower his self-esteem. You want to help him develop an "I can and I will" attitude.

You can help strengthen your son's self-esteem by affirming him in front of others. So often we reprimand and correct our sons around other people, but we affirm them much less. Regardless of his age, your son needs to hear your encouragement and positive reinforcement, and he needs others to hear you giving it to him. He needs to hear you say statements like, "I'm proud of you. Your performance was awesome. You have a great heart. I love you." If parents don't affirm their son in this way, then he will find another way to get that affirmation, often from peers or by smoking, drinking, or engaging in other dangerous behaviors when he is older. Build your child up by telling family or friends a positive story about him, send him an email with a photo or a great story about him, or simply send him a note in his lunch box that he can read.

These are additional suggestions you can use to help develop your son's self-esteem:

> ▷ When age appropriate, explain his ADHD and help him understand it.

▷ Read age-appropriate books about self-esteem with your son. Some good choices might include: *Don't Put Yourself Down in Circus Town* by Frank Sileo (ages 4–8), *Being Me: A Kid's Guide to Boosting Confidence and Self-Esteem* by Wendy Moss (ages 8–13), *Nobody's Perfect* by Ellen Flanagan Burns (ages 9–12), and *My Diary: The Totally True Story of ME!* by Gilles Tibo (ages 8–12).

▷ Engage him in extracurricular activities (e.g., music, art, drama, sports, computers) where he can find success.

▷ Be aware of your positive-to-negative comment ratio, and increase your genuine praise.

▷ Comment on his positive qualities rather than his negative ones.

▷ Try to reduce family conflict by establishing routine, consistency, and structure.

▷ Help him identify and build at least one good friendship.

▷ Try to help him establish a positive relationship with his teacher.

▷ Identify a mentor (e.g., at school, within a club or other organization) who takes a special interest in your son and helps build him up.

▷ Work with a counselor if you feel he needs professional help in building his self-esteem.

Points to Consider

1. You can expect the elementary years to be challenging for you and your son. The demands of school shine a new spotlight on his deficits in executive functioning skills and his difficulties with behavior, focus, and attention. What weaknesses do you recognize in these areas? Think about how can you put a plan in place to help him strengthen them.

2. Are you keeping a problem-solving perspective? Seek professional help when necessary and never give up.

Points to Consider, *continued*

3. How involved are you? Your son needs you to be involved at school to advocate for him and to work with his teachers to create interventions that will help him succeed at this critical time in his life.

4. Because your son is different than every other boy with ADHD, he may require interventions tailored to his needs. Can you think of any that might help him?

5. Is your son in a school and classroom where his needs are being met? If not, what steps can you take to improve the situation?

6. Your son's challenges spill over into family and community life. Are you helping him be his best self?

Action Steps

1. If you have not already done so, establish daily (or at least weekly) communication with your son's teacher if he is experiencing any difficulties.

2. Monitor your son's academic progress. Supplement where necessary.

3. Make sure you have a workable homework plan in place.

4. Try some of the techniques in this chapter to create a healthy home and community environment for your son.

5. If your son's self-esteem needs strengthening, think of some ways to develop his confidence. Put supports in place if he needs to grow in his ability to self-regulate his behavior.

6. Make sure you set up and enforce guidelines for playing video games.

Chapter 5

The Teenage Years

Your son is changing. His body is changing. His voice is changing. His emotions are changing, sometimes from minute to minute. He's entering that unfamiliar, sometimes unsettling phase of life—adolescence.

The adolescent and teen years are filled with new experiences and new responsibilities. If your son is attending a public or private school, imagine him walking down the hall of his new middle school or high school. The hallways are covered with posters for clubs he can join. It's loud. Inside each classroom there's a different teacher, and he knows the work is going to be hard. His interest in friendships and romantic relationships is growing. He's got a locker, and he has to remember the combination and where it is and which books and notebooks to bring to which class. He's nervous. Or excited. Or scared. Or confused. Or all of those things. If he is homeschooled or attending virtual school, he will have a different set of challenges. He will still have to juggle all of the different assignments with often less assistance from the teacher. Online and technology temptations can use up his academic time. Loneliness and social isolation may become a factor. However your adolescent son is receiving his education, there will likely be issues to be worked through and problems to be solved.

Adolescence these days can be extremely challenging on many fronts. On the global front, there is much instability among countries and in politics and healthcare. On an individual front, teens may struggle with family and/or economic instability, the impact of social media, constant bombardment with information, stress of standardized testing and school pressures, insecurities about their future, gender and sexuality issues, and many other concerns.

It goes without saying that it is a critical time for you to stay closely tuned in to your son. Because he has ADHD, you already know change can be a challenge for him. This is a time in his life when all of his familiar routines may be upset. He'll need to develop new strategies for success, and he'll need your help and support to guide him toward independence.

You can expect that this will be a time of tremendous growth, but not just for your son. As he learns to become an independent young man, your role transitions as well. You'll continue to be his biggest fan, his advisor, and his sounding board. But now, it's also your job to look for ways to start letting go. I know that can be a scary thought!

School Issues: A Time of Transition

Your son has many strengths that he'll take into his middle school and high school experience. Remind him of this, and take the time to explore areas you may not have considered before. Is he an especially sharp observer? Does he have an exceptional memory for intricate details? Is he gifted in music or art or math?

More and more, he'll have opportunities to use and develop his special talents and abilities. Everyone is different, but certain strengths have been identified in many individuals with ADHD. Maybe your son falls among them, if he is:

 ▷ a creative thinker,
 ▷ a good negotiator,
 ▷ a "big picture" thinker who doesn't get mired in the details,
 ▷ willing to take a risk to achieve a positive outcome,
 ▷ intuitive and perceptive, and
 ▷ able to focus intently on a subject or topic of extreme interest.

As a student with ADHD enters the upper grades, it is easy to dwell on the struggles he's likely to encounter. It's also important that you regularly remind your son of how he's unique and how far he has come. Encourage him to find ways to use and develop his natural gifts in the more adult world he's about to enter.

And it is a more adult world. In elementary school, the focus is often on the child. In middle school, the focus moves away from the student and onto the curriculum. With his ADHD, it's likely your son has trouble remembering things, paying attention, organizing his time, and controlling himself. Success in higher education requires lots of executive functioning skills—memory, attention, organization, and self-control—the very things that can be so difficult when you have ADHD.

> *Encourage him to find ways to use and develop his natural gifts in the more adult world he's about to enter.*

As I have mentioned before, these executive functioning skills can improve with maturity and support. Depending on the severity of their ADHD, boys may be delayed by as many as 3–4 years in problem-solving, attention, and memory functions that they need in a middle school or high school setting. Their social development may be similarly delayed. At one time, researchers studying ADHD believed that most children "outgrew" ADHD. Now we know that's not the case. Not all children with ADHD continue to struggle into their teen years, but a majority of them do. Many carry those challenges into adulthood as well. So you can see how important it is for boys to equip themselves with strategies they may need to use their entire lives.

As schoolwork gets more challenging and demands grow greater, the performance gap between students with ADHD and their friends without ADHD tends to widen. That can begin to happen in middle school. Sometimes, it doesn't manifest itself until high school, where there's even more to juggle, a quicker pace, and often, a less-friendly schedule. So, just as you've worked hard to make your son's elementary years productive, you and your son need to form a team to tailor his middle school and high school educational experiences.

Middle School

Your son is not a little kid anymore. In fact, he probably reminds you of that on a regular basis. As your son leaves the comfortable and more nurturing environment of elementary school, you naturally hope his past successes will carry over into his new learning environment.

Remember that middle school will be a chance for him to grow, to make different friends—hopefully ones who will be positive influences, and to try interesting things. It will be important for him to be surrounded by people who are going to be eager to give him a chance to shine. If he has experienced frustrations or problems before, it's a chance for him to start fresh. Your son probably takes a lot of cues from you. It's a big step, but if your first response is fear, it's very likely you'll convey that to your son, and he'll become worried and nervous, too. It's true that there will be challenges—there will always be challenges for a person with ADHD. But do your best to reassure him that you're prepared and that he will be, too.

Multiple Teachers

This may be the first time your son is changing classes and having more than one primary teacher. Suddenly, keeping in close communication with your son's school just got 6–7 times harder. How will you manage it?

Many parents begin planning the transition to middle school many months in advance. If you haven't, don't panic. You can still make a difference in his school year. You may request to meet with school administrators and guidance counselors to discuss the curriculum and teacher selection and to let your son introduce himself. More and more, your son needs to be involved in school meetings and speak on his own behalf. This will be easier for some students than others. Still, encourage your son to contribute. It's a skill he'll need to practice.

You may find you have less input on teacher selection as your son moves into the upper grades. Instead of making specific requests, you may wish to express your preference for a specific type of teacher for your son. This will benefit not only your son, but also, in the long run, the teacher and the class.

Generally, boys with ADHD do better with teachers who are:

▷ **Flexible:** This teacher grants occasional extensions when your son misunderstands a homework assignment, leaves his work at home, or simply forgets to do it.

▷ **Open to modifying assignments:** This teacher understands that the goal is to have the student grasp the ideas and concepts being taught. If a student struggles with a long essay but can demonstrate command of the material another way, like making a video or an art project, the teacher is willing to let the student do so on occasion.

▷ **Knowledgeable about ADHD:** Some teachers have far greater understanding of the disability and what to expect of a student with ADHD. They don't mistake poor executive functioning skills for laziness.

▷ **Attentive:** This teacher takes note when students seem to be falling behind and alerts their parents. This is especially important when students have ADHD and may not remember or be too embarrassed to keep their parents updated when they're having trouble.

▷ **Cooperative:** Many teachers are very willing to work with parents. Keeping lines of communication open remains important in middle school. Your son probably hasn't learned all of the skills he needs to be his own advocate. You'll need to stay in close touch with all of his teachers as much as possible. Keep in mind that being a teacher in today's environment is a very difficult job, so try to establish a working relationship rather than an adversarial one.

Maintaining communication with multiple teachers doesn't have to be as overwhelming as it sounds. You will, however, have to do a little homework. I suggest taking the time to learn how each of your son's teachers prefers to communicate, and honoring that. One may have a planning period at a certain time every day. Another may wish to receive only emails or text messages. One may give you a cell phone number and invite you to call anytime and leave a message. Just be respectful of their time and remember they have many students.

Be sure to establish a courteous, respectful relationship with your son's teachers and with the school's administration and guidance staff. Get to know them, and show your appreciation for the jobs they do. Together, you can form a powerful partnership on your son's behalf.

More Classes, More Work

In the confusion of changing from one classroom to the next, having to find books and notebooks and reports in his locker, and getting the right books in his backpack to take to the right classes, how's a kid with ADHD supposed to manage during the day? And what about Thursday night at 9:30, when he mentions the blockbuster science project that's due the next day? Here are a few coping skills:

▷ **Establish a routine.** Before school starts, see if you can get permission to walk the halls with your son if he is attending in person. Your son will probably balk at this, but it can be very helpful for him to be familiar with the setup and have a plan. If you have his schedule, help him map out a route for his day. Together, determine when it makes sense for him to stop at his locker to drop off and pick up books based on the location of his classes. Color-coding books and notebooks can help him know at a glance what he needs for each class.

▷ **Enlist a "coach."** Someone at school may be willing to serve as your son's coach or mentor on a volunteer basis. This could be a favorite teacher, his homeroom teacher, a guidance counselor, or a teacher's aide. This person's role would be to help your son stay organized while at school and stay ahead of assignments and coursework. Your son and his coach may need to meet in the morning and again before the end of the day, once a day, or weekly. You'll feel more confident that any small problems will be flagged before they become big problems, and he will have a little extra help staying on track.

▷ **Find out about big projects early.** Your son may be studying half-a-dozen subjects with many different teachers. There's a good chance you won't be kept personally informed on every single homework assignment. Keeping track of those needs to be his job. But you may wish to ask about any larger or more complex projects your son will be expected to complete during the semester or year. Boys with ADHD have a more difficult time with long-term planning and organizing multiple components. Larger school projects are going to require you and your son to establish a game plan. For the sake of family harmony, you want to avoid unpleasant surprises—like learning about a 10-page paper with accompanying 3-D maps and video—the night before they're due. A good technique is to use a calendar and enter the due date for the project. Then break the assignment down in to smaller components and decide a date when each should be due. In this way, the project doesn't seem so overwhelming and will appear more doable to your son.

The Handwriting Issue

Boys with ADHD show greater difficulty with handwriting and written work than in any other academic area. Your son's handwriting may be illegible, incomplete, and missing punctuation. He may take an hour or longer to write one paragraph. As children advance in school, they need to develop the ability to rapidly transfer thoughts and ideas to paper without becoming distracted by changing their minds or obsessing over small mistakes. This is a skill that many boys with ADHD have not mastered by the time they've entered middle school.

If the issue of handwriting hasn't already been a source of frustration for your son, there's a chance it could happen now. Written assignments are getting longer. Note-taking is becoming more important. Your son will be asked to express himself through writing in almost every subject he studies. Simply the thought of sitting down before a blank sheet of paper can cause fear and anxiety in some children with ADHD. Help him minimize and move past his fears of handwriting in the following ways:

▷ Discourage the student from interrupting himself while he's writing to correct grammar. Instead, allow time when he's finished to go back and correct his mistakes.

▷ Suggest that he read his work aloud. That can help him identify and correct any errors.

▷ Find a pen or pencil that feels comfortable in your son's hand.

▷ Allow him to use a computer for written work, even if you need to get special permission to do so. For many schools, this is already routine. (Another plus: If he loses his work between home and school, it will be backed up on the hard drive!)

Setting Reasonable Expectations

You have a right to have expectations of your son. He has a right to expect certain things of you, too. Your son isn't perfect. You can't demand more than he's equipped to give. At the same time, don't ever expect complete failure. Most of all, don't assume that the things your son does are deliberately designed to drive you crazy. They're not.

> *Your son isn't perfect. You can't demand more than he's equipped to give. At the same time, don't ever expect complete failure.*

What's reasonable to ask of your son and his classwork? It is important to set expectations and put supports in place to help him meet them. Some basic ones might include:

▷ Complete his homework on time, without a big struggle, and turn it in.

▷ Get acceptable grades. You need to define, together, what acceptable looks like. If he's extremely gifted in one subject, he might be expected to maintain an A average in that class. In other areas, a solid C might represent success.

What's reasonable for your son to ask of you?

▷ Begin to release control. Allow him to make some mistakes, understanding that boys with ADHD tend to take quite a bit longer than other children to learn from their mistakes. Be patient and support him to learn from his mistakes.

▷ Trust him. When he demonstrates that he can handle a little responsibility, allow him a little more.

High School

Much of what I've written about middle school holds true for high school as well. The academic and social challenges continue to increase year by year. If they hadn't kicked in before, his hormonal and physical changes are now readily apparent. He's a young man. But if ADHD is still impacting his functioning, certain skills and abilities haven't caught up to his lanky limbs and ceaseless appetite. These are the years when a young person should be moving into independence and self-reliance. It's no different for a kid with ADHD, just more challenging in many ways. He will need to be aware of supports that help him be successful and how to advocate for himself. This will be a major step for both of you, one of many during the teen years. But remember, your primary job as a parent isn't to get your son with ADHD through school. It's to prepare your boy to be a man.

Self-Advocacy

From the time they enter high school, I believe students should be present at all meetings that concern their disability. There may be obvious exceptions—conferences when other students' privacy is at issue. But your son is now old enough to be part of the discussion, and you need to encourage him to answer the questions that pertain to him. Resist the urge to answer for him. As boys gain more insight into their functioning, they sometimes come up with the most helpful accommodations. As he becomes more comfortable in this role, it's possible he may attend such meetings without you.

It is appropriate for your son to initiate discussions with his teachers about his ADHD. Many teachers respond well when a young man approaches them directly about his disability. High school teachers today have so many students that it takes months to learn about each one, so it makes their lives much easier if your son helps them understand his learning style. He should be prepared to describe what his ADHD means for him—what it might look like in the classroom, the kinds of assignments that have been hard for him in the past, and what has helped him succeed. He could talk to the teacher privately between classes or communicate via email. It might go something like this:

> Mr. Rodriguez? Can I talk to you for a couple minutes about something important? I don't know if you know this, but I have ADHD. I have trouble paying attention and remembering things the way other kids do. Sometimes in class you might see me daydreaming. It's not because I'm bored or because I don't want to learn. It's because I get distracted really easily. It's just part of the disability. Last year in history, Mrs. Williams gave me a copy of her notes before every class. That really helped me pay attention better. When we had a test, she also let me stay after school and answer my essay questions out loud. That really helped a lot because writing out long answers is really hard for me. I've lived with this for a long time, and I've learned what works for me. I don't mind talking about it, if I can answer any questions. Can we work together on ways to help me learn so my ADHD doesn't get in the way?

Much of this, of course, depends on the severity of your son's ADHD and whether he has any additional learning disabilities that may require your more active involvement. If he has a 504 plan or and IEP, many strategies like those above may already be in place. However, it is still better for your son to talk to the teacher in person.

And please don't misunderstand. I'm not suggesting you abandon your son and let him figure out everything on his own. As you may know, that could lead to a very bad outcome! Nationwide, educators report that lack of parental involvement is a major frustration, often leading to avoidable setbacks for children with ADHD. By reading this book, you've already proven yourself to be a concerned and caring parent. I'm simply advising you to step back when it's appropriate to do so and see how your son does when he gets the chance to take the reins.

Sleep and the High School Student

Most current research shows that a typical teenager's body is designed to stay up late into the night and sleep well into the morning. Our school systems, on the other hand, still run on up-with-the-chickens time. In many parts of the country, high school students are in class by 7:30 a.m. Studies suggest that half of all teens with ADHD have additional sleep challenges. They report finding it hard to quiet their brains and go to sleep. Their sleep can be restless, or they may wake frequently in the night. They often feel tired in the morning.

Your son can't learn well if he can't get proper rest. In addition to trying common-sense procedures at bedtime (e.g., no caffeine, no video games), you might explore the following:

▷ **Establish a reasonable bedtime.** Talk this through. For instance, he may observe that he often feels tired at about 10 p.m. but gets a "second wind" after 11 p.m. Together, you'll probably see that it would be wise for him to get to bed between 10:00–10:45 p.m.

▷ **Don't start projects after a certain time.** Whether they're school-related or just for fun, big projects can make a person with ADHD lose track of time. If he becomes absorbed, he might look up to see that it's 3 a.m.

▷ **Get plenty of exercise.** There's a lot to be said for taking a bike ride, a swim, or a run after school. Your son will work off the energy he stored up all day, and a tired body sleeps better.

▷ **Arrange the school schedule to avoid groggy times.** It may be possible to set up your son's school day so he has nonacademic classes (e.g., PE, art, music) early in the morning if it takes him a while to wake up. Or schedule them for the end of the day if he tends to run out of steam and lose focus.

Clubs and Sports

Extracurricular activities are a valuable part of the middle school and high school experience. Surrounded by other teens with similar interests, your son will have the chance to make new friends. This is especially important for those children with ADHD who struggle in social situations. He'll gain a sense of belonging. He'll have an outlet for the energy that builds up during the school day. His life will become more balanced as he gets to turn his focus temporarily from the challenges of school and homework. Kids with ADHD seem to want to be doing something all of the time, and extracurricular activities are a great, positive way to respond to that need.

I encourage parents to let their sons explore a wide range of activities, though not all at once. Try new things one or two at a time, and see what works for your son and your family. If a particular sport or group isn't a good fit, require that your son fulfill his commitment and then move on to something else. I've put together some guidelines for you and your son to consider:

▷ Be honest with coaches and group leaders about your son's ADHD if it is likely to impact him during the activity. This can be a very touchy subject for teens, so you will have to use your judgment about how to handle it. The best-case scenario would be for you and your son to talk to the coach together, but most teens I have worked with are very opposed to this. Many coaches will be unfamiliar with the disability. If you expect problems to occur, coaches would benefit from knowing what to expect from your son, and how (and when) to discipline him.

▷ Remember that every added activity is one more thing for your son's daily planner, and one more thing for him to remember. You probably already know that overloading a child with ADHD is a bad idea. Remember this when you're thumbing through his school's activity booklet or reading your city's online recreation flyer.

▷ Every boy with ADHD is different, but hand-eye coordination often tends to be less developed in these boys. This can make some team sports—like baseball and basketball—a challenge because they require agility in catching and throwing. Your son may have more success in sports that emphasize gross motor skills—swimming or track, for instance.

▷ If your son's ADHD impairment remains severe, he may still have difficulty paying attention to the rules of a game or the instructions of his coach. Talk through his choice of sports with him, and encourage him to choose sports and positions that are engaging. He might be a great soccer player but might not fare well at playing goalie, where there's a lot of downtime.

▷ Getting regular daily activity is a great way to improve the quality of your son's sleep, which may help him do better at school. If team sports aren't his thing, he may enjoy sports like skateboarding, rollerblading, or surfing. The martial arts can help develop discipline. Explore lots of options, and stay open to trying them yourself. Sharing a common love of a sport can be a powerful relationship builder.

Homework and Studying

In the families I see, homework causes more conflict than almost any other issue. The parent-child relationship can become volatile. Homework struggles lead to fights, nagging, exasperation, impatience, anger, and tears.

If you've spent years sitting beside your son at homework time, you're ready to turn the responsibility over to him. You wonder whether *he's* ready. You're eager to help him develop a study routine that works well for him. You want peace in your home.

That desire is neither unreasonable nor impossible. If everyone in your house dreads homework time, you need to believe it can change.

Why It's Tougher With Boys With ADHD. If he's like most young men with ADHD, your son may have difficulty seeing homework as a worthwhile use of his time. To him, it's boring. He probably doesn't feel as though he learns much from it. Boys lack the maturity to recognize the long-term value of their efforts. He knows he's been expected to sit in a seat at school all day, quite contrary to his active nature. Now he must sit some more.

Estimates vary, but at least 40% of boys with ADHD have additional learning disabilities, compounding an already serious problem.

Boys, especially boys with ADHD, can have a much more defeatist attitude toward school than girls. Girls with ADHD often overcompensate toward perfectionism. Boys with ADHD often simply "check out," especially if they've gone through years of struggle. Estimates vary, but at least 40% of boys with ADHD have additional learning disabilities, compounding an already serious problem.

Getting Him Off to a New Start. Helping your son get organized is the first step toward breaking old bad habits. Far more than their friends without ADHD, kids with ADHD need a way to keep track of every assignment, every report, every project, every swim meet, and every band rehearsal. Help your son set up a homework area so that all of the supplies he'll need will be within reach of a quiet, comfortable place he chooses.

I also suggest that you and your son spend some time brainstorming about an age-appropriate planner system he finds workable and interesting. Go shopping together and see what makes sense to both of you, based on his needs. He might think a new iPad would be just the thing, but if he tends to lose electronic gadgets, you're well within your right to suggest a less pricey alternative. Traditional paper planners are available in office supply stores. You can even download an app for his phone to keep him on track. *What* you get is far less important than *how* he uses it and *how faithfully* he uses it.

Once his system is in place, he won't have to spend a lot of time thinking about how to get started on his homework—he'll just do it. He won't spend 15 minutes looking for a pen, because his homework area will already be set up with everything he needs. He will be ready to go.

Establishing New Homework Routines. Wise parents need to take steps to restore and protect family harmony during the middle school and high school years, especially with so many other changes happening all at once. That means eliminating homework battles and shifting the responsibility for homework to the child. If you have a middle schooler, this may be a gradual transition, but the goal is to have your son be as self-directed as possible.

Your new rules need to emphasize this point: Homework isn't an option. Once again, putting a new routine in place requires you and your son to collaborate. Here are some guidelines:

▷ Let him set the time he's going to do his homework every day. Help him find a way to stick to it, whether he has a wristwatch alarm, a computer alert, or some other reminder.

▷ Establish a workplace where distractions are minimal. Some students with ADHD say it helps them to have music playing or some sort of white noise on in the background. You can give your son some leeway, as long as he's able to stay focused.

▷ Encourage your son to tackle his more difficult (or least favorite) homework assignments first.

▷ Help him learn to prioritize assignments in terms of their importance in the overall grade. If he can't get everything done, a project that is 50% of his grade is more important than something that is 5%.

▷ Short breaks may improve his efficiency. It may be effective for him to set small goals for himself (e.g., read one section, do 10 problems) and then assess whether he's fresh enough to continue. If he is, he sets another small goal. If not, he takes a short, timed break.

▷ You are not to do your son's work for him. Make yourself available if he has questions, but do not correct his work when he's done. Simply check to see that it's finished.

▷ If your school is not using digital versions of textbooks available online, investigate whether you can borrow or buy an extra set of textbooks for your home, especially if your son is prone to forgetting the books he needs.

▷ If he continues to have a problem recording or remembering assignments, see if your son can organize a study group of friends who don't have ADHD. They can help remind him of work requirements. Hearing discussions of the material will also help him learn.

When He Needs Extra Help. Your son may find that organization and routine are still not enough. If your son needs hours and hours to finish his homework every night, it may be time to bring in reinforcements. You want to be his loving parent, not a sentry who keeps him locked in his room at night slaving over his homework. Some solutions include:

▷ **A tutor:** If you can afford it, this is often a wonderful option for a student with ADHD. The one-on-one attention helps him maintain focus, and talking through the material is an effective learning method when a student has ADHD. Teachers and education professionals are obvious choices, but sometimes a special neighbor or college student can make a great tutor. A gifted tutor can build a strong relationship with your son, will see his value, and can help him realize his abilities. No less important, if there are struggles over homework, they're on someone else's watch. You're not the bad guy anymore.

▷ **An accommodation plan:** If your son is laboring over the sheer amount of homework he is given, ask his teachers about reducing his workload. With the appropriate paperwork (discussed in Chapter 6), he may be eligible for a 504 plan or IEP. It may be acceptable for him to complete only the even-numbered math problems, for example, as long as he can demonstrate mastery of the concepts. If your son's work is reduced, make sure he still has enough practice to learn the skill.

▷ **A deadline extension:** Occasionally, your son may need to ask for extra time to complete an assignment. If this is part of his accommodation plan, then it's already available for him to use. I stress that this should be the exception, rather than the rule. Many boys with ADHD tend to procrastinate, and being given extra time simply means their work piles up even more.

Planning for College and Career

Your son's high school years are the time for both of you to shift your focus from what's immediately before you to the future—college or additional career training, career, or other life plans. It's a time for the boundaries to expand again.

In high school, your son will be given the opportunity to choose the classes he wants to take. He'll start to consider where—and whether—to attend college. He'll think about what he wants to do for a living. He'll need your guidance, along with the input of other wise mentors.

Encourage your son to think about college or career training early, even during his freshman year in high school. He'll feel your support, and it will help keep him focused on his goals and the reasons he continues to work so hard in high school. One of my clients, Nick, offered this advice to other teens:

> Use college as a goal for motivation and not to fail. You have one part of your brain that says give up, but the other half says you'll feel worse if you give up so you have to try your best. You have to identify where you are, identify what you want, and figure out how

you are going to get there. Think of it as having a master plan.

If College Is an Option, Have Your Son Make a List of His Target and/or Dream Colleges

Not 30 schools. A half-dozen, maybe, and talk about why he's interested in them. Be objective and realistic. For instance, going to school 2,000 miles away from home is a legitimate draw for a young man seeking independence, but it may not be affordable or wise to be that far away. Remind him that a college with small class sizes, academic support, engaged professors, and an active Office for Student Disabilities is much more important than the athletic teams or where his friends are going.

Two colleges specifically for students who have learning differences and need support are Landmark College in Putney, VT, and Beacon College in Leesburg, FL. Many other colleges welcome students with ADHD and provide significant support:

- ▷ Northeastern University in Boston, MA, pairs students with expert counselors;
- ▷ Auburn University in Auburn, AL, has a semester-long SKILL Program that helps students adapt to college and involves weekly meetings with a counselor;
- ▷ University of Arizona in Tucson, AZ, features a Strategic Alternative Learning Technique Center (SALT) that provides ADHD coaches for a fee; and
- ▷ Saint Louis University in Saint Louis, MO, offers student success coaching.

If you and your son feel he may need a moderate level of support, find many more colleges by using a search engine to identify those with special programs to support students with ADHD.

After you have done some research on your own, make an appointment for the two of you to sit down with his high school guidance counselor and talk about his choices and what it's going to take to get into his target colleges. This will be a great opportunity for him to practice advocating for himself, something he will have to do in college. Even practice questions beforehand and help him be prepared with a list of potential colleges and questions for his counselor. Hopefully he will walk away with a realistic list of colleges.

Visit Potential Colleges When Possible

Just being on campus, sitting in on classes, and talking to students will help him see that college isn't just an extension of high school. It's a different world. He'll need different, new skills.

Begin to Coach Your Son on the Life Skills He'll Need

Teach him to do his own laundry and learn to fix some simple, nutritious meals. Help him manage his own schedule because he will have no oversight in college. Let him begin to navigate bureaucracy himself. Keeping track of and managing money is a big challenge for some boys, so make sure he can keep track of his money. One very important life skill is problem solving—what to do when things don't go as planned. He'll need to do those kinds of things, and many more, at college or when he's out on his own.

Help Him Stay on Track With His Classes

Teens with ADHD sometimes make impulsive choices. A student with ADHD might decide to take a class only because his buddy is going to be in the class, not because it is a subject that interests him. In high school, the choices your son makes about his curriculum will start to affect his potential for admission to college in general and to the colleges of his choice. He needs to understand what goes into wise, long-term decision making.

Some resources that may be helpful as you help your son plan for college include:

▷ ADDitude's "Questions to Ask Yourself Before You Choose a College," available at https://www.additudemag.com/adhd-college-accommodations-school-decision,

▷ *Making the Grade With ADD: A Student's Guide to Succeeding in College With Attention Deficit Disorder* by Stephanie Sarkis, and

▷ *AD/HD and the College Student: The Everything Guide to Your Most Urgent Questions* by Patricia O. Quinn.

Technical, Career, or Military Training

As I have said before, college isn't the answer for everyone's future plans. Many boys I know with ADHD have developed very successful careers by following their passions and interests in areas like culinary arts, construction, farming, landscaping, and horticulture, to name a few. There are many certification and diploma programs for training as electricians, plumbers, security technicians, and programmers. Apprenticeships offer opportunities for on-the-job training and mentorship. One young man who came from a long line of doctoral degrees decided college was not for him after struggling through high school. He had a great love for the water and is happily and successfully serving on a ship in the Coast Guard. Another young man who dropped out of high school has made an excellent career for himself in the Navy. Just as we know ADHD impacts boys in different ways, we would expect that their career paths would be just as variable. The most important thing is that they find an area where they can thrive and be successful, happy, and independent.

Home and Community Issues

As young people mature, society looks for them to take responsibility for themselves, for their actions, and for the choices they make. This extends across an ever-widening arc, from their social lives to the workplaces and onto the roadways. The troublesome part, as your son may know, is that teens with ADHD are still experiencing delays in impulse control, attention to detail, decision-making ability, problem solving, and social skills. In fact, they may be months or years behind their peers without ADHD. Your son still needs time, tools, and tactics to succeed.

Helping Your Son Win With People

What comes to mind when you think about the qualities that help you enjoy life? What about interacting and socializing with people? I believe our teens with ADHD must have good people skills in order to live life to the fullest. After all, building relationships is one of our primary functions as human beings.

If you are interested in a book that provides a format for helping your son refine his social skills, you might want to pick up *25 Ways to Win With People: How to Make Others Feel Like a Million Bucks* by John C. Maxwell and Les Parrott (2005). It's packed with practical ways to build relationships. The book is easy to read and not at all dense or technical. It includes many stories to illustrate the 25 key points. And the book is small. It won't overwhelm teens who are immediately turned off by thick, textbook-style volumes.

I encourage parents, grandparents, or any important adult in your son's life to read the book ahead of time or together with him. This allows for important common ground so everyone has the same information. That opens the way for discussion and shared experiences or ideas. How might your family work this valuable book into your routine? Here are two ways you might do so:

1. **Save this book for summer reading, when the academic demands of school lessen.** Read the book in advance, and let your son know that over the summer he'll be reading an excellent and potentially life-changing book called *25 Ways to Win With People*. For the first 25 weekdays of summer, he'll read a chapter a day. Reassure him that the chapters average fewer than 7 pages. It will take 5 weeks to complete the book. Each day, you'll ask him to write a short summary of the key points or discuss it with you, whichever he would prefer.

   For example, one way to win with people is to practice the "30-Second Rule." This rule simply states that within the first 30 seconds of a conversation, you say something encouraging to a person. Once your teen has presented his summary, ask questions about how he envisions himself using this rule. Teens with ADHD will understand this rule, but many won't know where to apply it. They will need a parent or adult's concrete guidance. If your son comes up blank, you might say something like,

   > I bet you can use this rule when we are at the grocery store. When we check out, the cashier usually looks at us and smiles. I think you could offer that person encouragement by saying, "Thank you for being so friendly." Do you think you can try this?

   Role-playing is another effective practice tool. You can practice his new skills within the supportive context of your home, where he shouldn't be as self-conscious as he might be in public. He might shock one of his siblings by saying something encouraging to them!

2. **Make learning and applying the 25 points a family project.** Together, the family agrees to read one chapter per week. Some parents set aside part of the day on Saturday or Sunday to have a short talk about the key points. For the

entire week each family member works on applying the step. Family members practice with each other as well as out in their school, work, or daily activities. If the family has dinner together, they should talk about their experiences.

Even though a new point is introduced each week, it's important to keep in mind that earlier points don't get discarded. Apply them as much as possible, especially if there are one or two you have found highly useful. This is what I call the "rent-to-own" philosophy. I like to teach teenagers to try the point out (or rent it) for a week. If he finds it useful, he continues to rent it and use it. At some point your son may decide that this point is so helpful that he'll decide to own it and apply it on his own because he has recognized its value in his life.

This is exactly what happened when Donald's son Jacob read the chapter on "Be the First to Help." He and his dad discussed this point and practiced it, and he tried it out for the first week. At first he found it was hard to apply in school, because he didn't want his friends thinking he was trying to be the teacher's pet. But then he did simple things like help a friend solve a tough math problem, pick up a girl's pencil when it fell on the floor, and stick up for a kid being called names. Jacob felt so internally rewarded that he said, "This is one way to win that really works like it's supposed to."

Clients typically report that the one-point-a-week method really helps the teenager understand, practice, and internalize the steps. Think about your family and decide which way would work best for you.

Getting a Job

Much like an extracurricular activity, finding a part-time or summer job can give your son a place where he can excel. There are many valuable skills and lessons he can learn in the workplace:

> ▷ employer, coworker, and customer relations;
> ▷ the importance of being on time;
> ▷ remembering and following directions;
> ▷ a sense of independence;
> ▷ money management; and
> ▷ building a resume for future positions.

If you and your son decide the time is right for him to find a job, talk through the kind of commitment it takes to be a dedicated employee. There are many entry-level jobs well-suited to a high-energy teen with ADHD, so take the time to help him find a job he can really get excited about. If he needs stimulation, a change of pace, and lots of physical activity, he should look for that in a job.

There are no careers a person with ADHD can't do.

He may learn more than he expects. It's not unprecedented for a boy to decide he eventually wants to go into a line of work that doesn't require a college degree. That idea can be pretty appealing to a boy with ADHD, who may have spent years struggling in the classroom. Spending a summer mowing lawns or flipping burgers might change his mind about the value of continuing his education. It may also help him realize he *does* want to work with his hands in some way. In that case, he may want to investigate vocational training or trade schools, so he doesn't get trapped in a minimum-wage job as an adult. Keep encouraging him. *There are no careers a person with ADHD can't do.* Remind your son he has what it takes to pursue careers in many different areas, but selecting areas he is passionate about and that utilize his strengths will bring greater commitment and job satisfaction.

Remembering some of the difficulties he may have had with teachers, your son may be concerned about having a boss. If you can't meet the person in charge, make every effort to have your son meet the supervisor he'll work with before he accepts a job. He needs to feel comfortable that this person will be flexible and understanding. Depending on the severity of his ADHD, it's up to you and your son whether or not his employer is informed of your son's disability. It will be important for his supervisor to offer support as he learns the job.

> Bobby was excited about starting a new job in an appliance repair shop. He was generally handy in fixing things because he understood how things worked. One thing he wasn't good at was understanding and processing verbal directions. He processed information more slowly than most people. When listening to multiple directions, he would often miss the second or third direction because he was still trying to understand the first one. He was embarrassed to let his employer know that he was most effective with written directions or those delivered to him orally with simple language and with time to process them. He was very reluctant to ask questions and tried to proceed with tasks the best he could. One day, he created a small electrical fire because he wasn't following proper protocols and was fired. His employer appreciated Bobby's willingness to help customers and his dependability in showing up every day on time, but felt he was too big a liability to keep on the staff. If Bobby had been more comfortable advocating for himself, the results might have been different.

Because working, even part-time, will be a new challenge, be prepared to help your son succeed. He'll need to establish a new routine and may need to practice some new skills before he feels comfortable tackling this big step on his own. For instance, you can help him:

▷ **Learn how to fill out a job application.** Help him collect and keep data often required on applications at his fingertips, such as important telephone numbers and information about his school. He might benefit from going through a few practice runs so he will understand the ways the information is being requested. Usually these applications will be online.

▷ **Understand the interview process.** If conversation is difficult for your son, practice this at home. He needs to be comfortable answering questions about himself. Together, you could role-play a typical interview scenario: Why are you interested in this job? Can you tell me about your strengths? What experiences have you had working on a team? Your son should also have some basic questions about the job. This indicates his interest level to a potential supervisor.

▷ **Learn to be on time.** Before it becomes an ingrained habit, you may need to wake him up or remind him it's time to leave for work. You don't want him to lose the job as a consequence of being late. Having a job is a confidence-builder and an important step toward independence. Also, arriving at his job 5–10 minutes early should become part of his routine. Especially at the beginning, do whatever you need to do to help him with this. That might mean setting two alarm clocks, leaving reminder notes on his mirror, or having someone call or text him when it's time to get ready for work.

▷ **Manage his clothing and work-related items.** He may have a uniform or other gear he always needs to have with him at his job. Develop a routine to make sure his work clothes get laundered and the other items are ready to go when he is. A teen with ADHD is just as likely to misplace his plastic name-tag as his homework. Having a specific place where these items are kept is a good habit to develop.

▷ **Work on his manners.** No matter where he goes, your son will need to be polite to the people he encounters. It's likely they won't know him. They won't know the background of his ADHD. If he blurts out inappropriate remarks, interrupts people, or chatters incessantly to his coworkers, he'll jeopardize his job. Employers need to see the same kinds of self-control he's been working to develop in other areas of life. Help him by role-playing and talking through situations that didn't go well on the job. He may be very sensitive to anything perceived as criticism, but keep reassuring him you are there to help him achieve the success you know he is capable of having.

▷ **Be a team player.** It's unlikely your son will be working alone. Having a job will be a wonderful experience for him to bring his unique perspective to a group effort, but he also has to be willing to consider other ideas and figure out how to work with people he might not like.

▷ **Learn the value of extra effort.** Your son is being paid to do a job. He can do it in an average way, or he can do it in an exceptional way that wins notice, praise, and an increased sense of self-worth. Talk with him about ways he can give a 110% effort.

Managing Money

Once your son has an income, he'll need your guidance in learning to manage his money. Together, you can begin to explore basic financial principles such as:

▷ how a checking account works and how to balance it,

▷ how compound interest works, and

▷ how to pay his bills and expenses on time. This is a little like homework. But in this case, if he fails to do it (or forgets), the penalty isn't failing the course. The consequences will be additional fees and eventually a poor credit score. A thousand reminders from you may not be as effective as the first $35 late fee that comes out of his pocket. Today there are many apps that make transfer of money so easy, like Zelle and Venmo, to name a few, but it is important to understand security issues unique to these services.

People with ADHD are especially vulnerable to spending their money impulsively. Saving is a very difficult concept for them to grasp because it's so abstract. Saving his money to buy something later is not nearly as stimulating as buying something—almost anything—right now. As he matures, your son needs to understand that the concepts of self-control and delayed gratification apply to his finances as well. Depending on the severity of your son's ADHD, he might be months or years behind his peers in his ability to handle his money soundly.

It's a fairly simple coping strategy, but if your son is saving for a big purchase, he should not take a wallet full of cash every time he goes with his friends to the movies or the mall. Restricted-access accounts are a great place to park money meant for a new set of golf clubs or another big purchase. Credit cards can be very difficult for a teen with ADHD to manage. They simply provide temptation to spend more than he has. If you feel your son needs to carry a card for emergencies, I recommend a card with a prepaid balance or a debit card you monitor carefully. Show your son that you trust him with a small amount. You can increase his access as he shows that he can handle it.

Dating

Much of what has come your way on the ADHD journey may have been a surprise. In the area of dating and your son's sexual development, you can anticipate some of the changes that are to come. You can discuss them openly. You can make sure he is as well-prepared as possible.

If a boy has a level of discomfort around others, how will he ever get up the nerve to ask someone out? One key might be simply lots of social interaction, and that can start long before he's of dating age. Many adolescent boys with ADHD benefit from participating in group activities with boys and girls. That helps dissolve some of the mystery and can help him feel more comfortable when the time comes.

Many boys begin to show interest in dating when they are 13 or 14. Because of their emotional immaturity, boys with ADHD still tend to act a little goofy. Many girls and boys don't generally like boys who still act so silly, so your son may not be ready to date until he's 15 or 16. Whatever his chronological age, though, you need to discuss your family's dating rules beforehand and ask questions. He will resent this intrusion but may need help and guidance in making good decisions. Having this discussion before he is actually ready to begin dating will help him know what to expect when the time comes. Topics can include:

▷ When can he go on dates and how often? You'll likely have different rules for the school year and for school holidays and the summertime.

▷ Who can he date? What if you don't know the person? Typically, he'll date a friend from his school, church, or community. But he might wish to date someone you don't know. Don't be reluctant to ask to meet them.

▷ Where are they going, what will they be doing, and who will they be with? Your responsibility to your teenage son doesn't end simply because he's on a date. If you would not permit him to attend unsupervised parties alone, he shouldn't be allowed to take a date to one.

▷ What are guidelines for having his friends or significant others come to your house? They should be welcome in your home. Whether you approve of them initially or not, try to get to know them and make them feel comfortable. If they're not right for him, he'll figure it out eventually. But he's never to have them over when he's home alone.

▷ What if he breaks a rule? Your son needs to know in advance that he will face consequences for breaking one of your rules about dating. Dating is a privilege that shows you trust him. If he loses that trust, take away that privilege for a week or so, and then return it for a trial period. For boys with ADHD, a short removal of a privilege is as effective as a long one.

For teens with ADHD, the line between dating and sexuality is a fine one. Dr. Russell Barkley (2020) has conducted exhaustive studies of children, adolescents, and teens with ADHD. His research showed that:

> ▷ 38% of teens with ADHD are involved in a pregnancy,
>
> ▷ teens with ADHD begin having sexual intercourse earlier than their average peers, and
>
> ▷ teens with ADHD have more sexual partners and are less likely to use contraception.

Parents, sit up and take notice. You already know that boys with ADHD have little self-control. They can be impulsive. They find it difficult to delay gratification. So from a physical perspective, the temptation to have sex is powerful. And there's a strong psychological urge as well. Because the teen boy with ADHD is delayed emotionally, he may seek out behaviors that may make him seem more mature—including sex—in order to fit in. Because he has trouble projecting long-term consequences of his actions, your son won't be as affected by fear of fathering a child or the threat of contracting a sexually transmitted disease.

I advise you not to turn a blind eye to the possibility that your son is acting on his strong sexual urges. Here are some tools and guidelines to help him:

> ▷ **Talk to him about the rest of his life.** He may not understand that millions of teens contract STDs every year and that for many of them, like HIV and herpes, there is no cure. He will take them into every future relationship he has. If he fathers a child, it will forever change him, no matter the outcome of the pregnancy.
>
> ▷ **Don't rely on school sex education classes alone.** Anticipate the physical changes he's experiencing and discuss them openly. If this is impossible or difficult for you or him, make sure he has access to good resources he can read or watch. Just because your son has ADHD and has had difficulty with reading material, don't presume he won't read a book about sex. Make sure to preview the book first to make sure it is in line with your family values.

▷ **Make sure he knows your family's moral code.** Many families want their sons to adopt the code "Dating = Love + Respect." It can be a dangerous and false assumption to assume boys easily adopt that view. Boys, including boys with ADHD, don't always view their early sexual experiences as being associated with respect and commitment. For them, it's more about excitement and maturity.

▷ **Teach consent.** He must understand that if someone says "no," he has to stop, no matter what has led up to that point.

A teen with ADHD has learned to expect his actions will be judged. Try not to judge him as he grows more mature and explores dating, relationships, and his own sexuality. Instead, be available to discuss—calmly and thoughtfully—any issues that come up. Remember, you *want* him to come to you.

One thing that makes your parenting job more difficult is that there are many teens out there whose parents try to be a pal rather than a parent. Don't fall prey to the old refrain, "Well, so-and-so can do it." Let your son know setting limits is not easy and is a sign of how much you love him and are trying to guide him in the best way you can. Pushback on parental limits seems to be part of coming of age.

Driving

Another major milestone for your son will be when he slides behind the wheel of a car. It represents freedom, independence, and being on the brink of adulthood. For you, it represents a major loss of control. Unlike many of the other obstacles you've navigated, this one truly is a matter of life and death.

Once again, I rely on Dr. Russell Barkley's research to suggest why parents of boys with ADHD need to be concerned. Working with Dr. Daniel Cox, Barkley (2007) found that young drivers with ADHD are:

▷ 2–4 times more likely to be involved in auto accidents,

▷ 4 times more likely to get speeding tickets,

▷ 3 times more likely to have injuries,

▷ 4 times more likely to be at fault, and

▷ 6–8 times more likely to have their licenses suspended.

It's hard to resist the temptation to assign cause for numbers like those. We know that distractibility and difficulty paying attention are traits of boys with ADHD. It's dangerous if you can't focus when you drive. Teens with ADHD also have a need for highly stimulating activities like risky, high-speed driving.

Whatever the reason, you may have a sense that your son may not be able to handle the responsibility of driving when his friends without ADHD begin getting their licenses. This is common. Many teens with ADHD wait 6 months, a year, or more before pursuing their drivers' licenses. This allows them a bit of additional time to mature and develop the necessary skills to operate a vehicle safely.

Some parents tell me, "I dread teaching my son to drive. He's so sensitive to correction." That's a valid point. Think back to the time when you were learning to drive. How many times did your own mom or dad stomp on the floor of the passenger side of the car, hoping to find that a brake had miraculously appeared? Your teen's driving experience will likely be tough for both of you. He'll be nervous and unsure. You'll be worried and tense. Remember, preserving your relationship is essential. This is a great time to enlist backup. If your school has a driver's education program, make sure he signs up. If it's in your budget, sign him up with a professional driving school. He's far less apt to act out with a stranger than he is with you and may listen much more closely to a driving teacher than he would to you. If that's not possible, maybe there's another trusted adult who'd be willing to teach him. Some communities and schools are even beginning to introduce high-tech driver simulation programs. Much like flight simulators, these machines expose inexperienced drivers to dangerous and unfamiliar situations to give them practice in safe driving techniques. They're expensive and not readily available, but they offer a wonderful way for learners to practice until they get it right, without risking anyone or anything in the process.

When you think your son may be ready to begin driving, here are some of the elements that need to be part of your family discussion:

▷ Do you believe your son is mature enough to drive?

▷ Does he feel ready to pass all of the parts of the driver's test? Does he need extra help with the written portion?

▷ Will he be expected to pay for the expenses associated with driving? Can he afford it?

▷ When he gets his license, how often will he be allowed to use the car? Will he be able to drive at night? In bad weather? With friends in the car?

▷ Can you trust him to honest with you? For example, if he is not permitted to drive with friends in the car, can you trust him to be honest about that?

▷ What happens if he breaks one of your rules?

This last point is an important one. You must have immediate, preestablished consequences for violating rules associated with his use of the car, and they need to be reasonable and proportionate. It's not reasonable to remove his car privileges altogether if he's a half-hour late getting home one day or if he forgets to fill the gas tank. That kind of offense might warrant loss of driving privileges for a week. But if you find he's been drinking and driving, the penalty needs to be strict and severe. If he drives with a friend in the car, becomes distracted, and has an accident, it could have dire repercussions. He needs to know this.

The day your son earns his license is a day he'll never forget. It's an enormous step toward manhood, and he should feel very proud. Celebrate this moment with him. But also emphasize that driving is a privilege, not a right. He needs to earn and continue to earn the privilege of driving a car.

As explained by Katz (2007), Dr. Russell Barkley has recommended a three-tiered graduated system for newly licensed teens with ADHD. I believe this is a fine idea. It allows your son to become more comfortable—and safer—behind the wheel. It also gives him time to earn your trust before you permit him more responsibility. Here's a basic summary of Barkley's ADHD Safe Driving Program:

▷ **Level I (0–6 months):** He drives only during the daytime.
▷ **Level II (6 months–1 year):** He drives during the daytime and until 9 or 10 p.m.
▷ **Level III (after he's had his license for 1 year or more):** Unrestricted driving according to parents' rules.

It's also recommended that a reminder of your family's driving rules be posted prominently in the car your son drives (Katz, 2007). Especially in the case of a young driver with ADHD, it's important to see that reminder every time he gets behind the wheel. I recommend that your list include the following:

▷ Absolutely NO alcohol or drugs.
▷ Keep music low.
▷ No wearing headphones.
▷ No texting. There are, in fact, apps you can download and built-in settings on some smartphones that will disable texting when he is behind the wheel.
▷ No talking on a phone, unless it's a parent calling. You may advise your son to pull off the road safely before he takes or returns your call.
▷ No other teens in the car. This is a smart rule for the first few months. But I believe that after your son has earned your trust, you should allow him to drive one of his friends if he is able to stay focused.

One of the reasons Barkley is such a proponent of limiting nighttime driving for teens with ADHD is that accident rates spike late at night and early in the morning. If your son takes medication to manage his ADHD, you need to be aware of the times of the day that his medication begins to wear off. Take precautions to see that he avoids driving when he may be more distracted or impulsive. Here are other preventative measures you can take:

▷ **If you can, provide your son with a big, slow car to drive.** It won't be cool, but hopefully it will be safe.

▷ **Figure out an "essential documents" system.** He'll need to remember his driver's license, registration, and insurance card for whatever car he's driving. Together, devise a routine to help him remember these every time he drives. That will be easy if he always carries a wallet. If he doesn't, you may need to put together a "car backpack" that always goes with him in the car.

▷ **Make sure he understands the long-term consequences of reckless driving.** This includes death to himself or others, injury, property damage, and loss of his driver's license.

▷ **Make sure your son knows what to do in case of emergency.** Does he know how to handle an accident? When a police officer pulls him over? A flat tire or other mechanical breakdown? Should he get in the car with a stranger who's pulled over to offer help? Does your family have a roadside assistance program? Go over the scenarios—not to frighten him, but to help him be prepared.

▷ **Consider having your son pay for his auto insurance.** The greater the risk he becomes, the more his insurance will cost. He'll have a financial incentive to stay safe.

▷ **Sign a safe driver contract with your son.** There are plenty of examples of these kinds of documents online, or you can draft your own. In a typical contract, the teen agrees that he and all passengers will wear seatbelts, that he will obey all traffic laws, and that he will not drive under the influence of drugs or alcohol. You promise to give him calm and respectful feedback on his driving, and you agree not to punish him if he calls you for a ride home because he's under the influence of drugs or alcohol. Often, such an agreement also outlines who is responsible for various car-related expenses. Posting your contract in a prominent place will help a teen with ADHD remember what he agreed to do.

▷ **Remember the "other stuff."** One mom told a story about her son, a new driver who had ADHD. The young man pulled into a service station to get gas. He put the nozzle into the tank and began to pump the fuel before deciding to run into the convenience store for a snack. He paid for his food, returned to his car, and sped off—forgetting all about the gasoline that was still pumping away. Help your young driver remember that he has to pay attention all of the time, not just when he's behind the wheel.

▷ **Set a good example for him.** If you want him to drive safely, make sure he sees you driving safely. Your behavior, in this or any situation, will always have a powerful impact on your son.

Discipline That Works

Your teenage son is almost a grownup—but not yet. Just as many of the other parenting strategies have evolved, you also need to find discipline techniques that are appropriate and effective. Your new approach needs to respect your son's increasing maturity and preserve your relationship with him. And it needs to help you keep your home a peaceful place.

Tall order? Maybe. But you may have been juggling life with ADHD for a long time. You know that things are constantly evolving and changing. You can do this, too.

The goal is to have your son look at situations that arise as simply another problem with a solution. By taking a problem-solving perspective, hopefully you and your son can develop a collaborative approach to solving the problem. For example, if he is consistently rude to a sibling, explore reasons that may be behind his negative feelings and what can be done to reduce the conflict. Perhaps the sibling is egging him on by purposely annoying him. If so, help him see the situation for what it is and figure out ways to resolve it. If, for example, he suggests trying to think of a funny response rather than getting aggravated, he can try that. Let him know that if that doesn't work, he will have to come up with another plan because disrespect just isn't part of your family's way of operating. You will ultimately be the one in charge but having him "buy into" the solution increases the likelihood of success.

Obviously I can't possibly foresee every situation you might encounter. Instead, I'd like to outline a handful of discipline strategies I've observed. I'll tell you what tends to work and what doesn't, and you can "rent to own" them for yourself.

Natural Consequences

A lot of mainstream child psychologists and many teachers suggest that a teenager be allowed to face the consequences of his own choices, without any intervention from his parents. If he neglects his homework, he'll fail his classes. If he annoys all of his classmates, he'll have no friends. If he can't remember to go to work, he'll get fired from his job. This advice assumes the teen has the full complement of skills that would enable him to accept responsibility. This may be effective in the general population, but boys with ADHD are much more easily discouraged and often need support as their executive functioning continues to develop. If he fails at any one of these things, he may convince himself that he'll never succeed at anything. Or, because his memory may be poor, he may not remember the consequences long enough for them to have the desired effect. He needs more encouragement and support than this form of discipline typically provides, particularly in more important matters like school performance.

Consistent, Mild Consequences

This tactic can be a more effective solution to chronic, mild discipline problems for a boy with ADHD. Instead of seeking a harsh punishment, look for the least restrictive, most lenient punishment that you feel will be effective. It is important for the consequence to follow the behavior quickly while the misdeed is still vivid in the teen's mind.

Teenagers with ADHD remember one thing: that they were punished. They don't tend to remember how long they were punished. Lengthy punishments often end up hurting the entire family, without any additional benefit. Teens with ADHD often repeat the unacceptable behavior, even when they've been punished. You may have to take away your son's iPad or cell phone for numerous 2-day periods over the course of a year, but eventually he'll get the point.

Grounding

It's rare for any teenager to escape getting grounded. But you need to proceed with caution if you're going to go down this road. Grounding your son will take him out of activities for a week, 2 weeks, a month—whatever sentence you've pronounced. That's a long time for a kid whose social network is already probably very fragile and whose social skills may need daily practice. If you isolate him, the effects could range from rebellion to depression. If a situation calls for this method of discipline, try it for short periods of time (1–2 days). I suggest that you warn your son ahead of time that this is the consequence he'll face for particular rule violations.

Losing Car or Phone Privileges

Neither of these are given rights, although your teenager might be surprised to learn this. It's perfectly reasonable to refuse him the right to talk on the phone for a period of time. You can also take the car keys for a week if he's chronically late getting home and it's become a major inconvenience. But don't take away the car for 2 months if his room is messy. That's an overreaction.

Negotiate

There should be room in your relationship for both of you to express your opinions about whatever you feel he did wrong. You both need to speak respectfully and calmly. For a boy with ADHD, this can be an empowering way to build conflict-resolution skills in a nonthreatening environment. It will be most helpful if he can understand the problems his behaviors might have caused or the implications they may have for the future. If the two of you can view the occurrence as a situation that needs a solution and then work toward that end, your son's follow-through will probably be much better.

Second Chances

Far more than other kids, boys with ADHD need plenty of second (and third and fourth) chances to regain your trust and prove they have learned whatever lesson you've meant to teach. If your son messes up, by all means, discipline him. But after a while, give him another chance along with a hearty dose of forgiveness and encouragement.

Admit You Don't Know It All

By now, your son has you pretty well figured out. He knows you're not perfect. Why not admit it every once in a while? When he makes a mistake, tell him about one of the dopey things you did when you were growing up, maybe something you never told your parents, but not something dangerous in case he decides to try it. Let him know there is a learning curve to growing up and also for parenting. When everybody gives it their best effort, things usually work out.

The Last Word on the Last Word

Your son may argue every point. Some teens with ADHD do. It can be a tremendous source of stimulation for him and next to impossible for him to resist. But it's a no-win situation for you. Try not to let yourself get drawn into pointless arguments with your son. If you do, either let him have the last word or simply refuse to discuss the matter until he stops arguing.

You've spent a lifetime—your son's lifetime—helping him. Now you're in the strange and uneasy position of needing to pull back a little here, a lot there. How will you know when to stop helping? One wise mom said, "I don't do things for my son that he can do for himself as a way to build his self-esteem. If I step in and do things for him, he gets the idea that I don't have confidence in him or that he isn't able to handle things on his own."

Your Son's Self-Esteem

The adolescent and teen years can be rough on any kid's self-confidence. As a boy grows and matures, he may experience moments of pure awkwardness he's sure no adult can comprehend. He may feel his peers are so much more successful and more mature, so unapproachable. He wants to be seen as cool, as fitting in—but how? His own body betrays him: His voice cracks, his arms and legs seem too long to control, his face breaks out. If only he could be taller, or shorter, or more athletic, or funnier, or have better hair. He's overflowing with emotions, but he doesn't have the inclination or the words to express them. So those feelings get stuffed inside, making him crazy.

And then factor in ADHD.

If your son has been struggling with his ADHD since he was a little boy, there's a chance his self-esteem may already have taken a hard hit. Many labels may have been attached to him over the years, and he may still carry the hurt from them. Just think of what he may have been called—or worse, what he may have called himself:

▷ lazy,
▷ disruptive,
▷ daydreamer,
▷ poorly behaved,
▷ dumb, or
▷ unfocused.

Is it any wonder that by the time they're in their early teens, some boys find it impossible to list even one of their strengths? Certainly, that's a worst-case scenario. As a caring parent, you can take measures to restore or protect your son's self-confidence. In fact, it's essential that you do so. His self-esteem is closely linked to his likelihood for success now and into adulthood.

Components of Self-Esteem

An individual builds self-esteem bit by bit, by succeeding in life, at school, with friends, and in relationships. True positive self-worth, particularly in the case of a young person with ADHD, needs to include a number of elements:

▷ **He believes he can identify and fix what's wrong.** Your son already knows that life with ADHD is extra challenging. If his self-esteem is healthy, he has begun to develop the ability to identify when there's a problem and to have confidence that he can, with effort, work toward a solution. If his grades have slipped, he's aware of the steps he needs to take and follows through. If he's had an argument with a buddy, he doesn't give up on the friendship. He figures out what went wrong and works it out. The key to this aspect of self-esteem is his *belief* that his efforts will be productive.

▷ **He tries.** Many teens with ADHD have become the unwitting victims of "learned helplessness." It's often quicker and easier for adults to do something for a child with ADHD than it is to teach that child to do it for himself. Sadly, when that child grows up, he believes there are many things he's incapable of doing on his own. That can result in an extremely low sense of self-worth. On the other hand, a young man who's willing to take a risk and attempt to figure things out—even if he's not successful all of the time—is likely to have much higher self-esteem. He will believe that trying may result in success, at least sometimes.

▷ **He views his ADHD not as a problem, but as something that makes him different but still capable.** Believing that he is unique is a key component to healthy self-esteem. As he grows older, your son may begin to see that there are components of his ADHD that can help him succeed in life. Maybe he is a big picture thinker and doesn't get mired in the details, or perhaps he can hyperfocus on something of interest to him. Some boys with ADHD have great people skills or are great problem solvers because they see things in a different way. Help your son realize strengths he has and feel good about who he is and how he's wired. Make sure he knows about the long list of influential, talented, and often brilliant people who have (or were believed to have had) ADHD, including Albert Einstein, Thomas Edison, Benjamin Franklin, Alexander Graham Bell, Abraham Lincoln, John F. Kennedy, Walt Disney, Henry Ford, Babe Ruth, Michael Jordan, Nolan Ryan, Michael Phelps, Pablo Picasso, and Sylvester Stallone.

▷ **He develops and maintains self-control.** As he grows toward adulthood, your son needs to know that ADHD is not in charge of him. A person with high self-esteem is in command of himself, his feelings, and his reactions. Although this ability may be naturally delayed in a young man with ADHD, it's a crucial part of self-confidence to know that he has strategies to help himself maintain control.

▷ **He acknowledges his own efforts and rewards himself.** If your son feels valued and confident, then he'll understand it's okay to give himself a pat on the back when he really tries hard at something. He might even buy himself a gift or do something fun to celebrate. If he's feeling good about himself, then he'll realize that it's the effort that earns the reward, not the outcome. He's not after perfection, which is unhealthy. He's rewarding persistence, which can be especially challenging for a boy with ADHD.

▷ **He has a parent or parents who support him, praise him, and love him for who he is.** Time and again, adults with ADHD report that their parents were their most consistent encouragers. As children and teens, they knew home was a safe place. They never doubted their self-worth, because they always felt loved by the people who mattered most in their lives. If you remember only one sentence from this book, remember this one: *The best predictor of success for a child with ADHD is having someone believe in him while he is growing up.* This finding comes from more than 15 years of research conducted by Gabrielle Weiss and Lily Trokenberg Hechtman, coauthors of book *Hyperactive Children Grown Up* (1993).

> *The best predictor of success for a child with ADHD is having someone believe in him while he is growing up.*

So what does healthy self-esteem look like? In this case, that may be better answered by discussing what it doesn't look like. Your son shouldn't be walking around feeling inferior every day of his life. But it's also a warning sign if he constantly brags that he's better than everybody else. That kind of false bravado can be a red flag for real difficulty with self-confidence lurking beneath the surface of his big talk. Your son should know that he has strengths and weaknesses, that he's wonderfully flawed just like the rest of us. Like everything in your walk with ADHD, the pursuit of healthy self-esteem is about balance.

Self-Esteem and Motivation

You can see that a young man who feels positive about his efforts is much more likely to believe he can grow toward mastering skills, even the ones that have eluded him because of his ADHD. Still, as you may have sensed, motivation itself can be a continuing challenge. An essential part of emotional maturity includes development of *internal motivation*. Internal motivation results when a young person no longer needs rewards or incentives to remain focused on a task and follow it through to completion. It's a kind of willpower that develops as we grow up. Boys with ADHD tend to struggle to achieve this kind of maturity and self-motivation.

You can also see how closely this can be tied in with a person's self-esteem. If your son believes he stands little or no chance of succeeding, he will have almost no motivation to apply himself, whether it's to a school project or to a relationship. His positive outlook that he can identify and fix what's wrong is essential in helping him remain motivated, especially as he matures, and that motivation needs to come from within.

Now is a great time to help him figure out what leads to situations where he is successful versus those that don't work out. Questions for you and him to consider include:

> ▷ Does he have a balanced life with adequate sleep, nutrition, exercise, and downtime?
> ▷ Does he have an understanding of his ADHD and how it affects him?
> ▷ When has he been successful, and what contributed to his success?
> ▷ Have any stumbling blocks to his success been identified?

Young adulthood is an excellent time to introduce role models and historic figures who have found a way to shine despite their ADHD. A small child might not be able to identify with the work of Albert Einstein or Thomas Edison. But your teen can understand that our world would be vastly different if those two men hadn't ignored the critics who labeled them as problem students. Or perhaps there's an adult in your life who's carved their own niche despite an ADHD diagnosis. Many teens with ADHD thrive in one-on-one mentoring situations. The idea is for your son to gain valuable motivational tools from people who inspire him. In my book *The ADHD Empowerment Guide: Identifying Your Child's Strengths and Unlocking Potential*, coauthored with Dr. James W. Forgan (2019), we provided a systematic way to go about identifying your son's strengths and provide information about people with ADHD who had a similar profile and what keys led to their success.

Self-Esteem Building Strategies for Teens

As your son matures, he becomes more capable of understanding how his own actions and thought patterns contribute to his self-esteem. Encourage him to boost his own self-esteem with strategies like the following:

▷ **He can develop "islands of competence."** This concept comes from Dr. Robert Brooks, educator and faculty member at Harvard Medical School. Everyone has some special gift, and some people have many. Your son needs to have at least one special area in which he can shine. It may be art, sports, music, computer programming, electronics, building, salesmanship, or in any of a number of other areas.

▷ **Inventory the life skills that will serve him well as an adult.** Ironically, the same qualities that are considered a drawback in a child with ADHD can be really beneficial to an adult in the workplace. It can be an eye-opening exercise to look at your son's individual characteristics and define which ones might be extremely valuable to him later in life. For example, his high energy level is frustrating when he's expected to sit still all day in school. But it will serve him very well if he decides to pursue a career in sales or as an engineer in charge of a production facility. Challenge him to brainstorm ways his gifts will help him in the future. You might also arrange to have him take an online inventory (like the Keirsey Temperament Sorter at https://www.keirsey.com or the Myers-Briggs Type Indicator at https://www.themyersbr iggs.com/en-US/Products-and-Services/Myers-Briggs) to help him determine his skills and personality strengths.

▷ **Good is great.** In many, many cases, boys with ADHD aren't striving to be the stars of the team or take home the blue ribbons. They just want to know they're good. This is really healthy thinking. Knowing he's good in at least one area will help him realize he can be good at many other things.

▷ **Set small goals.** It can be self-defeating to look at an over-whelming challenge, particularly for a kid with ADHD. It's far gentler on self-confidence to set smaller goals and feel the confidence boost that comes from achieving each one. Imagine your son thinking about saving enough money to buy a car. Now help him break that down into small, man-ageable pieces: $25 a month, for instance. Maybe you'll even match all (or a portion) of it if he's faithful to his goal. By meeting the challenge bit by bit, his confidence will build and he'll see he *can* do it.

▷ **Have hope.** Things tend to happen just a little later for peo-ple with ADHD. Encourage him not to lose sight of the fact that good things will still happen for him, even if he feels like ADHD has really messed up his life. Keeping a "gratitude journal" might not be right up his alley, but it doesn't hurt a guy's self-esteem to talk from time to time about the things that are going right. Sometimes we forget about them.

Self-Esteem Building Strategies for Parents

Your teenage son comes into contact with a lot of people, directly or indirectly—friends, teammates, teachers, coaches, and TV and movie characters. However, don't for a minute forget the influence *you* continue to have in building and nurturing his feelings of self-worth.

▷ **Love him unconditionally.** Love your son exactly as he is—his gifts, his talents, his quirks, his faults. His self-esteem depends upon knowing he's precious to you, not a bother, despite the wild ride his ADHD sometimes puts you through.

▷ **Make a list of his strengths.** Begin to list all of your son's gifts and talents. Once you start, it may be hard to stop. Find a quiet time to share your list with him, and make sure he has a copy of it. It may become one of his most cherished possessions.

▷ **Help him build on those strengths you have identified.** As a parent of a young man with ADHD, you need to keep him engaged and growing. Once his eyes have been opened to his many gifts, explore together how he can build upon them. Find seminars he can attend, books he can read, and volunteering or job-shadowing opportunities he can pursue.

▷ **Have fun with him.** Make sure to laugh together. Enjoy each other. Create memories.

▷ **Stay engaged.** As your son matures, continue teaching him the skills he needs to feel confident in life. He's old enough now to really grasp the consequences of his actions on *himself* and *others*, and you can coach him. For instance, helping him with anger management will keep him from destroying his own possessions (self) and alienating his friends (others). Continued work on time management will keep him from missing activities (self) and rudely keeping people waiting (others). Self-esteem stems from mastery of these kinds of skills.

▷ **Teach by example.** You cannot simply bestow self-esteem upon someone. You need to demonstrate how your choices and actions produce your own feelings of self-worth. Talk to your son about the sources of your self-esteem.

▷ **Praise him.** But do so genuinely. Like all kids, your son has a finely tuned "fake praise" meter. He'll know when he deserves praise and when he doesn't. If you gush with praise over trivial things, your true admiration will become meaningless. (And remember to praise effort, not outcome.)

▷ **Don't let your fears become his fears.** Many parents of boys with ADHD develop a worst-case mindset. They end up envisioning the darkest possible future for their sons. Most children are very perceptive. Watch the words you use, your tone of voice, and the looks you give. You can tell him a lot without ever saying a word. Be sensitive about not talking about him in front of others.

▷ **Listen when he speaks.** Especially for a boy, this may not happen often. He needs to know you're willing to put down what you're doing, look him in the eye, and hear what he has to say without interrupting him. Problem solve with him, and look for win-win solutions. Involve him in decisions. This goes a long way toward making him feel valued.

Remember, the most effective support he'll ever get comes from you when you say and believe with your whole heart, "I know you can do it." He is ready, or he will be. You have to think of your son as a whole, independent, capable person.

You've spent a lifetime—your son's lifetime—helping him. Now you're in the strange and uneasy position of needing to pull back a little here, a lot there. How will you know when to stop helping? Well, one mom puts it this way: "I'll stop helping when I'm no longer needed."

Points to Consider

1. Remember to nurture the relationship you have with your son. Nearly everything else is secondary.

Points to Consider, *continued*

2. There are no careers a person with ADHD can't pursue, and no jobs a person with ADHD can't do. Remind your child he has what it takes to succeed in any area he's passionate about, gifted in, and dedicated to pursue.
3. If your son has struggled with ADHD since he was a little boy, he may have been called a lot of hurtful names:
   ▸ lazy,
   ▸ disruptive,
   ▸ poorly behaved,
   ▸ stupid, or
   ▸ unfocused.

4. Be very, very cautious how you speak to and about your son, and what your expressions and body language say to him. He needs to know you see his value. Children who do best in overcoming the challenges of ADHD are the ones who can say, "Somebody believes in me." Don't you want to be that person for your son?

Action Steps to Take Now

1. Set reasonable expectations for your son's performance at school, at home, and in the community, and require him to live up to his end of the bargain.
2. Together with your son, explore sports, clubs, activities, volunteer work, and part-time job opportunities that are interesting and appealing to him.
3. Buy or borrow a copy of *25 Ways to Win With People* by John C. Maxwell and Les Parrott. Involve the whole family in reading and reviewing its principles.

Action Steps to Take Now, *continued*

4. Be sure you understand the significance of your son's ADHD as it relates to issues of sexuality and impulse control. Have open and honest discussions with him about dating.
5. Consider carefully your son's readiness to drive. When he does get his license, consider implementing a graduated driving system while he gains experience and builds confidence.
6. Make sure your son knows his strengths. This is an essential step toward reinforcing his self-esteem.
7. Praise your son when he tries, listen when he speaks, and love him all of the time.

Chapter 6

When More Support Is Needed

Sometimes even your most effective parenting tools, outside help including medication, and your son's best efforts are not enough to enable him to succeed in the classroom without interventions. Could your son use additional time on tests, frequent cueing to stay focused, some modification of assignments, permissible movement during the day, or a behavior plan? If so, how do you go about advocating for your son? Remember that ADHD is considered a disability. If your son's ADHD *significantly impacts* his life at school, there are two federal laws that could enable him to receive assistance if he meets the qualifications. I tell my clients that learning information about accommodations and services the school can provide is critical. Prepare for some complexity, but your knowledge will empower you to be able to communicate effectively with the school.

The first law relates to a 504 Plan—Section 504 of the Rehabilitation Act of 1973 (referred to as Section 504) and its companion federal laws—the Americans With Disabilities Act (ADA) and Americans

With Disabilities Act Amendments Act of 2008 (ADAAA). The second law relates to an Individualized Education Program (IEP)—Individuals With Disabilities Education Act (called IDEA), which began as Public Law 94–142, the Education for All Handicapped Children Act in 1975. Both have been amended multiple times with the last one occurring in 2017, which liberalized some of the standards for eligibility.

Sometimes the school will initiate the process for services and accommodations. Often, however, parents need to take the leadership role. Some schools are very accommodating and parent-friendly, but occasionally you will run into a school that is resistant to providing accommodations. In cases when you have to initiate and drive the process, you will need to understand the parameters of both Section 504 and IDEA to help you determine which best fits your son's needs. The following sections give you the information you will need to have a basic understanding of both 504 and IDEA. I have tried to simplify them as much as possible while making sure you have enough information to reach an understanding.

Section 504

What Is Section 504?

Section 504 is a federal civil rights law that protects children with disabilities from ages 3–21 against discrimination in public and non-religious schools, including colleges and technical schools receiving federal funds, and provides accommodations. However, it does not provide funding; it simply mandates accommodations and some services. The intent is to provide a level playing field so eligible students will have educational opportunities equivalent to nondisabled peers and so they will not be discriminated against. Section 504 states:

> No qualified individual with a disability shall, on the
> basis of disability, be excluded from participation in
> or be denied the benefits of the services, programs
> or activities of a public entity, or be subjected to dis-
> crimination by any public entity. (35.130, Subpart B,
> p. 549)

According to the Americans With Disabilities Act of 1990, the term *disability* means that an individual:

    a. has a physical or mental impairment that substantially limits one or more major life activities

    b. has a record of such impairment

    c. is regarded as having such impairment. (HR 3195 RH)

Your son could meet items B or C above and be guaranteed freedom from discrimination, but he would *not* be eligible for services and accommodations under a 504 Plan *unless* he had met the first requirement—"a physical or mental impairment that *substantially limits* one or more major life activities." In essence, your child can be diagnosed with ADHD by an outside source or can be suspected of having ADHD but still not be determined eligible for accommodations through a 504 plan because he demonstrates *no* substantial impairment in the school setting. A team of personnel from the school, which isn't tightly defined by 504 but usually includes parents, must determine if the ADHD *substantially limits* your child's access to an education on a case-by-case basis. If your son's ADHD is causing him to get in trouble at school, do poorly in his schoolwork or on standardized tests, or spend hours at home completing work he should have been able to finish at school, he could be considered to be substantially limited by his disability. In my district, a referral to the 504 team must be made for all children receiving medication at school to determine if they meet the eligibility requirements or not.

The impact of the American With Disabilities Act Amendments Act of 2008 (ADAAA) included the following changes:

▷ the definition of "disability" under Section 504 was broadened to include difficulties in "learning, reading, concentrating, thinking, communicating, and working" (Section 2A);

▷ it clarified that an impairment could limit one major activity but not others and could be episodic;

▷ it stated effects of medication and other forms of assistance should not be considered when determining if an impairment substantially limits a major activity (that means that if your son is receiving medication, the team should consider what his performance would be like without the medication. Why? If those supports were withdrawn, your son's performance might decline significantly); and

▷ broad interpretation is given to the term *substantially limits*.

What Does the 504 Process Look Like?

Most schools will follow similar steps to these to determine if your son is eligible under Section 504:

1. The school will gather information about your son's classroom performance, which might include teacher observations, grades, results of standardized assessments, and any outside medical or psychological information you might provide.

2. The school team may or may not require additional evaluation. As a parent, you have the right to request an evaluation of your child through the school district. Once permission is signed for the evaluation, it must be completed within 60 school days under current regulations.

3. An eligibility determination will be made by the 504 team. If the team determines that your son's ADHD substantially limits his academic performance or behavior at school, it would determine him eligible for a formal 504 plan.

4. A written 504 plan will be developed to delineate services and accommodations. It is to be reviewed every 3 years but

can be revisited at any time and is kept in place as long as needed. Even though a 504 plan includes strategies and assistance that an effective teacher would normally implement, it is always important to have it in writing. Without it, one year you may have a teacher who makes accommodations, and the next year you may have one who does not. If you change schools, you would want to transfer that information. Going forward, you want to ensure your son has the accommodations he needs and that they are provided consistently from classroom to classroom.

Belinda's son has a 504 plan for his ADHD that was established at the end of his kindergarten year. She had Billy privately evaluated by a psychologist and brought the paperwork to school. After reviewing the report, the school staff met with the parents and determined Billy was eligible for a 504 plan. Because Billy was struggling, there was no resistance from the school toward writing the 504 plan, and Belinda was pleased with the accommodations. Some of the accommodations written on his first-grade 504 plan included not taking away all of his recess, allowing reduced homework, providing spelling words on Friday instead of Monday, allowing frequent breaks, and letting him stand at his desk and work.

IDEA

What Is IDEA?

IDEA is the federal law that states that a free and appropriate education must be provided to all students who have a disability, meet their state's eligibility criteria, and have an *educational need* for special education services. At that point, an Individualized Education Program (IEP) would be written. IDEA provides funding for instruction, addressing your child's unique needs, usually from a special education teacher, and can provide related services like occupational therapy, physical therapy, or speech/language therapy if the child meets eligibility criteria or counseling when needed. The federal law specifies 13 disability categories. Other Health Impairment (OHI) is the eligibility category most often considered for children with ADHD. Other disability categories could be considered, depending on your son's specific difficulties. If he has academic problems, he may qualify under Specific Learning Disabilities. If your son has serious behavioral or emotional problems, he may qualify under Emotional Behavioral Disorder.

If a child is considered for services under the Other Health Impairment eligibility, he must have a disability (such as ADHD) that *significantly* impacts his ability to learn and perform in the classroom to the extent that he would require special education services. Factors other than his test scores should be considered. Those factors might include "grades, homework completion, independent work habits, alertness, sleeping in class, class participation and attendance, ability to complete schoolwork and tests within specified time frames, relationships with peers, and compliance with rules" (Durheim & Zeigler Dendy, 2006, p. 128).

How Is the Disability Category OHI Defined Under IDEA?

Federal law defines OHI as:

> having limited strength, vitality or alertness, including a heightened alertness to environmental stimuli, that results in limited alertness with respect to the educational environment, that:

    i. Is due to chronic or acute health problems such as asthma, attention deficit disorder, or attention deficit hyperactivity disorder, diabetes, epilepsy, a heart condition, hemophilia, lead poisoning, leukemia, nephritis, rheumatic fever, and sickle cell anemia; and

    ii. Adversely affects a child's educational performance. (IDEA, 1990, Section 300.8(c)(9))

If your son qualifies as having a disability under IDEA, then the school staff meets with you to write an IEP. IDEA requires that your child must be educated in the least restrictive environment (LRE), meaning that he must be educated in a general education classroom setting as much as possible. Schools have different options for delivering educational services. Many have inclusion classrooms where a special education teacher comes into the classroom for part of the day or the general education teacher is trained in techniques for instructing children with disabilities. Elsewhere, the child leaves the general education classroom for another classroom for a portion of the day to receive instruction in areas where he needs extra help.

What Would the IDEA Process Look Like?

The school may follow steps similar to these in determining if your child qualifies under IDEA:

1. The school would gather information about your son's classroom performance, which might include teacher observations, grades, results of standardized assessments, the amount of assistance and time required to complete homework, and any outside medical or psychological information you might provide.

2. A formal evaluation is required, either done through the school district or provided by you from an acceptable outside source or a combination of the above. As a parent, you have

the right to request an evaluation of your child. Once permission is signed for the evaluation, it must be completed within 60 school days.

3. An eligibility determination will be made by the IEP team. If the team determines that your son's ADHD is a disability that requires special education services, then it would determine him eligible for a disability category.

4. A written IEP would be developed to delineate services and accommodations. It is reviewed annually, and a reevaluation is considered every 3 years.

How Are 504 and IDEA Different?

Generally, children who qualify for IDEA are more impaired and require more services than those best served by a 504 plan. IDEA provides actual funding to schools for special education instruction specified in an IEP, while a 504 plan provides no additional funding to schools but affords your son accommodations and some services, such as a quiet place to work, use of educational aids such as computers, or small-group instruction. As you would expect, the qualification procedure is less stringent for Section 504.

IDEA requires the development of an IEP that specifies the student's current levels of performance, specific goals written for a year in all areas where he is below his grade-level peers (with specification about how these goals will be monitored), and details about where and for how long special education services will be provided. A 504 plan requires only written documentation of accommodations to be reviewed every 3 years.

Members of the IEP team under IDEA are specified by law and must include the parents; a teacher knowledgeable about the child; a special education teacher; an administrator (usually called a Local Education Authority or LEA), who is knowledgeable about the laws, disabilities, and general curriculum; and someone who can interpret test results, such as a school psychologist or speech and language pathologist. Members of the 504 team are not as clearly defined.

IDEA requires a formalized evaluation that might include a psychoeducational evaluation of the child's intelligence, academic levels, and processing abilities, and possibly behavior rating scales. Some schools require a diagnosis of ADHD. Eligibility criteria can vary by school district. 504 requires some documentation of the child's difficulties related to his disability, and it could include results of rating scales, teacher and parent information, and medical information.

IDEA requires consideration of reevaluation needs every 3 years. Many times those reevaluations might be results of assessments and written observations provided by the classroom teacher. If your son has a 504 plan, it does not have a specific 3-year reevaluation component but still needs to be reviewed every 3 years.

More specific parental rights come into play with IDEA, such as clearly defined due process rights when there is a serious disagreement between the school district and the parents over the need for an evaluation or determination of services. Section 504 provides for parent rights, usually left up to the discretion of local school districts, which are not as extensive but still allow parents to contest a 504 determination.

Paperwork required in IDEA is more stringent and requires specific written notice of eligibility or ineligibility. Under IDEA, an official IEP meeting is required before any change in placement can occur. The 504 requires no such meeting, but parents should be notified. Table 5 further outlines the differences between the two laws.

How Are 504 and IDEA Alike?

Both are based on federal laws requiring that a child with a disability receive a free and appropriate public education (FAPE). As I've said earlier, the laws attempt to level the playing field so that your son will have the same access to education as all of his peers. For example,

Table 5
How IDEA and Section 504 Differ

IDEA	504
Office of Special Education of the U.S. Department of Education responsible for enforcement	Office for Civil Rights of the U.S. Department of Education responsible for enforcement
Students' learning generally more impaired and requires more service	Students generally don't require special instruction
Funding provided based on disability category	No funding provided to schools, but schools receiving IDEA funds must meet 504 requirements
More stringent qualification procedure	Less stringent qualification procedure
Individualized Education Program (IEP) developed	504 plan written
Members of IEP team specified by law	504 team may vary by school district
Formal evaluation necessary	Some documentation of difficulties necessary
Reevaluation to be considered every 3 years	No reevaluation specified
More specific parental rights	Parent rights provided but not as stringent as IDEA
Official IEP meeting and parent permission required before change in placement can occur	No meeting required, but parent should be informed

if he processes information slowly or loses his focus so frequently that he can't finish his work in a specified amount of time, he may be given extended time to complete his work.

> *Both laws require that the child be educated*
> *in the least restrictive environment with*
> *nondisabled peers as much as possible.*

Both can provide accommodations, such as extended time to complete work, lessons broken down into smaller segments or "chunked," and copies of notes provided for the student's use.

Both require a formal eligibility process with paperwork that must be kept confidential. This allows the teacher and those working with the child to have knowledge of his disability and the required accommodations. Parents can request a review at any time of either a 504 plan or an IEP.

Both laws require that the child be educated in the least restrictive environment with nondisabled peers as much as possible. Both eligibilities transfer if your child moves to a different school, but they may have to be rewritten.

Due process rights are provided by both laws when a parent disagrees with a school district over a child being eligible or services provided. The due process in IDEA is specified by federal law, whereas the due process in section 504 is left up to the local school district. The similarities between IDEA and Section 504 are further summarized in Figure 7.

Students receiving ESE (Exceptional Student Education) services with an existing IEP are automatically eligible for 504 services or accommodations because their ESE eligibility automatically classified them as having a disability under Section 504. They would not need a written 504 Plan because all services or accommodations would be written into their IEP.

Figure 7
Similarities Between IDEA and Section 504

- ► Both are federal laws requiring a free and appropriate public education (FAPE).
- ► Both have accommodations and some services available.
- ► A formal eligibility process is required for both.
- ► Paperwork for both laws must be kept confidential.
- ► Under both laws, the child is to be educated in the least restrictive environment with their nondisabled peers as much as possible.
- ► Eligibilities under both laws transfer from school to school but may have to be rewritten.
- ► Under both laws, due process rights are provided when a parent disagrees with the school district.

What Determines Which Is Most Appropriate for My Son?

The decision will be based on the needs of your son and the extent of his needs. If he needs individualized instruction from a special education teacher, eligibility under IDEA should be considered. Remember that if your son is eligible for special education, the goal will be to have him remain in a general classroom as much as possible. With eligibility under IDEA, he could also access other services as needed, such as occupational or language therapy if he met criteria for those services.

Boys with ADHD often may be eligible under multiple categories. For example, a comprehensive evaluation may determine that he has a specific learning disability or an emotional and behavioral disorder. If so, his IEP would address those issues.

On the other hand, if your son is doing relatively well, he may only need accommodations in the classroom, such as being reminded to pay attention, permissible movement, or extended time, so his needs could be met through a 504 plan.

What Can Parents Do?

▷ Try to maintain good communication with your son's teacher(s).

▷ Advocate for your son and make sure the 504 or IEP team has a clear picture of your son and his struggles.

▷ Provide any outside documentation that might help the team.

▷ Request an evaluation if more information is needed. Put your request in writing and keep a copy.

▷ Try to understand the eligibility process and parental rights for your school district, often addressed on its website, and make yourself an integral part of the team by doing what you can do to help your son. Don't hesitate to disagree with the school and advocate for your son. Sometimes it helps to remind the school staff of all you are doing on the outside to help your son, whether is it providing medication, tutoring, counseling, or spending hours reinforcing school work and helping with homework. Some parents bring advocates or attorneys to the table, but my experience as a school psychologist has been that this is usually unnecessary. Be reasonable in understanding that teachers are responsible for many students, not just yours. The end result is that both you and the school want your child to be successful, so agreements can usually be reached on how to make that happen. Check with your school district to determine if parent liaisons are available to assist with problem solving and support if needed. As a parent, you have the option to request mediation or a due process hearing if you and the school cannot agree on what your son needs.

> *The goal of a 504 plan or IEP is . . . to enable him to receive the support he needs to be as successful as possible when he's at school.*

What if I Don't Want to Label My Child?

Some parents are reluctant to create a "paper trail" and formalize their child's disability in the school's records, but it is better for your son's problems to be understood for what they are—deficits in neurocognitive processes that affect his day-to-day functioning. It's not laziness, lack of ability, or obstinacy. At times, early intervention provided through accommodations on a 504 plan could prevent the need for special education services later. The goal of a 504 plan or IEP is not to provide a crutch or an easy out for your son but to enable him to receive the support he needs to be as successful as possible when he's at school.

When I worked with Jeremy, he was constantly in trouble in his first-grade classroom. His performance was falling further and further behind that of his peers. Jeremy was not completing his work, was making careless errors, and didn't seem to be able to answer simple comprehension questions about stories he had read. The school implemented a Response to Intervention (RtI) plan targeting one of his academic deficits, one of the first steps in most states to look at whether a child has a learning disability. His RtI plan involved small-group instruction by the classroom teacher in comprehension. His progress was monitored weekly over a 6–8 week period. With the additional assistance on reading, he showed improvement.

Because Jeremy seemed to be making progress, the school did not pursue formalized testing to determine if he had a learning disability. However, he was still having difficulty staying in his seat, doing his best work, and finishing assignments. I asked his parents and teachers to complete rating scales that assessed Jeremy's functioning as compared with other children his age. Those ratings showed significantly more inattentive and disorganized behaviors than would be expected given his age, so the school initiated a meeting to discuss his eligibility for a 504 plan. His parents brought in documentation of his ADHD diagnosis (not required but helpful), and the team developed a 504 plan. It included an individualized task-monitoring plan, which his teacher used to help Jeremy keep track of his responsibilities. He received a check for each item completed and turned in, for checking his work, and for self-monitoring his reading. He was able to earn special privileges, such as additional time on the computer, with the check marks he received. In addition, he received frequent cueing on tasks by his teacher and opportunities to move about the classroom to different stations when his work was completed. He showed progress and benefited from the provisions of his 504 plan.

The Importance of Establishing Eligibility Before College

Requirements for receiving accommodations on the SAT and ACT for students with ADHD have become more stringent in recent years. In addition to a diagnosis, the student must provide a comprehensive evaluation that is not more than 3 years old and was completed by a licensed professional. The testing companies look closely at requests for extended time on their standardized testing that come up in the months before the testing when the student hasn't needed that previously.

When students with ADHD get to college, they sometimes fall apart without those supports that served them well in high school, like the structure provided at home and the efforts of their teachers. If you suspect your son's ADHD might cause him significant difficulty in college, it is important to establish eligibility for 504 or IDEA before he leaves secondary school so that his needs and accommodations will already be documented. The eligibilities don't transfer to the college setting, but the paper trail can be helpful. If you don't have any eligibility from high school, it is still possible to get accommodations in college with the proper documentation. Postsecondary institutions have their own individual requirements for updated evaluations. Most colleges have Offices of Disability Support that handle eligibilities, accommodations, and other supports.

During his school-age years, Joseph never required a 504 plan or special education eligibility. There were times he could have benefited from some accommodations, such as being allowed to make up tests he had missed in a quiet environment or receiving extended time on complex testing, but his strong self-regulation skills helped him do well without any accommodation. His organization skills improved over time, and even though it was often a scramble at the end, he was always able to produce projects on time. His parents made sure he had a quiet place to work and tools that he needed, and encouraged him to break large assignments into manageable components well ahead of the due date. However, he seemed to work more effectively under the pressure of time and that adrenaline rush that came from barely completing an assignment on time. The summer prior to his senior year in high school, he attended a college preparatory camp where he had ample time to write his college essays. However, true to form, he generally completed each one the night before he mailed the application. Once attending college, he found the academic demands were much greater than in high school, and he needed the accommodation of extended time on classroom tests. He kept losing his focus on tests and wasn't able to finish them in the allotted time. His parents were able to have him evaluated by a clinical psychologist in the college town where he was living who diagnosed him with ADHD and referred him to a medical doctor who prescribed a mild stimulant. His college accepted the psychologist's and doctor's findings and allowed extended time even though he had no previous history of a diagnosis or support.

Accommodations and Supports Common in Elementary and Secondary Classrooms

As your son's advocate, you should be familiar with the universe of options that could be available to your son. Listed on the following pages are examples of some of the accommodations that can be made with either a 504 plan or an IEP (take note that it is not an all-inclusive list). Be realistic about what a teacher can be expected to do for your child and still manage an entire classroom. The best advice is to focus on the accommodations that you feel would be most beneficial to your son. The quality of the accommodations will likely be more effective than the quantity of interventions.

Classroom Structure

- ▷ Warnings provided by the teacher before transitions. For example, the teacher gives your son a 5-minute warning before he must put away his work and begin a new task. It is helpful for some children to be allowed to begin cleaning up a few minutes before the rest of the class, allowing extra time to improve organizational skills.
- ▷ Placement of your child's seating in an area that is as free of distraction as possible. For example, you wouldn't want your child's desk in an area where other students are constantly walking past it.
- ▷ A clean and clutter-free workspace to avoid distractions.
- ▷ Provision of a quiet workspace, such as a study carrel or quiet corner of the room, where your son could take his work if he can't concentrate in a group classroom setting.
- ▷ Placement near a positive role model.
- ▷ Scheduling accommodations. If there is an option, schedule more demanding classes earlier in the day and try to include some activity, such as physical education or recess, during the middle of the day.
- ▷ A dedicated place for turning in homework or the ability to email it to the teacher.
- ▷ Permissible movement, such as allowing your son to get out of his desk and go to another area of the classroom for a specific purpose—to get materials or a drink of water or to run an errand for the teacher. Gaining the self-discipline not to bother other children would be important.
- ▷ Permission to stand beside his desk and work.
- ▷ Specific classroom routines and structure, such as a specific routine for turning in homework.
- ▷ Having the teacher establish eye contact with the student when providing important information.

▷ Encouraging the teacher to ignore slight movement behaviors, like twirling a pencil, that do not interfere with classroom instruction.

Assignments

▷ Reduction in the amount of work to be completed. For example, in math, your son would complete the even-numbered problems rather than doing all of the problems if he had demonstrated he understood the concept being taught. A caveat here is to make sure he has enough practice to cement the skill being taught.

▷ Assignments presented in manageable chunks. Your son could be given an assignment in several different parts so he isn't overwhelmed by the amount of work.

▷ Masking his papers. In this strategy, the student is encouraged to use a plain sheet of paper to cover up a portion of the page he is not working on. This helps minimize the distraction from so much information on a page and can keep it from being overwhelming.

▷ Assistance in breaking down large assignments into manageable chunks.

▷ A monitoring plan to check work for careless mistakes before submitting it for grading.

▷ Having the teacher mark correct responses rather than wrong answers when grading papers as a way of providing some positive reinforcement.

▷ Use of highlighter for key words in reading or mathematical signs.

▷ Frequent checks to ensure that the student has understood directions. Sometimes it may be helpful for your son to repeat directions to the teacher.

▷ Watching for signs that the student does not understand the assignment and providing additional instruction.

▷ An example of what the finished product should look like.
▷ Multimodal instructions—visual and auditory instructions paired with hands-on learning when possible.
▷ Use of technology such as computer programs—often an effective way for a boy with ADHD to practice skills.
▷ Study guides in writing when possible, as well as copies of notes or board work.
▷ Access to word processing programs on computers to produce written work.

Self-Regulatory Skills

▷ Training in turn-taking, waiting in line, remaining seated, and identifying cause and effect, especially important in kindergarten and first grade.
▷ Opportunities to regain self-control by removing himself from overwhelming situations.
▷ Holding stress balls or fidget toys in his hands, especially if they enhance concentration.
▷ Assistance in organizational strategies, such as writing items in an agenda and keeping papers in their proper place.
▷ Opportunities to self-manage behavior. For example, your son counts and records a specific behavior with teacher assistance and receives positive, corrective feedback and some reward, such as verbal praise, a privilege, or a tangible item when he demonstrates a desired behavior.
▷ Placement on an individualized behavior management plan where the teacher monitors behavior in specific areas. Your son would have the opportunity to earn rewards, such as additional computer time, lunch with the teacher or a special friend, or tokens. These are most effective when the system carries over to the home and parents are reinforcing the same behaviors.

Memory

▷ Frequent repetition and review of previously learned material.
▷ Provision of cue cards that would outline steps, especially important in solving math problems requiring sequential steps like long division.
▷ Use of a calculator.
▷ Assistance in attaching new learning to previously learned material.
▷ Use of memory techniques such as mnemonics.
▷ Overlearning until it becomes firmly embedded in long-term memory. This may require intensive practice, repetition, and review.
▷ Assistance in organizing information into meaningful categories.
▷ Assistance in using verbal rehearsal (repeating information to himself) or using visual imagery to assist with recall.

Options When the Current School Setting Isn't Working

In some cases, boys with ADHD cannot function in a public school with special education eligibility or 504 accommodations or in a private school providing some support. Other alternatives can include a special day or private school specializing in ADHD, learning disabilities, behavioral difficulties, or all three; specialized boarding schools; homeschooling; or virtual school. All of these options will require extensive research to ensure that your son's educational needs will be met while preparing him for a successful future. It will be especially important to ensure that there is an adequate and robust curriculum.

Homeschooling

Homeschooling is legal in all 50 states, so if you are interested in your state's specific requirements, contact your state Department of Education or check with your local school district. Homeschooling may be an option if a parent can commit the time, patience, and knowledge necessary. It would require registering with your local school district, many of which have a separate office to handle homeschooling. There, you would be informed about state requirements, which usually entail annual evaluations to assess progress and documentation of the programs you will be using.

I believe that homeschooling can be a viable choice for boys with ADHD. There are many elements you must establish, including a structured and comprehensive curriculum, adequate supervision, and social opportunities with peers. Although homeschooling is not for everyone, it works for many. Homeschooling provides parents the ability to give their son an individualized curriculum, no homework, opportunities for hands-on learning, and the possibility for him to be more active. It can allow your son to gain academic confidence and build his self-esteem. Some families homeschool their sons because it does not require high-stakes testing and offers flexibility.

It is a myth that homeschooling is isolating and does not allow your son to have social interactions. Many communities have homeschool cooperatives (or co-ops) that you can join. There are also national, state, local, and online homeschool groups for you to investigate. Homeschooling affords your son the flexibility to interact with others as little or as much as you wish. My advice is to ignore the naysayer who makes statements like, "He won't have any friends," "You'll feel alone," or "Homeschooling doesn't work for boys with ADHD." I know firsthand that homeschooling can and does work for many boys with ADHD.

The homeschool movement is continuing to expand, and more resources are becoming available to support homeschooled boys with ADHD. These supports will include stronger curricula, improved approaches to teach executive functioning skills, and educational options.

> At the end of fifth grade, Kevin and his wife, Tamara, explored Jonathan's educational options and decided that a homeschool program would best suit his middle school needs. Because Kevin and Tamara both worked full-time in the education field, a homeschool center fit their circumstances far better than trying to have Jonathan complete his homeschool lessons at home. They chose a learning center that partnered with parents to facilitate and house instruction, monitor student progress, and mentor both the parent and the homeschooled student.
>
> At the school they chose, students attended the center Monday through Thursday. Each student worked on his specific curriculum and was taught by certified teachers. There were a maximum of six students to one teacher, and students had a daily rotation through their subjects. Fridays were designated for field trips, community service activities, or as an optional instructional day at the center.
>
> Besides the low student to-teacher ratio, things that appealed to them about this option included the lessons presented in small units and often with hands-on activities and discussion to reinforce the concepts, frequent breaks and opportunities for movement, and a structured but flexible environment.

In other cases, parents choose to provide the instruction for their son rather than use a homeschooling center. Although it is beyond the scope of this book to discuss specific curriculum choices, parents can choose between traditional, online, or virtual school homeschool experiences. When you are deciding, look for key features that include the quality of instructor resources for you, the types of hands-on activities offered for your son, the availability of computer-aided instruction, and the quality of the tracking system for recording your son's progress.

Of course, a prime secret for a successful homeschooling experience is having a good working relationship between the homeschooling parent and son. I use the term *working relationship* to emphasize that your son must be able and willing to complete schoolwork for you, the homeschool parent. You should have good organizational skills and the time to plan your instruction. It can be like a full-time job to adequately homeschool your son. Parents I have worked with have benefited from the support of networking with other homeschooling parents. Figure 8 includes pros and cons of homeschooling a boy with ADHD.

You can weigh the pros and cons of homeschooling your son by creating your own chart. Check resources in your community and determine if there are homeschool centers or co-ops nearby. I have seen homeschooling work and understand it can be a viable option for boys with ADHD.

Virtual Schooling

During the COVID-19 pandemic, virtual schooling grew in importance. The virtual learning offered by schools varied widely. Some were very organized in presenting teacher-led lessons throughout much of the day, which were instrumental in helping students establish a workable schedule. Others offered programming that almost ensured a parent would have to be heavily involved, such as having second graders do check-ins with their teachers at specific times, like 10:17 a.m. The results of this virtual learning seem to be very mixed; some students thrived, whereas others seemed to get further behind. One mother told me that her son became completely lost without a teacher standing in front of him all day directing the assignments, being readily available for his questions, and insisting that he complete and turn in his assignments.

Figure 8
Pros and Cons of Homeschooling

Pros	Cons
Customized curriculum	Parent as teacher (typically)
Online curriculum options	No paycheck for teaching your son
Flexibility	Patience required
Shortened school day	High structure necessary
Can work at a slower or faster pace	Difficult to stay disciplined and make progress
Increased opportunity for hands-on projects	Fewer social opportunities unless participating in a co-op
Opportunity for movement	Dealing with your and his academic frustrations
No high-stakes state testing	Slower work speed means progression through the curriculum takes longer
Teach to his learning style	Reduced freedom for the teaching parent
No homework	High burnout rate
Freedom to teach your religious beliefs	Requires teaching multiple subjects
Opportunity to teach more real-life skills	Record keeping required to monitor progress
Support of other homeschool parents	Can't take advantage of benefits of public school (e.g., intensive tutoring, teacher expertise) but can participate in school sports and clubs

Some students with ADHD are successful with computerized instruction because it can be faster paced than traditional classroom instruction, and much of the monotonous repetition can be eliminated.

Pre-COVID-19, most states were offering enrollment in virtual schools so that students could access courses online. This service is likely to continue and grow in importance. Some enroll in virtual school full time or elect to take specific courses while attending regular school or during the summer. I have known students who have taken calculus or even physical education virtually. Students have interaction with a teacher online and do the majority of their work on the computer. Some students with ADHD are successful with computerized instruction because it can be faster paced than traditional classroom instruction, and much of the monotonous repetition can be eliminated. It is usually more effective with children in the upper elementary grades, middle school, and secondary students. Attending a virtual school can require parental supervision and access to a computer with dependable Internet access. Contact your local school district for more information.

Specialized Day Schools

For some families, there comes a point when their son's academic and/or behavioral difficulties approach the disaster level. Some children with ADHD and learning disabilities do better in schools designed to serve students who learn differently. Or your son's ADHD may be so severe that he needs more than you or his current school can offer. This may be especially true if he has been diagnosed with ODD in addition to ADHD. His behavior may have escalated to the point that you don't know what to do for him, and you may be concerned for his safety and that of your family. He may be taking up the majority of your time and energy. Other family members may feel resentment or jealousy because of all of the time you spend on your son. This includes your time thinking and worrying about your son, talking to school staff, going to therapy, making and attending doctor's appointments, and doing online research. You likely feel exhausted and worn down. At times you may feel hopeless and worry that you might lose your temper and hurt him. When this happens, it is time to consider either a special day school or a boarding school.

You should do what is best for your child and your family. If your son attends a special day school or boarding school, try not to worry about what grandma, cousin, or aunt so-and-so is going to say about your decision. They don't walk in your shoes or truly understand how stressful your daily life has become. Some parents cope with their son's stress by nail biting, smoking, drinking, or just keeping him in so many activities that he is away from them and the family. These actions may provide a temporary escape, but in the long run, they do not help him or you.

> *You should do what is best for your child and your family.*

If you are considering a specialized day school for your son, look for one that offers these qualities:
  ▷ small classrooms with no more than 14 students (fewer is better),
  ▷ a student-to-teacher ratio of no more than 7 to 1,
  ▷ an environment with minimal distractions and unnecessary interruptions,
  ▷ a school philosophy of building upon strengths rather than just remediating deficits,
  ▷ an administrator who understands ADHD and provides teachers with ongoing professional learning,
  ▷ teachers with specialized training in teaching and understanding boys with ADHD,

▷ teachers who know how to make accommodations and provide differentiated instruction,

▷ a daily schedule that places academics in the morning hours,

▷ a schedule that includes recess or physical activity every day, and

▷ a curriculum that teaches study skills and organizational strategies and utilizes multisensory and hands-on learning techniques.

Boarding Schools

Despite your best efforts, your son's best efforts, and the efforts of school staff, you may feel that your son needs a more therapeutic setting or a more individualized academic program with more specific services than you are able to provide or obtain in your local area. His teen years are critical, so you want him to be in a positive environment structured to develop independence and prepare him for his next step, whether it be college or career. There are boarding schools around the country that provide additional support for boys with ADHD and their accompanying academic or behavior problems. In some large metropolitan areas, there are educational consultants who specialize in boarding school for boys with ADHD who can make your search much easier. In my practice, the main reasons parents have chosen boarding schools include:

▷ family history of attending boarding school,

▷ complex family structures that can't provide the needed support,

▷ significant academic problems that can't be handled locally,

▷ behavior problems that are becoming increasingly severe and resistant to intervention, or

▷ involvement with a negative peer group.

It is helpful to consider pros and cons when making any important decision. (It's also important to teach your son how to make decisions

Figure 9
Pros and Cons of Boarding Schools

Pros	Cons
Small class size	Expensive tuition
Increased individualized attention	May be isolating
Counseling services may be available	Emotionally difficult to separate from your son
Fresh start	Lack of appropriate role models
May increase his self-esteem if the program is structured to help him build on successes	Cost of travel to and from home for holidays, weekends, etc.
Mentoring	Family separation
Highly structured, around-the-clock supervision	Requires adjustment to new environment

based on pros and cons.) Although any decision is always more than a simple count of pros versus cons, it provides a starting point and reassurance that you have considered all options. Always consider the extraneous factors in your life and focus on the most important issues to your particular circumstances. Figure 9 lists the potential pros and cons of your son attending boarding school.

One concern I hear from parents is that the boarding school will not know their son as well as they do. Most parents ask endless "what if" questions. What if he gets into a fight? What if his medications get mixed up? What if he doesn't go to the bathroom for weeks on end? What if he gets sick? What if he misses us so much that he cries himself to sleep? What if he feels abandoned? What if he hates us for doing this? To overcome this, you have to do your research and ask countless questions.

After telling your son of your decision to investigate boarding schools as a strong possibility, expect pushback, resistance, and possible tears. Transition is never easy, especially for boys with ADHD. Often the unknown is very frightening to them. They may wonder how they will survive without you, whether or not they will be able to make friends, and/or how they will handle the academic and behavioral demands. Explain that you love your son and genuinely feel this will help him develop into his best self.

Whether or not you are working with an educational consultant, consider some of the following questions when speaking with boarding school admissions directors. Make a chart with these questions on the left side and columns to the right where you can place each school's answers.

▷ Does the curriculum follow state guidelines?
▷ What kinds of academic support are available?
▷ How many counselors, psychologists, and/or psychiatrists are on staff at one time?
▷ What is the student-to-teacher ratio?
▷ How long does the average teacher stay employed with the school? Are they certified or licensed?
▷ How will my son be disciplined? What is the school's discipline plan?
▷ Is physical restraint used with students?
▷ Are parents encouraged to have their son take ADHD medication?
▷ What does a student's typical daily schedule look like?
▷ How frequently do parents get to talk and email with their son?
▷ How long is your average student's stay?
▷ Is your school accredited, and will my son's coursework transfer to another school?
▷ What happens on weekends, long weekends, and holidays?
▷ What is the history of illegal drugs being used by students at your school?

You may consider involving your son in the process of researching schools. Ask him what he thinks of two different schools, both of which are acceptable to you. Show him the schools' websites and literature to teach him about what they offer. This can create buy-in and help your son believe he has some input and that his opinions are valued.

After you narrow your decision to the top two, visit each school's campus before making a final selection. Your son should definitely attend the campus visit with you. Take a look at their facilities, student population, staff, curriculum, values orientation, food service, medical facility, support services, and level of communication with parents. If possible, try to talk to parents or current students or graduates of the school. The school may sound like the perfect fit when you talk with staff on the phone, read the catalogue, and study the website. Seeing the campus in person and talking to students will help finalize your decision. The process and transition will not be easy, but finding the right support for your son can pay big dividends.

Points to Consider

1. If your son's ADHD is impairing his school functioning significantly, he could meet the criteria for a 504 plan or Individualized Education Program (IEP).
2. Even though the disability perspective is difficult to accept, isn't it better for people to have an understanding of the neurobiological nature of his ADHD than to think he is just being difficult or lazy?
3. You are your son's most important advocate and always will be.
4. What specific struggles does your son have in his current classroom?
5. Are homeschooling or virtual school viable options for your son, and what resources exist in your community?

Action Steps to Take Now

1. Continue to educate yourself about your child's legal rights within the school system.
2. Think about your son's learning style, strengths, and weaknesses. What does he need in the classroom in order to do his best?
3. If he is struggling behaviorally or academically in the classroom with no support, contact the school about the necessity of a 504 plan or IDEA eligibility. Make sure you educate yourself so you can be a good advocate for him.
4. Develop a good working relationship with his teacher(s) and with other staff members who could assist him.
5. Be a positive and strong advocate for him and help him learn to advocate for himself.

Chapter 7

The Dynamic Action Plan

*T*hroughout this book I've given you action steps at the end of each chapter. Whether or not you've had the opportunity to apply them, my message to you is the same: Your son needs you, for you are his advocate, his champion, and a constant presence in his life. You realize that sitting idly does not help either of you, and by reading this book, you are working in the right direction. The Dynamic Action Plan is a reflective tool to help you prioritize your steps. As a parent myself, I understand how it feels to become overwhelmed by the demands of parenting. You worry about what lies ahead. Despite his challenges, your son is a unique person with a special purpose in life. You know there is hope for his future. You can help your son discover his purpose and grow in his journey.

The Dynamic Action Plan is a fluid and ever-changing document that you can complete and revisit as needed. I suggest you keep it in a visible location and review it monthly. The key is to begin by reflecting upon where you see your son 5 years from now, and if he's mature enough, to ask him to consider his next 5 years as well. Together, think about his future in the following ways:

- ▷ How old will he be?
- ▷ What will he physically look like?
- ▷ What will his personality be like?
- ▷ What do you expect from his behavior?
- ▷ How will he feel about himself?
- ▷ What will his ethics and character be like?
- ▷ Will he be able to make good decisions?
- ▷ What type of school will he attend?
- ▷ What interests and hobbies will he pursue?
- ▷ Who will his friends be?
- ▷ Will he have a job?
- ▷ Will he be taking medication?
- ▷ What strategies will he be using to manage his ADHD?
- ▷ What kind of support will he need at school? From his family?

Download a printable version of the Dynamic Action Plan at www.routledge.com/Raising-Boys-With-ADHD.aspx.

I find that thinking about and predicting what your son will be doing in 5 years is an interesting exercise. For you it will stir various emotions, and you'll realize just how fast those years will pass. Now is the time to help him chart his course and lay the groundwork for skills that will help him in his life's journey.

After your time of reflection and discussion, select the areas that you feel should be the object of your focus, and put them in writing. Creating a written, permanent document is an important part of your Dynamic Action Plan's success. If it's not written down, you are less likely to refer back to your plan, and today's thoughts won't be as clearly defined. Also, your son will find many of these topics and responses encouraging, and I believe that making this Dynamic Action Plan a centerpiece in your life will provide tangible evidence of your commitment to his success. Try to identify broad 5-year goals for your son and use intermediate steps to work back to today. Consider all aspects of his life—school, family, friends, leisure time and extracurricular activities, health and fitness, religion, etc.—as you complete these sentences:

▷ In 5 years, I/we see my son doing/being . . .

_____

_____

_____

_____

▷ In 3 years, I/we see my son doing/being . . .

_____

_____

_____

_____

▷ In one year, I/we see my son doing/being . . .

_____

_____

_____

_____

In order for my son to achieve the vision I/we have for him at the 5-year mark, I need to do the following.

▷ Today:

_____

_____

_____

▷ Tomorrow:

_____

_____

_____

_____

▷ Within one month:

_____

_____

_____

_____

▷ Within 6 months:

_____

_____

_____

_____

In order for my son to achieve the vision I/we have for him at the 5-year mark, he needs to do the following.

▷ Today:

_____

_____

_____

_____

▷ Tomorrow:

_____

_____

_____

_____

▷ Within one month:

_____

_____

_____

_____

▷ Within 6 months:

_____

_____

_____

_____

I/we believe my son's strengths include:

1. _____

2. _____

3. _____

4. _____

5. _____

I/we need to communicate these strengths to him as well as to the following people:

1. _____
2. _____
3. _____
4. _____
5. _____

Fill in this statement and share it with the people listed previously.

I/we can use his strength in _____

to help him _____

_____.

In order for my son to achieve the vision I/we have for him at the 5-year mark, I/we need to obtain the support of the following individuals or professionals:

1. _____
2. _____
3. _____
4. _____
5. _____

When I/we become discouraged or frustrated with his behavior or performance, I/we need to remember these things:

1. _____
2. _____

3. _____

4. _____

5. _____

6. _____

When I/we become discouraged or frustrated with his behavior or performance, I/we can count on these people for support:

1. _____

2. _____

3. _____

When my son becomes discouraged or frustrated with us or with his ADHD, he needs to remind himself of these things:

1. _____

2. _____

3. _____

4. _____

5. _____

When my son becomes discouraged or frustrated with us or with his ADHD, he can turn to the following people for support (other than myself):

1. _____

2. _____

3. _____

I'd like to close by thanking you for your effort and for the hard work you are doing on behalf of your son. I understand your journey because I've traveled similar paths. Each day you work hard at raising your son, and one day he'll realize this. Helping your son make the most of his capabilities will be an accomplishment you can cherish all of your life. I can assure you that it will be worth every ounce of effort you put into it. My compassion and hope for your future go out to you.

References

Agnew-Blais, J. C., Polanczyk, G. V., Danse, A., Wertz, J., Moffitt, T. E., & Arseneault, L. (2018). Young adult mental health and functional outcomes among individuals with remitted, persistent and late-onset ADHD. *The British Journal of Psychiatry, 213*(3), 526–534.

Alderson, R. M., Rapport, M. D., Hudec, K. L., Sarver, D. E., & Kofler, M. J. (2010). Competing core processes in attention-deficit/hyperactivity disorder (ADHD): Do working memory deficiencies underlie behavioral inhibition deficits? *Journal of Abnormal Child Psychology, 38*, 497–507. https://doi.org/10.1007/s10802-010-9387-0

Alexander-Roberts, A. (2006). *AD/HD parenting handbook: Practical advice for parents from parents.* Rowman Littlefield.

American Academy of Child and Adolescent Psychiatry & American Psychiatric Association. (2013). *ADHD parents medication guide.* https://www.aacap.org/App_Themes/AACAP/Docs/resource_centers/adhd/adhd_parents_medication_guide_201305.pdf

American Academy of Pediatrics. (n.d.). *Family media plan.* https://www.healthychildren.org/English/media/Pages/default.aspx#home

American Psychiatric Association. (2013). *Diagnostic and statistical manual of mental disorders* (5th ed.). https://doi.org/10.1176/appi.books.9780890425596

American Psychological Association. (2012). *Memory training unlikely to help in treating ADHD, boosting IQ.* https://www.apa.org/news/press/releases/2012/05/memory-training

Americans With Disabilities Act of 1990, 42 U.S.C. § 12102 *et seq.* (1990). https://www.ada.gov/pubs/adastatute08.htm

Armstrong, T. (1995). *The myth of the A.D.D. child: 50 ways to improve your child's behavior and attention span without drugs, labels, or coercion.* Penguin.

Bailey, E. (2007). *ADHD in young children.* http://www.healthcentral.com/adhd/children-40947-5.html

Barkley, R. A. (2000). *A new look at ADHD: Inhibition, time, and self-control.* Guilford Press.

Barkley, R. A. (2007). School intervention for attention deficit hyperactivity disorder: Where to from here? *School Psychology Review, 36*(2), 279–286.

Barkley, R. A. (2015). *Attention-deficit hyperactivity disorder: A handbook for diagnosis and treatment* (4th ed.). Guilford Press.

Barkley, R. A. (2016). *Managing ADHD in school: The best evidence-based methods for teachers.* PESI.

Barkley, R. A. (2020). *Taking charge of ADHD. The complete, authoritative guide for parents* (4th ed.). Guilford Press.

Barkley, R. A., & Cox, D. A. (2007). A review of driving risks and impairments associated with attention-deficit/hyperactivity disorder and the effects of stimulant medication on driving performance. *Journal of Safety Research, 38*(1), 113–128.

Bower, B. (2006). Med-start kids: Pros, cons of Ritalin for preschool ADHD. *Science News, 170*(18), 275.

Breaden, M. (2007, September 12). Preschoolers with ADHD. *Education Week, 5.*

Brier, N. (2010). *Enhancing academic motivation: An intervention program for young adolescents.* Research Press.

Brown, T. E. (2013). *A new understanding of ADHD in children and adults: Executive function impairments.* Routledge.

Brown, T. E. (2017). *Outside the box: Rethinking ADD/ADHD in children and adults.* American Psychiatric Association.

Centers for Disease Control and Prevention. (2020, November 16). *Data and statistics about ADHD.* https://www.cdc.gov/ncbddd/adhd/data.html

Chang, Z., Lichtenstein, P., Halldner, L., D'Onofrio, B., Serlachius, E., Fazel, S., Långström, N., & Larsson, H. (2014). Stimulant ADHD medication and risk for substance abuse. *Journal of Child Psychology and Psychiatry, 55*(8), 878–885. https://doi.org/10.1111/jcpp.12164

Children and Adults With Attention-Deficit/Hyperactivity Disorder. (n.d.-a). *About ADHD.* https://chadd.org/understanding-adhd

Children and Adults With Attention-Deficit/Hyperactivity Disorder. (n.d.-b). *Neurofeedback (EEG biofeedback).* https://chadd.org/about-adhd/neurofeedback-eeg-biofeedback

Dawson, M. M. (2007). The ideal versus the feasible when designing interventions for students with attention deficit hyperactivity disorder. *School Psychology Review, 36*(2), 274–278. https://doi.org/10.1080/02796015.2007.12087944

Dawson, P., & Guare, R. (2009). *Smart but scattered: The revolutionary "executive skills" approach to helping kids reach their potential.* Guilford Press.

DuPaul, G. J. (2007). School-based interventions for students with attention deficit hyperactivity disorder: Current status and future directions. *School Psychology Review, 36*(2), 183–194.

Durheim, M., & Zeigler Dendy, C. A. (2006). Educational laws regarding students with AD/HD. In C. A. Ziegler Dendy (Ed.), *CHADD educator's manual on attention-deficit/hyperactivity disorder: An in-depth look from an educational perspective* (pp. 125–134). CHADD.

Forgan., J. W., & Richey, M. A. (2015). *The impulsive, disorganized child: Solutions for parenting kids with executive functioning difficulties.* Prufrock Press.

Forgan, J. W., & Richey, M. A. (2019). *The ADHD empowerment guide: Identifying your child's strengths and unlocking potential.* Prufrock Press.

Goldstein, S. (n.d.). *What do we want from children with ADHD? Keeping a moving target in mind.* http://samgoldstein.com/resources/articles/general/what-do-we-want-from-children-with-adhd.aspx

Goldstein, S. (2011). Attention-deficit/hyperactivity disorder. In S. Goldstein & C. R. Reynolds (Eds.), *Handbook of neurodevelopmental and genetic disorders in children* (2nd ed., pp. 131–150). Guilford Press.

Harvard Health Publishing. (2007). *Preschool ADHD.* https://www.health.harvard.edu/press_releases/preschool-adhd

Individuals With Disabilities Education Act, 20 U.S.C. §1401 *et seq.* (1990). https://sites.ed.gov/idea/statuteregulations

Katz, M. (2007, December). AD/HD safe driving program: A graduated license plan. *Attention,* 6–7.

Kofler, M. J., Rapport, M. D., Bolden, J., Sarver, D. E., & Raiker, J. S. (2010). ADHD and working memory: The impact of central executive deficits and exceeding storage/rehearsal capacity on observed inattentive behavior. *Journal of Abnormal Child Psychology, 38*(2), 149–161.

Kubik, J. A. (2010). Efficacy of ADHD coaching for adults with ADHD. *Journal of Attention Disorders, 13*(5), 442–453. https://doi.org/10.1177/1087054708329960

Loo, S. K., & Barkley, R. A. (2005). Clinical utility of EEG in attention deficit hyperactivity disorder. *Applied Neuropsychology, 12*(2), 64–76. https://doi.org/10.1207/s15324826an1202_2

Mattox, G., & Vinson, S. (2018). Culturally competent approaches to ADHD: Issues in African-American populations. *Psychiatric Times, 35*(9). https://www.psychiatrictimes.com/view/culturally-

competent-approaches-adhd-issues-african-american-populat
ions

Maxwell, J. C. (2007). *Talent is never enough: Discover the choices that will take you beyond your talent.* Nelson.

Maxwell, J. C., & Parrott, L. (2005). *25 ways to win with people: How to make others feel like a million bucks.* Nelson.

McConaughy, S., Volpe, R., Antshel, K., Gordon, M., & Eiraldi, R. (2011). Academic and social impairments of elementary school children with attention deficit hyperactivity disorder. *School Psychology Review, 40*(2), 200–225. https://doi.org/10.1080/02796015.2011.12087713

Merriman, D. E., & Codding, R. S. (2008). The effects of coaching on mathematics homework completion and accuracy of high school students with attention-deficit/hyperactivity disorder. *Journal of Behavioral Education, 17,* 339. https://doi.org/10.1007/s10864-008-9072-3

Monastra, V. J. (2014). *Parenting children with ADHD: 10 lessons that medicine cannot teach* (2nd ed.). American Psychological Association.

Monastra, V. J., Lynn, S., Linden, M., Lubar, J. F., Gruzelier, J., & LaVaque, T. J. (2005). Electroencephalographic biofeedback in the treatment of attention-deficit/hyperactivity disorder. *Applied Psychophysiology and Biofeedback, 30,* 95–114. https://doi.org/10.1007/s10484-005-4305-x

Monastra, V. J., Monastra, D. M., & George, S. (2002). The effects of stimulant therapy, EEG biofeedback, and parenting style on the primary symptoms of attention-/hyperactivity disorder. *Applied Psychophysiology and Biofeedback, 27*(4), 231–249. https://doi.org/10.1023/A:1021018700609

Morgan, P. L., Staff, J., Hillemeier, M. M., Farkas, G., & Maczuga, S. (2013). Racial and ethnic disparities in ADHD diagnosis from kindergarten to eighth grade. *Pediatrics, 132*(1), 85–93. https://doi.org/10.1542/peds.2012-2390

National Institute of Mental Health. (2006). *Preschoolers with ADHD improve with low doses of medication.* https://www.nih.gov/news-

events/news-releases/preschoolers-adhd-improve-low-doses-me
dication

National Institute of Mental Health. (2009). *The Multimodal Treatment of Attention Deficit Hyperactivity Disorder Study (MTA): Questions and answers.* https://www.nimh.nih.gov/funding/clinical-re search/practical/mta/the-multimodal-treatment-of-attention-deficit-hyperactivity-disorder-study-mta-questions-and-answ ers.shtml

The Neurofeedback Collaborative Group. (2020). Double-blind placebo-controlled randomized clinical trial of neurofeedback for attention-deficit/hyperactivity disorder with 13-month follow-up. *Journal of the American Academy of Child & Adolescent Psychiatry.* https://doi. org/10.1016/j.jaac.2020.07.906

Parker, H. C. (n.d.). *Accommodations to help students with attention deficit disorders.* https://www.addwarehouse.com/article4.htm

Pelham, W. E., & Fabiano, G. A. (2008). Evidence-based psychosocial treatments for attention-deficit/hyperactivity disorder. *Journal of Clinical Child & Adolescent Psychology, 37*(1), 184–214. https:// doi.org/10.1080/15374410701818681

Pharmacological and behavioral treatments for ADHD in preschoolers. (2009, April). *The Brown University Child and Adolescent Behavior Letter, 25*(4), 1–8.

Pliszka, S., & AACAP Work Group on Quality Issues. (2007). Practice parameter for the assessment and treatment of children and adolescents with attention-deficit/hyperactivity disorder. *Journal of Clinical Child & Adolescent Psychiatry, 46*(7), 894–921. https:// doi.org/10.1097/chi.0b013e318054e724

Rapport, M. D., Bolden, J., Kofler, M. J., Sarver, D. E., Raiker, J. S., & Alderon, R. M. (2008). Hyperactivity in boys with attention-deficit/ hyperactivity disorder (ADHD): A ubiquitous core symptom or manifestation of working memory deficits? *Journal of Abnormal Child Psychology, 37*(4), 521–534.

Rief, S. F. (2008). *The ADD/ADHD checklist: A practical reference for parents and teachers* (2nd ed.). Jossey-Bass.

Section 504 of the Rehabilitation Act, 29 U.S.C. § 706 *et seq.* (1973).

Taylor, J. F. (2001). *Helping your ADD child: Hundreds of practical solutions for parents and teachers of ADD children and teens* (3rd ed.). Three Rivers Press.

Taylor-Klaus, E. (2020). *The essential guide to raising complex kids with ADHD, anxiety, and more.* Fair Winds Press.

Teeter, P. A. (1998). *Interventions for ADHD: Treatment in developmental context.* Guilford Press.

Vitiello, B., & Sherrill, J. (2007). School-based interventions for students with attention deficit hyperactivity disorder: Research implications and prospects. *School Psychology Review, 36*(2), 287–290. https://doi.org/10.1080/02796015.2007.12087946

Weiss, G., & Hechtman, L. T. (1993). *Hyperactive children grow up: ADHD in children, adolescents, and adults* (2nd ed.). Guilford Press.

Wendling, P. (2008, December 1). Full exam guides ADHD diagnosis in preschoolers. *Family Practice News, 26.*

Williams, N. I., Zaharieva, I., Martin, A., Langley, K., Mantripragada, K., Fossdal, R., Stefansson, H., Stefansson, K., Magnusson, P., Gudmundsson, O. O., Gustafsson, O., Holmans, P., Owen, M. J., O'Donovan, M., & Thapar, A. (2010). Rare chromosomal deletions and duplications in attention-deficit hyperactivity disorder: A genome-wide analysis. *The Lancet, 376*(9750), 1401–1408. https://doi.org/10.1016/S0140-6736(10)61109-9

Wolraich, M. L. (2007, August). Preschoolers and AD/HD. *Attention,* 8–11.

Wright, P. (2009). *Four rules for raising children.* http://www.wrightslaw.com/nltr/09/nl.0106.htm#4

About the Author

Mary Anne Richey, M.Ed., is a licensed school psychologist with degrees from Virginia Tech and Florida Atlantic University. In 2012, she was named Florida School Psychologist of the Year. She worked for the school district of Palm Beach County and now maintains a private practice. She also has experience as a middle school teacher, administrator, high school guidance counselor, and adjunct college instructor. She has been a featured speaker at many national and international conferences. It has been Mary Anne's pleasure to assist many students with ADHD and their families over the years.

In addition to *Raising Boys With ADHD*, she has coauthored four other books, which include *Raising Girls With ADHD*, named as one of the Eight Great Books on ADHD by Book Riot and as one the Best ADHD Books of All Time by Book Authority; *The Impulsive, Disorganized Child*; *Stressed Out!*, named the 2018 Book of the Year in the parent category by the National Association for Gifted Children; and *The ADHD Empowerment Guide*.

Throughout *Raising Boys With ADHD*, Mary Anne helps parents manage the issues they face and incorporates strategies to help their sons succeed in school and life. She shares an integrated perspective on ADHD based on her experience as a parent and professional, her academic research, and her interactions with so many other parents raising boys with ADHD.

Printed in the United States
by Baker & Taylor Publisher Services

Printed in the United States
by Baker & Taylor Publisher Services